New Loss Prevention

New Loss Prevention

Redefining Shrinkage Management

By

Adrian Beck

With

Colin Peacock

First published 2009 by
PALGRAVE MACMILLAN

Palgrave Macmillan in the UK is an imprint of Macmillan Publishers Limited,
registered in England, company number 785998, of Houndmills, Basingstoke,
Hampshire RG21 6XS.

Palgrave Macmillan in the US is a division of St Martin's Press LLC,
175 Fifth Avenue, New York, NY 10010.

Palgrave Macmillan is the global academic imprint of the above companies
and has companies and representatives throughout the world.

Palgrave® and Macmillan® are registered trademarks in the United States,
the United Kingdom, Europe and other countries

ISBN-13: 978-0-230-57583-7   hardback

This book is printed on paper suitable for recycling and made from fully
managed and sustained forest sources. Logging, pulping and manufacturing
processes are expected to conform to the environmental regulations of the
country of origin.

A catalogue record for this book is available from the British Library.

A catalogue record for this book is available from the Library of Congress.

Printed and bound in Great Britain by
CPI Antony Rowe, Chippenham and Eastbourne

To Sue with Love

Contents

List of Figures and Tables

Figures

Tables

List of Abbreviations

ABRAS   Association of Brazilian Supermarkets
AP   Asset Protection
CCTV   Closed Circuit Television
CPTED   Crime Prevention Through Environmental Design
EAS   Electronic Article Surveillance
ECR   Efficient Consumer Response
EPoS   Electronic Point of Sale
FMCG   Fast Moving Consumer Goods
FMEA   Failure Mode and Effects Analysis
GCI   Global Commerce Initiative
LP   Loss Prevention
NRSS   National Retail Security Survey
ORC   Organised Retail Crime
POS   Point of Sale
RFID   Radio Frequency Identification
RIS   Retail Information System
SKU   Stock Keeping Unit
UPC   Uniform Product Code

1
Introduction

The term 'shrinkage' usually refers to something becoming smaller or a gradual contraction over time – an impact not considered to be serious or of much concern. Within the world of retailing and loss prevention, however, it has a much more significant meaning although achieving agreement on precisely what that meaning is, as will be discussed in this book, has proven highly illusive for those working in the field or studying the subject. Generally speaking it is used as a catch-all phrase to categorise the financial losses that retailers face through spoilage, damage, error and theft. It incorporates a highly disparate group of activities ranging from apples going out of date to organised gangs of thieves clearing shelves of high value ink jet cartridges. Its scale is truly extraordinary and rarely fails to shock the uninitiated. For instance, the Global Retail Theft Barometer, a survey of retailers which covered 36 countries in Africa, Asia Pacific, Europe, North America and Latin America, provides a relatively recent attempt to measure the scale of the problem and concluded that the annual cost of shrinkage in these countries was $104.5 billion (Bamfield, 2008). Such an enormous number is difficult to comprehend until you consider that it is almost equivalent to the combined Gross Domestic Product (GDP) of two countries – Luxembourg and Vietnam (World Bank, 2009). In simplistic terms, every year the retail communities in 36 countries could buy the entire output of two nations with the amount they lose through shrinkage! And as we reveal in this book, total global losses from shrinkage are probably much higher, perhaps equating to as much as $232 billion a year.

It is also a problem that has proved to be stubborn and resistant to the many and varied attempts to reduce its impact on retail profits. Within the industry, shrinkage is usually reported as a percentage of

1

retail turnover and one of the most authoritative and long running shrinkage surveys undertaken by Hollinger and others in the USA shows that the rate of shrinkage has remained relatively unchanged over the last 16 years. His first study in 1991 recorded an overall rate of loss for retailers in the US of 1.79 per cent and the most recent survey covering 2007 calculated that it was 1.44 per cent – a historic low but still a relatively modest reduction compared with the first survey (Hollinger & Adams, 2008). However, it has not been a straightforward downward linear progression and this annual security survey has shown much fluctuation in the cost of shrinkage with a peak in 1994 of 1.95 per cent. And if we head back a little further in time, studies undertaken in the second half of the last century reported rates not that dissimilar to some of those that have been completed in the last few years with averages of between 1.5 per cent and 2 per cent (Curtis, 1960, 1983; Baumer & Rosenbaum, 1984; National Supermarket Research Group, 2003).

Understanding why shrinkage has proven to be such a resilient and long lasting problem for the retail industry is one of the main reasons for writing this book. The loss prevention industry is a multi-billion dollar global business that is increasingly developing and making use of some of the most sophisticated and cutting edge technologies, including biometrics, surveillance systems, digital recognition and data analytics. Our estimates suggest that globally, retailers could be spending as much as $46.4 billion a year on trying to tackle the problem of shrinkage, which when combined with our estimate of the cost of shrinkage, would produce a total shrinkage bill of some $278 billion a year, almost equivalent to the GDP of Denmark. Why does shrinkage cost so much and why do the current approaches to deal with the problem seem to be at best holding back the tide of loss? Perhaps more importantly, is there a better way to deal with the problem of shrinkage that may have a more lasting impact on the scale and extent of the problem? These are the key questions that this book would like to address.

So why have we called it *New Loss Prevention* – what makes it different from the other texts that have charted the problems faced by the retail industry and the security professionals employed by them? Well, this book does not intend to dwell upon the details of how you deliver a loss prevention strategy, such as how many cameras you should install in a retail store, how to draw up a work plan for a store detective or guard, or what is the best way to interview a suspected member of staff. We leave that to those who have far more experience in that area than we can ever presume to have. This book is much more interested in exploring the true nature of the problems faced by the retail community and developing an overarching theoretical framework that will enable practitioners and scholars alike to think about the problem of shrinkage in a different way. It is premised upon developing a systemic and systematic understanding of the root causes of shrinkage rather than the current approach which is predominantly reactive and fire fighting in nature, primarily targeting external theft. It also seeks to recognise the powerful relationship between operational failure and opportunity, with the former creating the latter which in turn enables theft by internal and external thieves and the day-to-day losses caused through poor execution of retail practices.

Too often, many loss prevention practitioners have become fixated with 'solving' the problem of external theft (shop theft) without ever understanding the true causes or indeed whether it is the actual cause of the problem in the first place. Partly this has been driven by technology providers who have often found it easier to pedal their 'technological panaceas' when the focus is kept narrow and simplistic (i.e. shrinkage is primarily about external theft). But it is also due to some practitioners not getting to grips with understanding the true causes of shrinkage in their business, primarily through not having good quality data but also by not casting their net sufficiently wide to incorporate all the potential reasons why shrinkage might occur. *New Loss Prevention* is about challenging the existing preconceived ideas about not only what constitutes shrinkage, but also the approach that should be adopted to deal with it. It is firmly rooted in the use of evidence, analysis and the selection of shrinkage 'solutions' that are fit for purpose. This requires the industry to move away from preconceived ideas about what causes shrinkage and what can be done to manage it, and to challenge existing boundaries concerning ownership and location of the problem, and embrace new ideas and approaches that are based less on presumption and guesswork and more on rigorous assessment and detailed analysis.

This book also provides the reader with a guide to implementing *New Loss Prevention*, a major part of which is the *Loss Prevention Pyramid* – a structured approach to delivering a more strategic way of dealing with the problem of shrinkage. Based upon the experiences of some of the best performing retailers in the world, and the extensive research undertaken by the Efficient Consumer Response (ECR) Europe's Shrinkage Group, the pyramid focuses upon the key areas that need to be developed in order to tackle shrinkage effectively. This includes amongst others securing senior management commitment, the effective use of data, the development of operational excellence, and generating store management responsibility. Ultimately, *New Loss Prevention* is concerned with developing a framework that relies upon redefining the role of the loss prevention practitioner away from a reactive thief catcher to one that is primarily an 'agent of change' ensuring that the rest of the organisation is engaged, enthused and accountable for shrinkage. The *New Loss Prevention* manager is somebody who fully recognises the broader retailing context within which they operate and how effective shrinkage management can make a lasting and highly significant contribution to retail profitability.

Research methodology

This book is based upon research carried out over the past ten years undertaken primarily, but not exclusively, through the auspices of ECR Europe's Shrinkage Group. ECR is an initiative that seeks to develop understanding and insights relating to the common challenges faced by retailers and manufacturers alike in their quest to increase profits and customer satisfaction. Since its inception in 1993 it has focussed upon a wide range of themes including continuous replenishment, efficient promotional practices, efficient assortment, efficient new product activities, and shrinkage (Kent & Omar, 2003). The ECR Europe Shrinkage Group, which is co-chaired by a retailer and a manufacturer, has conducted a large number of projects designed to address critical concerns as perceived by the industry representatives sitting on the committee, such as: staff dishonesty; developments in Radio Frequency Identification (RFID) and shrinkage; understanding shrinkage hot spots in supply chains; measuring the value of technological loss prevention innovations; and methodologies for understanding root causes of shrinkage more effectively, in particular the Shrinkage Road Map, which will be discussed in detail later in this book. Much of this work adopted a case-study approach involving researchers visiting over 100 retail locations and supply chains, both in Europe and the USA.

In addition, the research work which helped develop the Loss Prevention Pyramid, adopted a multi-case-study approach, focusing on five retail companies based in the US (Beck, 2007a). Making use of a variety of data collection techniques this approach is considered to be one of the most powerful research designs available to researchers (Burns, 2000; Yin, 1993). More specifically, the project undertaken by Beck utilised 'sequential analysis', where the analysis process is an integral part of the data collection phase enabling further data collection to take place as a consequence of initial interpretation (Yin, 1993). The method used to select the companies to be case studies utilised the 'reputational' approach (Burns, 2000), whereby a group of experts, key practitioners and academics made recommendations based upon personal and experiential evidence.

Panellists were requested to select their top five US retailers in terms of known levels of shrinkage, innovation in the approach adopted and recent success in dealing with the problem. From their responses, a composite list was generated and these companies were then contacted and all agreed to take part in the project. For each company data was collected in three ways: interviews with key members of staff, particularly the head of loss prevention but also other staff within the loss prevention team and employees working in the stores; where it was made available, secondary analysis of company documents and data; and finally observation through visits to stores to talk to staff and look at how policies, procedures and approaches were operationalised.

As with any research methodology, the approach adopted is not without its problems. Using a expert panel to select the 'best' retailers can be problematic – have the right experts been chosen, on what basis are they making their selections and is there a danger of past history selection i.e. they were good in the past but are they still high performing retailers? To overcome this, two strategies were adopted: the first was to get as many experts as possible to participate to reduce the effect of any single respondent, and the second was to purposefully exclude those 'experts' that did not have sufficient experience of the retail environment in the US. Problems can also arise when collecting information through semi-structured interviews as they can be open to interviewer bias and interpretation. In addition, there is a danger that the rhetoric spoken by senior managers may have little connection with what is actually done on the ground in the stores and the distribution network. Both of these problems were addressed through the use of a relatively detailed interview schedule that took each respondent through a series of questions, but at the same time allowed for new topics to be raised by the respondent if they considered them important. Secondly, by undertaking store visits and talking to staff who worked there, it was possible to do some form of 'reality' check against the comments made by senior managers.

Structure of the book

This book is organised around ten chapters. After this introductory chapter we move on to chart the developments in retailing over the past 100 years or so and how this has had an impact upon loss prevention.

We feel this is important because any attempt to develop new ways of dealing with such a stubborn and long lasting problem as shrinkage needs to recognise the broader and in many ways revolutionary changes that have taken place, and will continue to take place, within the retail sector.

The next chapter will then focus on what we understand the term shrinkage to mean. While it is a term that has been in use for over 100 years, there is as yet no industry agreed standard on what should be included or excluded in this term, how it should be measured or indeed valued. Chapter 3 will look in detail at these issues and offer some insights into how organisations might develop a better definition in the future, enabling more comparable benchmarking to be undertaken. Chapter 4 then goes on to map out what is know about the scale and extent of the problem of shrinkage, focusing particularly on the various surveys and other research studies that have been completed in recent years. Building upon this, Chapter 5 will then offer a detailed insight into the four areas that are generally considered to account for shrinkage looking first at the issue of external theft, then internal theft and inter-company fraud and finally the issue of process failures.

Chapter 6 moves on to consider how shrinkage has been managed to date focusing on the traditional methods adopted by many retailers and arguing that for the most part this has been a tale of failure, with losses remaining much the same despite enormous investments in 'solutions'. The following chapter then seeks to map out what we see as the important and significant relationship between operational failure and opportunity and how this in turn creates shrinkage. Making use of a range of criminological theories it will argue that operational failures play a leading role in creating the environment within which retail losses can occur. Chapter 8 then introduces the Shrinkage Road Map – a tool developed to enable retailers to quickly and easily identify operational failures within their organisations and subsequently identify appropriate interventions designed to deal with them. The next chapter then goes on to put forward the key components of *New Loss Prevention* including a detailed description of the various elements that make up the Loss Prevention Pyramid. The final chapter will then offer an overview of the key themes covered by this book and some considerations on how *New Loss Prevention* can be implemented by retail practitioners.

New loss prevention

Ultimately, this book is an attempt to develop fresh thinking on a problem that continues to significantly affect retailers and their customers across the globe. We would like to argue that traditional approaches to managing shrinkage have at best merely kept a lid on a problem that is constantly threatening to get out of control. We believe that a new approach, what we have termed *New Loss Prevention*, is much more likely to succeed in meeting the challenges of shrinkage management in the 21st century. It is an approach that ensures that organisational responses to shrinkage are premised upon a detailed understanding of the root causes of stock loss and that the role of operational failure in providing the opportunities for deviant behaviour is fully recognised. Above all, this approach is concerned with organisations developing a much more systemic and systematic methodology for responding to shrinkage and recognising that all parts of the business (and indeed those organisations that they deal with) need to be engaged, with the loss prevention function acting as 'agents of change' – providing information, expertise and enthusiasm. We believe the *New Loss Prevention* manager is much more a business leader than a thief catcher, more concerned with monitoring process adherence than Closed Circuit Television (CCTV), and measures success in increased profitability not the number of suspects appearing in the local court of law. Above all, the approach outlined in this book is concerned with encouraging those engaged in managing shrinkage to recognise the vital role that ensuring operational excellence can have upon keeping shrinkage at a level which maximises sales and minimises losses.

Acknowledgements

We would like to thank all those who made this book possible through offering access to their companies, reading early drafts of chapters, and offering advice and reassurance. Your help is very much appreciated. In particular, we would like to thank: Sean Bowen, Brad Brekke, Paul Chapman, Ernie Deyle, John Fonteijn, Martin Gill, Paul Jones, Brian Moore, Walter Palmer, Martin Sayer, and Paul Stone. We would also like to thank all those who have represented their companies on the ECR Europe Shrinkage Group over the past ten years including Katrin Recke for her long serving administrative support to the group. Your thoughts and ideas are the foundation for much of the work presented in this book.

2

Retailing and Shrinkage in Context

In this chapter we intend to put the issue of shrinkage within the broader context of developments in the retailing industry. We think this is a worthwhile exercise for a number of reasons. First, as we will discuss below, retailing has gone through a series of dramatic changes in the way in which it is organised and operates and these changes have undoubtedly had an impact upon the way in which not only shrinkage affects retail companies, but also the way in which they respond to the problem. The growth of mass merchandising, consumerism, open sale formats and many other changes have all had an impact upon how shrinkage affects retail organisations and we feel it is important to outline what these are in terms of managing shrinkage. Secondly, these changes have informed the way in which we have developed *New Loss Prevention* – it would be naive to propose new ways of managing shrinkage unless this broader context was fully recognised and understood, particularly in terms of how retailing and shrinkage management is likely to evolve in the future.

The chapter starts with a short history of retailing highlighting some of the key developments in the last 100 years or so, but focusing particularly on the radical changes witnessed in the last 30 years. It then goes on to look at some of the key changes that we feel have an impact upon the management of shrinkage: the consequences of customer self selection, focusing upon changing consumer expectations and the relationship between accessibility and sales; the challenges of complexity in modern retailing, looking particularly at the changing nature of retail operations; the growth of specialisation within retailing and the impact of increased competition on managing shrinkage; the impact of technologies, both in terms of the retail operation and responding to shrinkage; and the growing trend toward globalised retailing and the associated challenges it presents.

Before we begin it is perhaps worthwhile reflecting on what we mean by the term 'retailing' – this may seem strange as we all think we know what retailing looks like when we see it. But it is, to a certain extent, a contested term and can mean different things to different people (Dawson *et al.*, 2008a; Peterson & Balasubramanian, 2002). For most of us retailing is epitomised by the retail store itself and the provision of goods to the consumer, but retailing is much more than this. It encapsulates a broader array of activities which could include: the design and manufacture of goods; their shipment along increasingly lengthy and complex supply chains, spanning different continents and modes of transport; the use of various forms of technology to monitor and control their progress; and indeed their marketing to the eventual consumer. Indeed, retail stores probably employ only a relatively small proportion of those engaged in the process of enabling customers to buy the products they want (or at least they think they want). For the purposes of this book we intend to adopt a relatively broad definition of retailing encompassing all the activities necessary to bring a product to the consumer. We do this because a key element of *New Loss Prevention* is recognition of the opportunities for shrinkage that can occur throughout the life cycle of a product and indeed how ameliorative actions can be taken long before the product reaches the shelf in the retail store. As we will detail in Chapter 6 there is often a danger that shrinkage is seen as a problem that mainly occurs and needs to be addressed in the retail store, when in fact this may simply be the location where the shrinkage is most easily identifiable and loss prevention approaches (particularly technologies) more readily applied.

A short history of retailing

Retailing has a very long history and the trading of goods can be charted back to some of the earliest times in human history. The earliest forms of exchange can be found in the development of local markets where local produce was sold to those living in close proximity (Winstanley, 1983; Tse, 1985). The 18th century saw the gradual development of shops as larger population centres attracted a range of artisans offering specialist services to customers, such as cobblers, bakers and tailors with products being sold from their workshops. This is the start of the roots of modern retailing as independent specialist shops began to emerge. The 19th century saw the emergence of what we now would recognise as retail shops, in particular the creation of the Department Store, albeit initially focused only upon clothing but gradually offering a range of discrete sections within one building covering a wide range of different product types (Abelson, 1989). In the UK and the US in the mid 1850s onwards such places became a favoured destination for the growing middle classes, especially women, who would combine shopping, browsing, social-ising and stealing within these new retail spaces (Winstanley, 1983; Tse, 1985). For many this was the start of the consumer society and the growth of the department store has been used by a number of his-torians as a mechanism to reveal the complexity of the social process of consumption (Abelson, 1989; Glennie & Thrift, 1996).

The industrial revolution had an important impact on the development of retailing in the UK: the new industrialised working class demanded mass consumer goods; the emerging middle classes demanded a better shopping experience; new supply chains developed as a dwindling agri-cultural sector could not longer meet the growing demand or compete with cheaper imported produce; mass production techniques began to develop and real income per head began to grow rapidly (Young, 2004). The 20th century saw this movement continue at a pace with the inex-orable growth in the size of retail organisations, the establishment of retail brands and the growing importance of retailing as a vital part of the economic development of many countries. Some have described this as the dawn of 'new commerce' (Cohen, 2003; Dawson, 2001) as the scale and size of the sector grew dramatically, moving away from small scale retailing toward much larger businesses that required significant changes to the way in which they were organised and how people worked. Arguably from this time onwards retailing has become much more important to people, moving away from something that was essentially functional towards something that is much more significant to the way people carry out their lives – 'a switch from satisfaction of needs through acquisition of goods to the satisfaction of desires through the meaning and symbolism attached to goods and to the places (shops and towns) from where they were obtained' (Dawson *et al.*, 2008a: 10).

The 1970s onwards saw significant changes to the way in which food retailing in particular began to be organised and grocers began to recog-nise the full benefits achievable from economies of scale and a trend began that has continued almost relentlessly ever since – the decline in the total number of shops and an increase in average store size. For example, over the period 1971–79 the total number of grocery shops in the UK fell from 105,283 to 68,567, a decline of 35 per cent (Young, 2004). This was also the period which saw an acceleration in the dev-elopment of the shopping mall and out of town shopping as retailers recognised the rewards possible from creating shopping environments specifically designed to meet the ever growing voracious consumer appetite. These 'machines for selling' (Cohen, 2003; Guy, 1994) have arguably transformed the social and cultural geography of many towns and cities in developed countries across the globe.

But it is in the last 30 years that retailing, perhaps more than any other economic sector, has been transformed fundamentally, both economically and culturally (Dawson *et al.*, 2008a). The 1990s saw the trend towards fewer retailers radically accelerate with the large supermarket chains expanding further through the absorption of smaller retail chains and the creation of a wide range of store formats (such as large out of town mega stores through to local convenience style outlets). For example, supermarkets in the UK now control over two thirds of the grocery market and have significant shares in others, including clothing, books, electronics, petrol, financial services and pharmacy. In 1950, supermarkets had only 20 per cent of the grocery market in the UK while small shops and cooperatives had 80 per cent. By 1990, this situation had more or less been reversed (Blythman, 2004). The decline in independent grocers in the UK fell from 116,000 in 1961 to only 20,900 in 1997 (Department for Environment, Trade and Regional Affairs, 2000). And researchers at Manchester School of Management have predicted that if current trends continue there might not be a single independent food store left in the whole of the UK by 2050 (Mitchell & Kyris, 1999).

The growth of the 'big' retailer is best exemplified by what is now regarded as the largest company in the world – Wal-Mart. In its short history, this company has grown exponentially and has had a major impact upon how retailing has developed in the past 60 years. Wal-Mart is not only the biggest retail company in the world it is also the largest company in the world. From its humble beginnings back in the 1940s when Sam Walton, its founder, opened his first 'five and dime' store in Newport Arkansas, it has grown dramatically both within the US and globally, with a presence in 15 countries and a turnover in excess of $430 billion (dwarfing its nearest rival Carrefour whose turnover in 2008 was estimated at $160 billion) (Planet Retail, 2009). To put this in context, if Wal-Mart were a country, then it would be ranked 21st in the world in terms of GDP, just below Sweden (World Bank, 2009). The scale of the operation is vast employing over two million people (twice as many as the US army) in over 7,800 stores worldwide with over 1 million items available on their online website (Edemariam, 2009; Wal-Mart, 2009). Not without its critics (for instance see Quinn, 2000; Young, 2004) it has become a hugely dominate force in retailing claiming to have a customer base of more than 100 million (Wal-Mart, 2009).

In the early years of the 21st century, retailing has continued to evolve at a pace with the rapid growth in on line shopping and the expansion into ever more market segments by the big retailers being but two examples of this on going change. In the last 200 years retailing has fundamentally changed from its humble beginnings in the trade of local goods to meet local needs to a \$14.07 trillion global leviathan intrinsically intertwined with the social, cultural and economic fabric of societies throughout the world (Planet Retail, 2009). Shopping is no longer about buying what we need, it has for many become a fundamental part of their daily lives – something which offers entertainment, pleasure and excitement (Kent & Omar, 2003). Consumers have become increasingly fickle as they demand ever greater choice, availability and lower prices, which in turn has made retailing an ever more competitive and demanding concern. It has also become a key factor in the economic well being of many countries, for instance 11 per cent of the UK workforce is employed in retail and this sector accounts for 8 per cent of the countries GDP (British Retail Consortium, 2009). In the next part of this chapter we will focus on some of the key structural developments within retailing and consider how they have impacted upon the management of shrinkage.

Help yourself – Self selection in retailing

The early part of the previous century saw a radical change in the way in which many retailers began to organise and run their stores – the introduction of self selection by customers. Pioneered initially by the departmental stores in the US and gradually adopted by all forms of retailing throughout the world, it is difficult now to imagine retailing organised in any other way. But at the time, it was a radical departure from how the sector had been run in the past as the prevailing expectation was that customers who wanted particular products would be provided with them by a member of staff, usually across a counter. This meant that customer access to products was strictly controlled and levels of staffing had to be relatively high to ensure that customers did not have to wait unduly long for the products they wished to purchase.

The move to self selection, where customers take responsibility for finding, selecting and eventually paying for the items they want at a designated check out area, was part of broader changes in consumer behaviour, some of which were retailer inspired, while other elements were as a consequence of changing customer expectations and demands. Early adopters of this model of retailing quickly realised (once customers had been 'taught' how to do it) the economic benefits of this approach – fewer staff were required, the store operation could be radically redefined to maximise the display of products, but must importantly, it led to increased sales. It also triggered a whole host of other consequential developments in packaging, store design, cash register technologies, refrigeration and promotional techniques (Du Gay, 2004). Retailers began to realise that what the products looked like and how and where they were displayed in stores could have a profound impact on the likelihood of people to buy them. In this respect, self selection was a key part of the rise of the consumer culture referred to earlier. Retailers began to understand the way in which customers' behaviours could be influenced, particularly in terms of impulse purchasing, through the ability to touch, taste or hear products without the need for a member of staff to be present (Kent & Omar, 2003).

While self selection was a revolutionary change in the nature of retailing and is something we now take for granted, it also had and continues to have a profound impact upon the problem of shrinkage (Curtis, 1971). Giving all customers unparalleled access to all the products in a store, often with reduced levels of staff supervision inevitably leads to increased theft and damage. As we detail in Chapter 7 opportunity is a critical variable in explaining why people steal and self selection retailing provides a plethora of opportunities for this to happen. Customers are positively encouraged to pick up goods, handle them and in some circumstances try them on in the privacy of their own changing room. If we view retailing as a delicate balancing act between selling and security – encouraging customers to purchase goods they desire but not steal them – then the rise of self selection can be seen as a watershed where the balance tipped dramatically towards selling (Beck & Willis, 1998). Some have argued (such as those employed in law enforcement) that retailers are to a certain extent the architects of their own downfall and therefore perhaps should not be that surprised when they give unfettered access to often highly desirable and in some cases unattainable products to literally anybody who enters their stores, to discover that some of them get stolen or damaged. In no way are we trying to act as apologists for those that steal from retail stores (including store staff who may use self selection as a convenient cloak to cover up their own offending), far from it, but at the same time those that create the environment within which crime can take place need to reflect upon their responsibilities and the impact changes introduced (in part) to increase sales may have on the likelihood for theft to occur. Self selection dramatically changed the way in which products could be protected by the retailer – it opened a Pandora's box of opportunities for 'customers' and staff to literally help themselves to the products available. While for the most part this leads to a legitimate transaction between the consumer and the retailer, and increased sales (i.e. the customer pays for more and more products they want), there is undoubtedly a fine line between increasing sales and also increasing the cost of shrinkage through more products being damaged and stolen by staff and customers alike.

One of the primary reasons why this is the case is that the redesign of the retailing environment to accommodate self selection significantly increases the ease of stealing, dramatically reduces the perceived risk of being caught and can also trigger a series of neutralising behaviours. Much criminological research has shown that the propensity to steal is a function of the amount of effort required compared with the anticipated reward, the perceived likelihood of being caught, and the perceived severity of the subsequent punishment (Cornish & Clarke, 1986) (See Chapter 7 for a more detailed discussion). If the would-be offender thinks that the amount of effort required is modest compared with the reward they are likely to get, and/or the risk of being caught is low, and even if they are caught they are not likely to face much of a punishment, then they are highly likely to offend (especially so if they have been previously caught and have experience of the way in which they are likely to be dealt with).

Within a self selection retail context one of the perceived benefits for the retailer is markedly reduced staff costs as less people are required to serve customers. The side effect of this is that the level of guardianship over the products is also significantly reduced – thieves therefore feel that it is much less risky because there are few people around likely to react to their offending behaviour (a number of studies have shown that 'thieves' consider vigilant staff to be the biggest deterrent, see for instance Butler, 1994). One of the key challenges therefore in the self selection retail space is to consider how the mindset of would-be offenders can be changed – how can the degree of effort required to steal products be made sufficiently high to put them off, and how can the perceived risk of being caught and subsequently punished be increased?

In addition, the layout of most self selection stores (where large quantities of stock are on open display) can trigger the neutralisation of moral reasoning on the part of offenders (Sykes & Matza, 1957). In other words the sheer volume of stock available can lead to a sense that the theft of just 'one' item will make little difference, or that the sheer scale of the operation means that this loss will be hardly noticed – 'the retailer is obviously making lots of money and can easily afford it', or that 'there is no obvious victim' (it is the organisation that loses and not a person) and so the theft hurts nobody. Dealing with such attitudes is another challenge presented by the rise of self selection in the retailing environment.

What is interesting about each of these factors is that while we have been considering them mainly with respect to customers, in many respects they are equally applicable to the staff who work in the stores as well, and this is something we will consider in more detail in Chapter 5. Self selection is not going to go out of fashion as a means of organising the retail environment in the very near future (despite the inexorable growth in Internet-based shopping); if anything it is becoming more pervasive (such as the increasing trend towards self checkouts), and so modern loss prevention needs to recognise the challenges that it presents and how they can be minimised and managed.

Challenges of complexity

For those not intimately involved in the world of retailing, it is difficult to begin to comprehend the scale and complexity of most modern retail operations. Whilst obviously not typical, Wal-Mart gives a sense of the scale – operating in 15 countries, a turnover in excess of $430 billion, employing over two million people in over 7,800 stores worldwide, over one million individual items available on their online website and a retail database that is second only to the Pentagon's in capacity (Time, 1998; Wal-Mart, 2009). The numbers for the UK-based retailer Tesco, are equally stratospheric – operating in 14 countries, a turnover of nearly £52 billion, and employing over 440,000 people in over 3,700 stores (Tesco PLC, 2009). This company is now engaged in a plethora of activities hardly imaginable when the company was first started as a food market stall in 1919: from offering mortgages, bank accounts and insurance, to the provision of pharmacy services, dry cleaning, cash machines, travel shops, and petrol stations (Tesco PLC, 2009). As one commentator put it, 'our largest supermarket chains have become multi-tasking retail monsters with voracious appetites...' (Blythman, 2004: 305). More broadly, the scale of operations is equally huge: IGD estimate that in the UK alone, five billion cases of products are distributed through 35.9 million square feet of warehouse space every year, and that journeys between distribution centres and stores account for 991.9 million kilometers a year (IGD, 2009). This complexity can be summarised in a number ways: growing availability and product ranges; expanding supply chains; and a broader array of stores locations and formats.

Availability and product ranges

In the not too distant past, availability of products was very much dictated by seasonality and consumer location. Some food products would only be available depending upon the growing season of the local producers – such as strawberries in the summer and root vegetables in the winter. Similarly, some types of products would only be regularly available depending on the proximity of the manufacturer – for those based far away from the point of production supplies could be highly spasmodic and unpredictable. Equally, the range of products available was often limited and retailer specific – footwear was purchased from a shoe shop, bread from a bakery and so on. Of course today things are very much different and the larger supermarket giants in particular have transformed the range and availability of products considerably. No longer are food products dependent upon the local growing season – consumers now expect (or have got used to) having a range of fresh foods available at any time of year – availability is no longer associated with seasonality. Similarly, the range of available products has expanded enormously – where once a consumer might expect to be able to choose between say two types of apples, they now have a choice of ten. Where there were once perhaps only one or two types of washing powder, there are now more than a dozen. Offering the consumer choice is the new mantra of large parts of the retail sector.

In addition, consumers not only now have a greater range of choices within types of product, they can also expect a broader range of products to be available under one roof (or retail brand). Once again, this change can be seen most graphically with respect to the large supermarket companies who have relatively recently expanded well beyond their original food-based remit and now offer everything from TVs to clothing (the ultimate one stop shopping experience). A company like Tesco will now have in excess of 76,000 different types of product in their large format stores equating to more than 1.5 million separate items with a value of over £4 million (pers comms). Both Asda Wal-Mart and Sainsbury's hold similar quantities of stock in their large format stores and each of these companies will have literally hundreds of millions of separate items spread throughout their organisations. Keeping control of such vast inventories is not easy, particularly when each store could be selling as many as one million items a week (pers comm.). Indeed, to the uninitiated, current estimates of shrinkage may seem remarkably low given the sheer volume of stock movements undertaken by many of the largest retail companies and the myriad of opportunities for things to go wrong that are present within complex modern retail supply chains.

Expanding supply chains

The ability to offer such large ranges of products throughout the year has only been achieved through major developments in retail supply chains, both in terms of their length and their reach. Whilst there are growing populist movements to try and get major retailers to source their products more locally, the reality of most modern retailing is that products are frequently sourced many thousands of miles away from where the consumer eventually purchases them. A quick scan of the 'fresh' produce in your local supermarket will reveal a geographical lexicon of points of production encapsulating countries across the entire globe. The same can be said of non-food items as well as countries such as China and India have become the new manufacturing power houses of the 21st century producing a significant proportion of all the products now consumed globally. As a consequence, many products have a lengthy and arduous journey before they reach the shelves of retail stores crossing multiple national borders and encountering numerous transport and distribution nodes. Not only has the length of supply chains increased, but they have also deepened for the large retailers. As exemplified by the likes of Tesco and Wal-Mart, the number of stores these companies now operate has grown considerably generating a complex web of retail operations not only spanning countries but also stretching across continents. Developing a supply chain that can make as many as 70,000 different products (many of which will be manufactured on the other side of the globe and some will be highly date sensitive) constantly available in between 4,000 and 8,000 geographically dispersed locations is an extraordinary feat of modern retailing and once again under lines the complexity inherit in such businesses.

Store location and retail format – From corner shop to dot.com

But it is not only the number of stores that many large retailers now operate, it is also the increase in the different types of format and location that further add to the complexity of modern retailing. In a country like the UK, where large retail developments are relatively strictly controlled and opportunities for future growth are being increasingly curtailed by revised planning regulations and resident protests, the large supermarket retailers in particular have sought to grow through acquisition. For instance, Tesco in 2002 bought the T&S chain of convenience stores enabling them to 'open' 450 of their new Express stores without any of the planning wrangles they would have inevitably faced if they had tried to develop so many new sites (Blythman, 2004). Currently they now have over 800 Express stores with a further 500 OneStop shops focused on the convenience part of the retail market (Tesco PLC, 2009). Like many of its competitors, Tesco have driven growth through broadening the areas in which they operate, with the convenience market being a good example. But this has also led to further complexity as most of these sites are situated in busy town and city centres with limited space and delivery access. But expansion has not only taken place physically, many retailers have now moved into 'cyberspace' offering customers the opportunity to shop online through dedicated websites. In 2009, this market is estimated to be worth $90 billion (Planet Retail, 2009). For food retailers the growth of the Internet has also led to them offering home delivery services – personalised shopping delivered to the door of the consumer on a regular basis. The consumer simply selects the products they want and pays for them online, a member of staff then selects the stock from the store and this is then delivered at an agreed time. Such a breadth of store formats creates many challenges, not least varying degrees of risk associated with different locations and types of store, but also the inability to have a one size fits all approach to managing shrinkage.

Complexity and shrinkage

This less than exhaustive review of some of the main changes in modern retailing has been done to show the range and depth of the complexity in modern retailing – it is a phenomenally multi-faceted environment that creates a plethora of challenges to managing shrinkage. In theory the concept of retailing is relatively straightforward – getting the right products at the right time and price to the consumer. But given the scale outlined above, this is increasingly a less than simple task and is riddled with opportunities for things to go wrong. Products can be delivered to the wrong place; they can be delivered at the wrong time leading to products that are highly date sensitive to be written off; they can be priced incorrectly; they can get damaged as they move through multiple supply chain nodes; and they can be prone to theft by the staff employed to manage the process. Indeed, the possible types of errors are so numerous that it would take pages to list them all. As we will detail later in this book all of these factors can be viewed as potential operational failures that in turn can lead to shrinkage. Not only appreciating, but also getting to grips with the plethora of opportunities presented by the complexity of modern retailing is an important part of *New Loss Prevention*.

Specialisation and competition

As retail organisations become bigger, they inevitably lead to the compartmentalisation of functions within the business – buying, marketing, distribution, store operations, audit and so on all become necessary as the complexity of the business increases. Indeed, large retailers now employ small armies of people who operate behind the 'scenes' ensuring that the goods arrive at the store at the right time, at the right price and in the right condition (Kent & Omar, 2003). This has been described as the bureaucratisation of retailing as more and more specialised functions are developed to enable the business to meet the challenges of increased competition and deliver profitability (Dawson *et al.*, 2008b). However, this has also led to problems in terms of managing shrinkage. In the early days of retailing a single store manager would more than likely be responsible for most of the functions of the business (deciding which stock to purchase, when to order it, how it would be delivered and received, how many staff to employ and so on) and be aware of any adverse consequences of decisions made (such as over ordering). In today's retail goliaths, most administrative and managerial decision-making is now highly segregated by function and each of them will have their own priorities, motivations and reward systems. This can lead to decisions being made for perfectly valid departmental reasons but which can have unintended and negative consequences for the management of shrinkage. For example, and something we will discuss further in Chapter 7, store operations may decide to change the level of staffing within particular stores, or the audit function may reduce the level of checking undertaken by till supervisors – both decisions taken because it will save the business money. However, this could lead to increased levels of shrinkage as the remaining store staff may no longer be able to provide the necessary level of customer vigilance to minimise shoplifting, or till operators will be provided with increased opportunities for stealing from the till because they think they are less likely to get caught. Therefore, the growth of discrete specialist functions within retail organisations can lead to higher levels of insulation between decisions taken in one part of the business and their impact on other functions. In order to deal with this problem some companies use 'balanced scorecards' designed to communicate and link business strategies developed across organisations as well as facilitate future learning on how to meet future strategic targets (Kaplin & Norton, 1996). The issue of how loss prevention departments can work to embed shrinkage within the rest of the business will be discussed further in Chapter 9.

Alongside the growth of specialisation, retailing has also become increasingly competitive (certainly amongst the larger retailers) as companies fight not only for the same consumers but also often for the same products to sell and the best sites to sell from (Dawson *et al.*, 2008b). This is especially the case in the food retailing sector where companies can sometimes be operating on profit margins of between just 1 and 3 per cent (Hughes, 1996). The growth of Internet-based companies has also seen many 'traditional' retailers having to operate in ever more challenging commercial environments and at the time of writing, this is being further compounded by a severe global economic downturn which is seeing all forms of retailing having their profit margins put under considerable pressure. The consequence of growing competitiveness is that many retail companies are increasingly looking to internal efficiencies to sustain growth. As with the growth in specialisation, this pressure can also have an impact upon the management of shrinkage. Companies looking to save costs will seek to minimise investment in those functions seen to be marginal to delivering core business functionality. As we will discuss in Chapter 6 loss prevention has often been viewed in this light leading them to be seen as something which is not integrally associated with profit production, and indeed sometimes viewed rather disingenuously by other retail functions as 'profit prevention'!

Technologies and retailing

Much of the complexity detailed above would not be possible without associated developments in technology and many of the largest global retailers have been some of the biggest investors in IT systems over the past 30 years. Most companies now have a Retail Information System (RIS) which can be viewed as the spine of the business – the operational backbone which enables them to locate, gather, process and utilise retail information (Kent & Omar, 2003). Increasingly, data is viewed as a key strategic asset of the business enabling retail businesses to sustain and improve competitive position, increase sales income, reduce retail costs, and improve operational flexibility (Gilbert, 1999). It is used to manage stock, staff and space, and to make complex supply chains more responsive. There are few parts of modern retailing that are not highly dependent upon IT: financial control, credit card verification, stock management, distribution, staff productivity and of course recent developments in e-commerce.

Where it has played a significant role has been in developments in Electronic Point of Sales (EPoS) – the collection of sales data at the till enabling businesses to more accurately control their inventories and automate their stock ordering processes. This information can then be used not only by the retailer but can also be passed on to their suppliers to enable them to more accurately forecast demand and manage the supply chain more effectively. The use of EPoS has also improved the shopper experience as queuing times have been reduced as till operators are able to process transactions more quickly. More recently developments in Self Scan technologies have sought to further respond to this problem. Essentially two types of this technology are currently in use: one which provides the shopper with a hand held product scanner which they use as they put goods in their shopping trolley (they then present the scanner to a member of staff who then downloads the data and arranges payment); and the other which requires the consumer to scan the goods themselves at the end of their shopping trip, put the products into bags and arrange payment themselves.

Technologies relating specifically to managing shrinkage have also developed markedly in the last 30 years spawning a major industry in itself. Some of the most obvious examples include: developments in Electronic Article Surveillance (EAS) which is a system designed to make the theft of items more difficult; Closed Circuit Television (CCTV), to, amongst other things, enable remote monitoring of retail spaces; and data mining technologies, which are focused on analysing EPoS data to look for incidents of staff theft or error.

Technologies and shrinkage

In many respects developments in retail technology can be viewed as a double-edged sword when it comes to managing shrinkage. On the one hand, developments in EPoS data have begun to provide greater levels of transparency within the retail businesses enabling the root causes of shrinkage to be more fully understood. This is certainly the case where item level data can be generated by the RIS. As we will discuss in more detail later in this book, without accurate and detailed data on loss any shrinkage 'solutions' are likely to be misconceived and prone to failure when they are premised principally upon guesswork and intuition. In addition, information collected at the check out can also offer a valuable window on possible incidents of staff dishonesty, including theft and collusion (Beck, 2008).

On the other hand, retail technologies can also cause shrinkage problems. For instance, if a member of staff incorrectly sets up a new product on the RIS, such as not entering the correct price or quantity, then shrinkage can be 'hard wired' into the business – losses will occur with few if any staff noticing. Similarly, incorrect electronic adjustments to store inventories can also lead to shrinkage. For instance, a member of staff may be manually updating an inventory because they have wrongly assumed that there is insufficient stock in the store (when in fact the stock is located elsewhere in the store). This will then trigger the automated ordering system to send more stock, which could lead to overstocking and the need to write-off stock (where it is perishable) or increase the likelihood of it being damaged or stolen by staff.

Developments in self scan technology have also raised concerns about the potential impact new forms of retail technology can have on shrinkage. Currently there is little consensus on what the effect is and certainly more research is required in this area. For some, self scan is nothing more than a licence for customers to steal – taking the concept of self selection to its natural conclusion enabling people to not only choose the goods they want but also which they want to pay for. Others suggest that customers are likely to be more vigilant than store staff in scanning products correctly and hence losses will be the same or possibly less.

In terms of technology relating to shrinkage itself, current research is very mixed on its performance mainly due to inadequacies in the way in which most studies measuring their effectiveness have been carried out in the past. There is certainly a case to be made that to date many loss prevention practitioners have been overly reliant on them – using them as a technological 'crutch' targeted more at the symptoms rather than the root causes of shrinkage (Beck, 2007b). Certainly much more research needs to be done in this area and the issue of security technologies will be returned to throughout the remaining chapters in this book. As with self selection, the use of technologies is now a fundamental part of virtually all retail operations and indeed the degree of complexity outlined above would simply not be possible without it. However, it also brings major challenges and yet further opportunities for a range of shrinkage events to occur.

Going global – Shrinkage across frontiers

Whilst not a new concept, the internationalisation of retailing has accelerated at a pace in the last two decades and has been a significant feature of the development of the retail sector from the late 20th century

(Dawson, 1994; Howard, 2000; Dawson *et al.*, 2008c). The reasons why companies decide to operate in countries outside their home territory vary although many companies have been forced to 'strategically reassess their accumulation strategies in order to counteract the declining opportunities within their domestic markets and to consider international diversification' (Shackleton, 1996: 144). Indeed, international expansion now plays a key role in the corporate strategy of many of the large retailers operating around the globe and for some it is no longer an option, but a necessity – those that do not face the risk of marginalisation within their traditional territory (Akehurst & Alexander, 1995; Simpson & Thorpe, 1995). In the past 25 years the number of the top 100 retail companies operating in ten or more countries has increased from five to 34 – 'operating internationally for the major retailers has become by early in the 21st century, the standard situation and is now not so much a key to success as a key non-failure factor for large retailers' (Dawson *et al.*, 2008c: 343).

In Europe the opening up of central and eastern Europe in the early to mid 1990s saw a number of the large western European retailers moving into this market, including Carrefour, Delhaize and Tesco, while US retailers have increasingly sought to establish their operations in Latin America, Europe and the Far East, such as Wal-Mart, Best Buy and Target. While for the most part, such international forays have been successful, some have proved more challenging (such as Wal-Mart in Germany and Ahold in Latin America (Wrigely & Currah, 2003)). In terms of managing shrinkage, operating beyond the home territory of the retailer brings with it a wide range of issues that need to be carefully considered and managed. What many companies have found is the need for the adaption of management practices and processes in response to the cultural character of the host country and it is perhaps worth reflecting on some of these issues and how they relate to managing shrinkage.

At the most obvious level this can be reflected in differences in language and the impact this can have on the way in which the incoming retail company communicates with its customers and staff. But perhaps as important is the broader social, economic and political context within which the retailer will be operating and how this may affect attitudes towards responding to issues of shrinkage. For instance, the host population may be used to a significantly different retailing environment than that being proposed by the incoming retailer. Certainly within many of the countries in central and eastern Europe prior to the collapse of the Soviet Union, retailing was seriously underdeveloped with little choice and availability, and using retailing practices resembling those found in the 1930s and 1940s in Western Europe and the US (little self selection and high levels of staffing). The introduction of 'modern' methods of retailing such as large product ranges, open sale, self selection and reduced staffing levels by international retailers can lead to higher levels of shrinkage in such circumstances. Customers and staff may need to be 'educated' in the way in which this 'new' way of retailing works. Moreover, customers and staff may be used to a particular level of security – in Eastern Europe the employment of numerous (often armed) security guards in retail stores is very common and new retailers not adopting this approach may be at risk of being seen as an 'easy touch' by would-be thieves (both internal and external). In contrast, some types of security may not be viewed as culturally acceptable such as the use of CCTV in certain countries.

Importing company processes and procedures may also prove challenging, particularly when expansion is being undertaken through the acquisition of an existing retailer. Previous operating routines and modes of working may be very difficult to change in the short term and the mis-match between differing ways of doing work could lead to problems of shrinkage (Kiesi, 2008).

In addition, prevailing attitudes to managing shrinkage may be very different from that found in the host country. Managers and their staff may not perceive this to be their responsibility (it is something that security staff deal with) or their understanding of what constitutes shrinkage may be significantly different. For instance, they may adopt a traditional perspective which sees the problem as principally that of external theft rather than appreciating the broader range of possible causes of the problem. Recognising the culturally context of a country and how this may affect levels of shrinkage and the adoption of loss prevention strategies is an important facet of international expansion.

The prevailing legal framework may also affect how a business is able to respond to issues of shrinkage. Laws relating to the detention and prosecution of offenders may vary considerably between different countries. More broadly, governmental regulation of retailing may also present challenges such as those relating to health and safety, working practices and employee-employer relations.

Finally, securing new supply chains in new territories can present major challenges, particularly in terms of negotiating cross border arrangements with governmental officials and ensuring that local logistics providers meet the minimum standards required in terms of product protection (Kiesi, 2008).

International retailing and shrinkage

The opportunities for increased profits through international expansion are clear and have certainly become a key strategic approach for many of the largest retailers operating today. But developing operations in other countries is not easy and can present those organisations undertaking this type of expansion with a series of shrinkage challenges, some of which have been outlined above. What seems clear is that those tasked with managing shrinkage in new territories need to develop a keen understanding of the social, cultural and political context within which they intend to operate and to recognise that simply parachuting in processes, practices and policies from the host country is less than straightforward. In addition, when a company is moving into new territories, its primary focus is often going to be on how to establish market presence and grow sales, which can lead to shrinkage management being sidelined within the business, adding yet further to the challenges of controlling loss in new international locations.

21ˢᵗ century retailing and shrinkage

In this chapter we have attempted to offer a broad overview of the retail context within which shrinkage needs to be viewed. In the last 30 years retailing has gone through some considerable changes. Its scale is breathtaking with some of the larger retail companies having total sales greater than the GDP of many countries. They are increasingly operating in thousands of outlets across numerous countries, which are frequently stocked with tens of thousands of different products that may have been on long and complex journeys before they eventually reached the shelf. In order to achieve this, hundreds of thousands of people are employed and their customer base is increasingly calculated in the tens of millions. Moreover, retailers are now wholly dependent upon increasingly complex retail operations held together by a swathe of technologies. For those that get it right the rewards can be significant but competition for many parts of the retail sector is becoming ever fiercer and profit margins increasingly thinner.

Within this context, managing shrinkage has become even more important, but it has also become much more challenging. It is more important because as we will discuss later, losses incurred through shrinkage impact directly on bottom line profitability and any small changes in its rate can result in dramatic changes to company profits, particularly where profit margins are at best slim. But is it much more challenging principally because of the complexity inherent in modern retailing and the opportunities that this presents for shrinkage to occur. Maintaining control in the large retail leviathans that are increasingly dominating the consumer landscape is certainly not easy and requires loss prevention practitioners to develop a range of skills that their fore-fathers would not have envisaged. Indeed, as Sam Walton himself noted, once you move beyond 100 stores, maintaining control becomes increasingly difficult (Walton & Huey, 1993). But there is an ongoing tension between maintaining sufficient control (or at least being perceived to have control) over the myriad of activities that make up modern retailing and reducing costs to improve profitability. While the former is not always a consequence of the latter, there is a danger that this relationship is not always fully appreciated or understood throughout retail organisations, and the outcome therefore can be short term gains followed by longer term shrinkage losses. One of the key components therefore, of *New Loss Prevention* is recognising the wider landscape within which loss takes place and how a more effective response requires a broader and more deep-seated organisational commitment to addressing the problem.

What it also recognises is the need for a detailed understanding of the plethora of ways in which shrinkage can be caused, in particular those due to operational failures. The starting point for doing this is to first understand what we mean by the term 'shrinkage' and it is to this subject that we turn to next.

3
Defining Shrinkage

The purpose of this chapter is to reflect upon what we understand the term 'shrinkage' to mean and how it is being used and measured by the retail sector. This may seem like a rather obvious set of questions but as we outline below, currently there is little consensus and interpretations vary widely between different parts of the retail industry and between different countries about what the term shrinkage means. This has made benchmarking highly problematic, and as we will discuss in the next chapter, seriously undermines the efficacy of the various surveys that are regularly undertaken to try and ascertain the scale and extent of the problem. This chapter will look at the ways in which shrinkage has been defined looking particularly at what is generally included or excluded and how it is measured. We will then consider the various typologies used to describe shrinkage and go on to suggest that a more meaningful way of considering the problem is to categorise it in terms of its maliciousness (those types of shrinkage which are a consequence of malicious activity compared with those which are due to non-malicious actions), particularly when considering ways of reducing its impact on retail companies. The chapter will then go to reflect upon the various ways in which shrinkage is valued and presented both internally and externally, before concluding with some suggestions on how a more standardised interpretation of the term might be developed.

What is shrinkage?

Consensus is hard to find on what shrinkage means and what should be included and excluded when this word is used within a retail context. The term 'shrinkage' itself seems to have a long tradition within retailing with the term being used as early as the turn of the 20th century to describe inaccuracies in inventory (Abelson, 1989), although the origin of the term seems unclear. Others refer to 'shortages' (Curtis, 1960) 'inventory shrink', 'inventory shortage' (Sennewald & Christman, 2008), 'retail inventory loss' (Hayes, 2007), or simply 'loss' (Shapland, 1995) rather than 'shrinkage' although they all seem to be essentially trying to describe the same thing. Definitions vary, for instance Sennewald and Christman describe it as 'the difference between book inventory (what the records reflect we have) and actual physical inventory as determined by the process of taking one's inventory of goods on hand (what we count and know we actually have)' (xxiv). Purpora defines it more specifically as 'the amount of merchandise that disappears due to internal theft, shoplifting, damage, mis-weighing or mis-measuring and paperwork errors' (1993: 103). Shapland focuses more on the value of goods and considers it to be 'the disparity between the financial value of stock acquired and sold and the financial value of stock left on the shelves' (1995: 273). Other texts on retail loss prevention simply ignore the issue altogether and offer no definition whatsoever (for instance see Jones, 1997; Hayes, 2007). However, the three examples above give an indication of the varying interpretations and levels of specificity that exist within the world of loss prevention when it comes to deciding what shrinkage means. Within this book we intend to use the following definition: *intended sales income that was not and cannot be realised* (Chapman & Templar, 2006a). We feel that this relatively straightforward description neatly summarises the broad parameters of the shrinkage problem faced by retailers. However, agreeing what should be included and excluded within this, what the various component parts should be called and how it should be measured and valued is certainly much more problematic.

The four 'buckets' of shrinkage

When considering why sales income might not be realised, a review of the existing literature on shrinkage suggests that most typologies are based upon four broad categories of loss, although the words used vary slightly. A good starting point is the terms used by the ECR Europe Shrinkage Group which described them as: External Theft; Internal Theft; Process Failure; and Inter-company Fraud (Beck *et al.*, 2003). These categories are similar to those used by a number of other authors with only slight variation in the terms used. For instance, Guthrie (2003) refers to Administrative Error rather than Process Failure and Theft by Suppliers rather than Inter-company Fraud. Hollinger and Langton (2004) and Oliphant and Oliphant (2001) also prefer to use the term Administrative Error and refer to Vendor Fraud rather than Inter-company Fraud. Hayes in his book entitled *Retail Security and Loss Prevention* uses a slightly different but relatively similar typology for three of the four types (Employee Deviance, Shoplifting and Vendor Theft and Error) but he does not refer at all to Administrative Error/Process Failure (2007). Bamfield in his series of global surveys on retail theft refers to losses broken down by those caused by 'supplier-vendors', 'internal error', 'customer thieves', and 'employees' (Bamfield, 2008), although he sometimes refers to employee theft as theft and fraud by employees, and losses from supplier-vendors as 'supply chain fraud'.

Overall, these differences are relatively minor and these four categories of shrinkage seem to be widely accepted in the industry. Part of the 'success' of this typology undoubtedly comes from its applicability and simplicity (the four elements are often referred to as the 'four buckets' of shrinkage) – it has proved to be a typology that is both easy to explain and understand and continues to be used across most surveys carried out on shrinkage. However, there is little published literature on what constitutes each of these elements and how they should be defined. The ECR Europe Shrinkage Group offered a broad overview of what it thought these terms mean when it conducted a shrinkage survey in 2004: **Internal Theft** – the unauthorised taking of goods by staff employed by the company; **External Theft** – the unauthorised taking of goods by customers or other non-company employees; **Inter-company Fraud** – losses due to suppliers or their agents deliberately delivering less goods than retailers are eventually charged for by them, or retailers deliberately returning fewer goods to manufacturers/suppliers than agreed/specified; and **Process Failures** – losses due to operating procedures within an organisation (Beck, 2004a). For the most part, the first three terms are relatively straightforward to understand and interpret although each raises a number of issues. It is the fourth element, Process Failures, which raises most issues as for the most part this terms provides for the greatest degree of latitude of interpretation. Detailed below is a breakdown of each of these types of loss as they relate to shrinkage and what can generally be considered to be their constituent parts.

But before we move on to consider these four elements of loss, it is worth quickly reflecting upon an area which has generated some confusion and misinterpretation – whether the loss of cash should be included in the definition of shrinkage or whether it should be viewed as a separate area of loss. In our view, cash loss is not part of shrinkage and should be recorded as a separate form of loss. So for instance, if a thief runs into a store and steals money from an unattended cash register, this would be recorded as a cash loss by most retailers. However, it is not always this straightforward. For instance, if a thief returns a stolen item to a retail store and successfully receives a cash refund, the retailer has the stolen item back, but has now lost cash. Would this be viewed as shrinkage or cash loss? Retailers seem to vary on how this would be categorised within their businesses – some would continue to record the loss as shrinkage while others would convert the incident to a cash loss event. For the most part, we consider shrinkage to exclude the direct costs of cash stolen from retailers and see shrinkage as being concerned principally with the loss of products and their associated value.

Internal theft

Internal theft is concerned with the loss of goods carried out by people directly employed within the organisation. So for instance, theft by official visitors to a place of work would not be viewed as internal theft, but what about those employed by others but working permanently within the business, such as contract or agency staff? In addition, employees may not just steal goods; they can also steal 'time', what Hollinger and Clarke (1983) termed production deviance. Moreover, should incidents of collusion, where a member of staff assists a customer to steal, be included in this category?

In our view, the term internal theft should only include incidents where the theft of products takes place by somebody directly employed by the business (including those carried out by staff contracted with another company but who are working almost exclusively for the host business, such as contract guards or cleaners), including incidents where they have colluded with outsiders to enable them to steal. This includes the direct removal of products from the store, eating stock while at work (which is termed grazing) or using other products while at work for personal gratification, such as health and beauty items.

External theft

This is the area that is perhaps most well defined as it dominates the loss prevention agenda. Various terms are used, including shop theft, shoplifting and customer theft, but all refer to the unauthorised taking of goods from a store at any time of the day or night by customers or other non-company employees. This includes: incidents of goods being stolen while the store is open (commonly called shoplifting), such as the direct removal of products from the store, eating stock while in the store (grazing) or the use of products in the store, such as administering pregnancy tests in the retailers' toilets; the fraudulent return of goods (such as removing an item from the shelf and then taking it to the returns desk and demanding a refund) (see above for how some types of refunds can be viewed by some retailers as cash loss and not shrinkage), and burglary (breaking and entering a store whilst it is closed) and stealing stock.

Inter-company fraud

Most definitions of shrinkage prefer to use the term 'vendor fraud' when discussing this issue, putting the responsibility for offending firmly with the supplier to the retailer. This is seen as losses due to suppliers or their agents deliberately delivering less goods than retailers are eventually charged for by them or delivering products of a lower quality than originally agreed. However, losses can also be suffered by the supplier when retailers themselves decide to deliberately return fewer goods to manufacturers/suppliers than agreed/specified. For instance, this type of activity could be used by some store managers to 'mask' shrinkage problems in their stores – using any surplus stock derived from defrauding suppliers to cover their tracks.

Process failures

While the first three forms of shrinkage are relatively straightforward to understand and classify, the fourth area, process failures, or administrative losses as some call it, is much more challenging and open to a wide range of interpretations. In many respects this is clouded by the debate concerning the extent to which known and unknown losses should be included within the term shrinkage and is something we will turn to below. But, the scope for inclusion and exclusion is extremely broad and is probably a major factor in explaining why such wide fluctuations can be found in the various shrinkage surveys undertaken around the globe in the past ten years (see Chapter 4 for more details on this). Few surveys offer much guidance to respondents about what this term actually means. For instance, the Global Retail Theft Barometer questionnaire offers a rather loose interpretation: 'Administrative error/Process errors loss/waste (includes damage, & errors in pricing, transactions, receiving etc)' (Centre for Retail Research, 2008). The annual National Retail Security Survey undertaken by the University of Florida offers even less advice to respondents and simply provides a category of 'administrative and paperwork error' (elsewhere in the survey respondents are told to exclude waste and spoilage from their shrinkage estimate so it must be assumed that these categories are also excluded from this category as well but it is not clear) (University of Florida, 2007).

Perhaps the most inclusive seems to be the definition offered by the ECR Europe shrinkage survey in 2004, which provides respondents with the following advice on what process failures include: 'Losses due to operating procedures within the organisation including products which have become out of date, or have been reduced in price; incorrect pricing; product identification errors; incorrect stock counting; products which have been damaged; scanning errors; and errors in deliveries to the stores (e.g. short deliveries due to errors in picking and dispatch from distribution centres)' (Beck, 2004b).

It is perhaps worthwhile reflecting more on what process failures include as this is a key part of *New Loss Prevention* and an area we feel that has consistently been ignored or sidelined by the loss prevention community in favour of the other types of loss outlined above (in particular external theft). We think there are nine areas that need to be considered when thinking about process failures:

Damage: goods that have been damaged during the process of delivery, storage and merchandising of the goods which means they cannot be sold for any value. Examples would include: a pallet of sugar that is left outside in bad weather; cartons of washing powder crushed by a forklift truck; pears/bananas that have been badly bruised; or bottles of wine that have been smashed.

Wastage/Spoilage: products that have reached their expiry date or gone beyond agreed temperature parameters and are no longer safe to sell to consumers or staff. Examples would include: fresh meat and vegetables, fish, ready-made meals, frozen foods, dairy produce, bread, flowers and so on.

Reductions: the original price of a product is reduced in order that the product is more likely to be sold, such as goods about to reach their sell by date, or have been partially damaged or have been discontinued. Examples would include: ready-made meals close to their expiry date; end of line clothing; and partially damaged boxes of washing powder. This calculation excludes planned reductions over the life of a product, such as intended markdowns on fashion lines and price reductions over time on electronic products. However reductions on these same lines that fall outside the plan would be included.

Pricing: losses caused by errors in the way in which goods are priced and sold in the business. Examples would include: head office setting up a promotion incorrectly but advertising it nationally meaning the stores have to discount locally; goods coded incorrectly on the store inventory system; staff incorrectly pricing product in the back room areas or on the shelf; a mismatch between agreed and actual selling price; or a member of staff entering the wrong price at the till.

Missed Claims: a failure to claim for refunds/rebates on items being returned to a supplier. Examples would include: newspapers and magazines not sent back within an agreed time to the distributor.

In auditing: errors in the audit process, such as stock being incorrectly counted – including annual stock checks and periodic cycle counts. An example would be the incorrect counting of packs of batteries that are located at multiple locations within a store/distribution centre.

At the checkout: errors occurring at the point of sale that lead to a positive or negative discrepancy in the store book stock. Examples would include: a till operator entering the wrong code for a product; entering a single code for multiple varieties of a product such as tinned pet food; not scanning free products as part of a promotion such as buy one get one free offers; a till operator forgetting to scan goods such as items at the bottom of a trolley or those removed from keepers/safer cases; or a till operator using a 'dump' code to sell items that are not easily scanned/identified.

Product movement: errors generated by the movement of goods within the business. Key areas of vulnerability would include mistakes made in the receiving of goods, the transfer of goods and returns/refunds. Examples would include: shortages in deliveries to a store directly from a manufacturer or a distribution centre; transfers to others stores incorrectly recorded; products for use within the store not recorded properly; goods returned to the store by the consumer that are not entered back onto the system, or cannot be returned to the supplier.

Data errors: errors in the recording of stock on company systems. Examples would include: retail buyers/suppliers incorrectly inputting item set up details that lead to stores receiving less items than identified on the system; items that are not correctly associated with the book stock database, such as promotional items not linked with items in the main assortment; and products registered on the store inventory that have not been delivered.

As can be seen, the potential scope of process failures is considerable and yet we feel it is an area that is largely ignored principally because it has not been well defined within the industry. It is often sidelined as not something that loss prevention should be concerned with because it can often be categorised as 'known' shrinkage, and it is to this issue that we next turn.

Known and unknown shrinkage

Deciding whether estimates of shrinkage should include 'known' and 'unknown' losses (Beck *et al.*, 2003) or as Grasso (2003) defined them: 'retail crime losses' (known) and 'unexplained stock losses (unknown) is a contentious area within the loss prevention industry. Known losses are those that can be readily identified, recorded and processed by the business, for example, incidents of shop thieves who have been caught red handed and the goods they attempted to steal recovered but could not be subsequently sold (if they have been damaged for instance). The costs of such incidents can then be recorded as shrinkage due to external theft. More common examples of known shrinkage are when products get damaged in the supply chain (and either they are sold at a reduced price or cannot be sold at all), or when food items go beyond their sell by date (these too can be marked down in price or have to be disposed of without any sale taking place). Retail organisations often have elaborate systems in place to record such incidents as they can account for a significant amount of a company's turnover. However, such processes can also be a source of unknown losses if staff forget to follow the systems in place or incorrectly record items of loss. They can also be potentially used by dishonest staff to mask their own offending.

Unknown losses, as the name implies relates to those losses where the cause is not known. These losses are mainly identified when organisations undertake regular stock audits and realise that there are differences between what the book stock suggests should be in a store and what an actual physical count of the stock identifies. The difference between the two numbers is defined as unknown shrinkage. For example, if a store's book stock states that there are 20 packets of baby formula in the store but the physical count only reveals 15, then the difference (five units) will be recorded as unknown shrinkage. The difficulty then arises in determining the cause of the missing five units, i.e. were they stolen? (by a member of staff or a customer), were they deliberately never delivered to the company in the first place? (inter-company fraud by a supplier), were they sent to the wrong store or simply never left the retailer's distribution centre, or were the items not scanned correctly at the checkout and allocated to a 'dump code' because the bar code could not be scanned? (process failure). As we will see below, attempts are frequently made to try and assign unknown losses to particular causes and numerous surveys have been completed trying to do this (see for example the University of Florida annual security surveys; Beck, 2004a; Bamfield, 2008). What the results from these surveys tend to do is offer observers a snap shot of how retailers are currently *thinking* about and *prioritising* their shrinkage problems rather than giving a true *measure* of the causes of unknown shrinkage. Inevitably, these results are for the most part based more upon gut instinct and prejudice rather than hard evidence and as such they need to be treated with caution (see Chapter 4 for more details about the way in which the various surveys collect data on shrinkage).

Few surveys have been completed that have attempted to gauge the number of retailers that include or exclude known losses from their shrinkage calculation although Beck (2004a) completed a survey of European retailers operating in the Fast Moving Consumer Goods (FMCG) sector in 2004 which asked respondents what they included in their shrinkage calculation. This study found that 90 per cent of retailers claimed they included both known and unknown losses in their overall shrinkage calculation, although there was considerable variance in what they considered to be known loss (for instance some retailers excluded product mark downs and stock going out of date as known shrinkage while other included them) (Chapman & Templar, 2006b). Once again this goes to the heart of the problem of measuring shrinkage where different retailers may be using the same terminology – in this instance known and unknown loss – but their interpretation of these terms differ markedly, making any comparisons or benchmarking exercises highly problematic.

Some attempts are being made to try and standardise these terms, such as the Global Commerce Initiative (GCI) Global Scorecard (Global Commerce Initiative, n.d.) but agreement is proving difficult and as yet there is no industry standard for measuring shrinkage (Yake, n.d.). The same ECR survey carried out by Beck also found that European FMCG retailers estimated that 51 per cent of their losses were unknown – the majority of shrinkage could not be categorised, with the causes remaining unknown to the respondents (Beck, 2004a). It may not be the case that this figure is representative of the retail sector globally, but even if it is close to the truth then the regular annual shrinkage surveys that are published potentially have an enormous error rate when it comes to deciding what the causes of shrinkage are – respondents are, for the most, likely to be in the dark about what causes the majority of their losses.

In our view, shrinkage should include both known and unknown loss. As we will document later in this book, many of the losses which are traditionally viewed as process failure-related known shrinkage tend to be sidelined by loss prevention practitioners, often viewed as something not core to their activities. Yet, any failure in the recording of process failure losses can have a dramatic impact upon the degree of transparency of the shrinkage problem within the organisation. This in turn may lead to unknown losses being wrongly assumed to be theft when in fact they are due to operational failures in the way in which other forms of shrinkage are recorded by the business. Moreover, many of the solutions to common process failure-related shrinkage problems can be much quicker, cheaper and easier to develop and implement than those focused on the various forms of theft suffered by retailers. Unless loss prevention teams adopt a systemic interpretation of the term shrinkage (which includes all forms of known and unknown loss), and use this to guide their work, they will struggle to identify and respond effectively to the key shrinkage priorities within their businesses.

Malicious and non-malicious shrinkage

While the four areas of loss provide a convenient and user-friendly way of thinking about the problem of shrinkage, we believe that it can also be useful to consider them based upon the maliciousness of the event. Malicious events represent those activities that are carried out to intentionally divest an organisation of goods, services and ultimately profit. Non-malicious events occur within and between organisations that unintentionally cause loss, through poor processes, mistakes, bad design and so on. Like the former, this has a dramatic impact upon the profitability of an organisation.

The importance of understanding the intentionality of a shrinkage occurrence is the impact it has upon the approach adopted to tackle it and the expected longevity of the results of an intervention. Malicious losses are intentional and occur deliberately with a degree of forethought. To a certain extent such losses occur when existing systems have been found to be vulnerable – sometimes by accident, often by 'probing' – and are duly 'defeated' by the offender. For example, the use of electronic alarm systems to prevent thieves may have a short term impact as thieves are initially deterred by the new intervention but as familiarity grows and the systems are 'tested' and defeated, any long term impact on levels of shrinkage may be limited. As such, remedial action to deal with some types of malicious activity will have a 'half life' where their effectiveness deteriorates over time as offenders find new ways to overcome them. Remedial actions can also lead to displacement where offenders target different products, locations, times or methods (Clarke, 1997; Felson & Clarke, 1997).

Unintentional or non-malicious shrinkage is usually less dynamic and more responsive to lasting ameliorative actions. For example, damage caused by loads shifting during transport can be addressed by employing new methods of pallet stacking and methods for restraining loads inside the vehicle. While they may require similar levels of vigilance (for instance to make sure staff are continuing to follow procedures) they are less liable to be anything like as evolutionary in nature as their malicious counterparts.

Understanding the causes of shrinkage in terms of 'maliciousness' also ensures that the in-built bias within the traditional shrinkage typology is less evident – for instance, three of the four categories are concerned with malicious shrinkage (internal theft, external theft and inter-company fraud) and only one covers non-malicious activities (process failure/administrative error). As stated at the start of this book, the key premise of *New Loss Prevention* is to redefine how shrinkage as a business problem is both viewed and responded to by the organisation, recognising that poor processes and lack of process adherence create opportunities for deviant behaviour which in turn creates shrinkage – what we describe as operational failures. We believe that the nature of the typology traditionally used to describe shrinkage has developed a mind set which is drawn to dealing with the causes of malicious shrinkage far more than the causes of non-malicious shrinkage.

Contextualising shrinkage

When reviewing the published literature on how retail organisations manage and contextualise shrinkage the most common way in which it is discussed is in terms of its cost as a percentage of retails sales, so for instance the most recent National Retail Security Survey (NRSS) concludes that shrinkage is costing US retailers 1.44 per cent of retail sales (Hollinger & Adams, 2008). As we will go on to describe, there are different ways in which one can quantify the absolute value of shrinkage, however what is common is that the value of shrinkage is almost always expressed as a percentage of total sales. This is a critical distinction for it frequently determines how organisations prioritise and develop their shrinkage strategies. Broadly speaking, organisations can potentially reduce shrink when measured as a percentage of sales in three ways. They can

Table 3.1   The Relationship Between Sales and Shrinkage

		Loss Prevention Strategies			
	Current Situation	Sell More, Lose More	Sell More, Lose Less	Sell Less, Lose Less	Sell Less, Lose More
Units Sold	100	200	200	90	50
Units Lost	10	15	5	8	11
Loss as Percentage of Sales	10%	8%	3%	9%	22%

lose less and sell less, they can lose less and sell more and finally they can lose more and sell more. Clearly what they most certainly do not want to do is lose more and sell less (see Table 3.1 for an example).

Understanding the broader relationship between shrinkage and sales is important for loss prevention practitioners; to simply target shrinkage without considering its association with sales can generate the wrong outcomes for the business as a whole. For instance, aggressively targeting shrinkage to the point where sales are severely impacted (beyond the original cost of shrinkage) is not something most retail businesses would consider a positive outcome. As one UK loss prevention manager wryly noted, 'it is very easy to solve retail shrinkage; you simply lock all the doors, and sack all the staff; end of problem. Not sure the sales director would be too keen though...' (pers comm.). As we will discuss later, there is a delicate balance to be struck between sales and security and the inter-relationship between the two needs to be keenly managed in order to maximise sales and minimise losses – it is a symbiotic relationship where any change to one can have profound impact on the other. It can also be difficult to manage for those interested in only one part of the relationship (or measured on it) and produce highly counterintuitive outcomes, such as it can sometimes be worthwhile losing more stock, because the approach adopted actually leads to greater sales and hence increased profits – lose more but sell even more. Therefore, how we measure and value shrinkage is vitally important if this is to be fully recognised and it is to this topic that we turn to next.

Putting a value on shrinkage

While recognisable accounting rules and procedures, such as the Statement of Standard Accounting Practice and International Accounting

Standards, exist for defining the value of a product as it moves through a manufacturing process, there is less guidance when it comes to goods that have entered the retail sphere. Three different methods are used by retailers to put a value on the goods that they have lost through shrinkage. The first is to value the lost stock at sales value (the price the retailer would have received had it been sold to a customer). The second option is to value the product at purchase price (the price that the retailer paid for the product from the supplier). The third option is called transfer cost or cost plus, which is the value determined by the purchase price plus an additional amount to cover the cost of handling the product (such as labour costs, storage costs etc) (Chapman & Templar, 2006b).

Each method has strengths and weaknesses associated with them. The first option (sales value) certainly presents the largest value for the lost product but some retailers who purposefully build in discount factors to their product ranges (such as the clothing sector) consider this an unrealistic representation of the cost to the business as initial prices have very high profit margins which are often designed to be reduced to attract customers at sales time. The second option (purchase price) is often favoured by the audit and finance functions within retailers as it offers a prudent measure consistent with the philosophy of valuing goods at the lower of cost or market value, in line with common accounting practice (Upchurch, 2002). Critics, however, argue that it fails to take account of all the on costs that have inevitably been incurred as the product moves through the supply chain. The final option (transfer cost or cost plus) is seen to be the most accurate reflection of the actual cost of lost stock as it not only accounts for the actual original cost of the product but also the additional costs incurred by the business as the product moves through the supply chain, but unfortunately, it is also the most difficult to calculate.

Once again, there is little published evidence on the extent to which different retailers use these various approaches to calculate the cost of shrinkage. The survey by Beck (2004a), however, did ask this question of the FMCG sector in Europe. He found that 52 per cent of respondents stated that they used the retail sales value method, with 39 per cent opting to use the purchase price approach and just 3 per cent used the third option of transfer cost or cost plus (the remaining 6% chose the 'Other' category). The Food Marketing Institute's Supermarket Security and Loss Prevention survey asked a similar question (2007) and found that 42.1 per cent used the retail sales value method, with a further 42.1 per cent using both the retail sales method and purchase price, and 15.8 per cent only using the purchase price method (they did not have a third category of transfer cost or cost plus). The low percentage using only the purchase price was perhaps a reflection of the mix of respondents in the survey as all retailers will book shrinkage in the company's annual accounts at purchase price.

So both these studies suggest that most retailers opt for calculating shrinkage at retail sales value, although a significant proportion choose to calculate shrinkage at purchase price. Our view is that for the majority of the time measuring shrinkage at retail sales value is the most appropriate method to adopt, certainly when communicating internally the scale of the problem – it is relatively simply to calculate, it accurately reflects and compensates for the myriad of consequential costs that are associated with the loss of a product, such as the actual loss of sales, handling and storage costs and product protection costs (such as buying security tags and the additional in-store labour costs to apply them), and it is likely to generate greater interest in shrinkage within the business following the simple truth that bigger numbers attract greater attention!

However, there is a strong argument to suggest that to fully understand the impact of shrinkage on the 'value' of a product, the profit margin needs to be factored into the equation. For instance, where a product has a very high profit margin, then the business can in theory tolerate a higher level of shrinkage than on a product where the profit margin is much smaller and therefore shrinkage is much more impactful. Table 3.2 provides a simple example of how profit margin and shrinkage are intrinsically intertwined.

Table 3.2   Impact of Profit Margin and Shrinkage on Profitability

Factors	Low Margin Item	High Margin Item
Selling Price	$10	$10
Number of Items Sold	100	100
Unit Cost	$9	$1
Total Sales	$1,000	$1,000
Shrinkage Rate (Units Lost)	10	10
Value of Shrinkage (at Cost)	$90	$10
Profit After Costs and Shrinkage	$10	$890
Percentage Profit	1%	89%

In this example, each item retails for $10 and both products have a rate of shrinkage of 10 per cent. However, the difference is that the low margin item costs the retailer $9 to purchase while the high margin item costs only $1. Using the retail sales valuation method, the cost of shrinkage for both items would have been the same – $100. However, using the cost method reveals that in fact a very modest profit is made on the low margin item compared with a very healthy level of profit for the high margin item. Simple logic would suggest that loss prevention resources would be more wisely used on the low margin item than the high margin item.

For every low margin item lost through shrinkage, the retailer has to sell a further nine just to cover that cost, while for every high margin item lost, the retailer has to sell less than one to cover the original purchase cost of the product. Sennewald and Christman (1992) in their text on shoplifting highlighted a similar conundrum where they offer an example showing how a company with a 2 per cent profit margin and annual losses of $1 million would have to sell a further $50 million worth of product to cover the loss.

Considering the margin on a product is a crucial component in not only understanding the impact of shrinkage but also how products should be protected within the retail environment. For instance, in the example above, the retailer clearly needs to be more mindful of the shrinkage relating to the low margin item than the high margin item despite the fact that they both have the same rate of shrinkage. This could lead to different processes and procedures being put in place to protect the low margin item, such as improving the security of the supply chain as it relates to this product or reviewing the type of packaging used or the location of the product within the retail space. Either way, using only the shrinkage figure in this example would not have provided a sufficiently nuanced appreciation of which products required particular attention. While some would argue that a 10 per cent rate of shrinkage is unacceptable on any product, understanding the actual impact of that 10 per cent on the business is an important calculation in deciding how to focus finite loss prevention resources.

What is key is that in isolation, the total loss figure, expressed either as cash value or as a percentage of sales only provides a partial picture of the problem and can lead to actions that may be inappropriate. Gaining an appreciation of what the actual 'cost' of shrinkage is needs to be suitably nuanced in order to take into account the impact sales figures and profit margins may have upon any understanding of the problem. Ideally, retailers want a situation where they can sell more and lose less rather than one of sell less and lose more. The reality in some situations may be one based upon the potentially rather morally ambiguous outcome where retailers lose more, but they sell even more.

Reframing shrinkage

Given the prevailing evidence, it would seem that an uneasy consensus on what shrinkage is would seem to be that it is made up of four elements: internal theft, external theft, process failure/administrative error, and inter-company/vendor fraud, and that it is calculated for the most part at retail sales value and includes both known and unknown losses.

However, we believe that this over simplifies what is a relatively complex and multi-faceted problem, particularly when it comes to understanding the impact of process failures. Indeed, it requires the user to delve much deeper into each 'bucket' before any real notion of what constitutes the causes of these types of shrinkage becomes apparent and also causes enormous difficulties when trying to compare data collected from different shrinkage surveys. There is a need for a shrinkage typology that begins to address much more than these overarching areas.

As mentioned above, the current typology tends to overemphasise the problem of malicious shrinkage and while most survey work suggests that malicious forms of shrinkage do indeed account for a significant proportion of stock loss (see Bamfield, 2008; Beck, 2004a; Hollinger & Adams, 2008), the 'four buckets of loss' classification, by not detailing the myriad of opportunities for loss presented by process failures (non-malicious shrinkage), suggests that malicious shrinkage far and away constitutes the majority of the problem.

An effective shrinkage typology needs to recognise that shrinkage is much more than just the theft of stock by external thieves – it is a resolutely complex and interwoven problem that transcends company and departmental boundaries and requires a much more multi-faceted and coordinated approach to its successful management (Beck & Peacock, 2006). Secondly, a more detailed typology will enable data sets to be created that will allow more accurate and genuine benchmarking across the industry. By adding a greater degree of granularity to the measurement of shrinkage, and offering a more concrete definition of what each component part contains, retailers should begin to be able to compare and contrast their data more reliably. Thirdly, a more robust typology would enable retailers to more readily identify the real causes of shrinkage within their organisations and subsequently develop solutions to respond to them. To date, too much solution selection has been premised upon guesswork and presumption.

Finally, by creating a much more transparent typology of shrinkage, which prioritises the importance of measuring the problem in detail, and highlights the myriad of non-malicious causes of loss, it raises important issues about what the necessary skills and competencies of those tasked to reduce and manage shrinkage within the retail environment need to be. To date, much of the loss prevention world has been dominated by a focus on external theft characterised by a reactive, security-oriented approach (See Chapter 6). What a more detailed typology would show is the many and varied components that make up shrinkage – the vast majority of which may have little or nothing to do with thief catching. This requires loss prevention specialists to fully understand the retail environment and develop solutions that may be much more about effective and robust retail processes and procedures than they are about tagging goods and arresting shoplifters. The next chapter goes on to begin to chart in detail the various causes of shrinkage and what the current research tells us about the scale of the problem.

4
Scale and Extent of the Problem

Getting to grips with the scale and extent of the problem of shrinkage is not an easy task – information is often patchy, scarce and of variable quality. This is further compounded by the fact that the issue tends to be dominated by the crime components of shrinkage, in particular external theft and the use of technologies to counter this particular problem, while other areas such as losses caused by process failures receive relatively little attention. This chapter will focus upon reviewing the existing information on what we know about the problem of shrinkage to date, focusing particularly upon the findings from various shrinkage surveys carried out around the globe and other research studies undertaken in this field.

Scale of the problem

Because of the myriad of definitional issues discussed in the previous chapter, it is not difficult to imagine that creating an accurate picture of the scale and extent of the problem of shrinkage as it affects retailers across the globe is less than easy. Depending upon the sector of retailing surveyed and the definition of shrinkage adopted, figures will and do vary enormously. Detailed in Table 4.1 are some of the most recent surveys (2002–2008) that have been undertaken by academics, representative bodies and private consultancy/research companies seeking to measure the overall cost of shrinkage (expressed as a percentage of retail turnover). It is not clear from the available information the extent to which definitions of shrinkage differ between these different surveys although they all seem to have collected data relating to the 'four buckets of loss' described earlier (internal theft, external theft, process failure/administrative error, and inter-company/vendor fraud). Certainly the

Table 4.1   Ten Recent Surveys on the Cost of Shrinkage as a Percentage of Retail Turnover

Year	Source	Sector	Estimate (%)
2003	National Supermarket Research Group (US)	Supermarket	2.32
2005	ABRAS Supermarket Shrinkage Survey (Brazil)	Supermarket	2.05
2004	ECR Europe Shrinkage Survey (18 European countries)	FMCG	1.84
2003	Retail Council of Canada	All	1.75
2007	Food Marketing Institute (US)	Supermarkets	1.52
2002	ECR Australia	Supermarkets	1.52
2003	New Zealand Survey of Retail Theft and Security	All	1.50
2008	National Retail Security Survey (US)	All	1.44
2008	Global Retail Theft Barometer (36 countries)	All	1.34
2003	Eurohandelinstituts (Germany)	All	1.23
	Overall Average		**1.65**

extent to which known and unknown shrinkage is included is very unclear as is what is included or excluded within the term administrative/ process failure – the NRSS study undertaken by the University of Florida certainly excludes losses caused by wastage and spoilage, while the Global Retail Theft Barometer includes these types of losses (University of Florida, 2007; Centre for Retail Research, 2008).

Considerable caution does need to be exercised when reviewing the data from these surveys, not least because of the difficulty of getting accurate data from a reliable sample of retailers in any given geographic area. The sharing of information relating to shrinkage with external groups is not common and the data is generally viewed as highly sensitive and something to be closely guarded by companies (Shapland, 1995). It is sometimes difficult to understand why this is the case – other major business metrics are regularly shared with shareholders, the stock market and the media, such as profit and loss data via annual reports and press releases. But in terms of rates of shrinkage, this is certainly not the case and it is very rare that a company will openly disclose how and the extent to which they are affected by the problem. This makes the job of the

researcher difficult and the response rate to surveys on shrinkage is notoriously low. For instance, the Global Retail Theft Barometer undertaken in
2007 represents only 16 per cent of retail sales turnover in Europe, 13 per
cent in North America and just 5 per cent in the Asia Pacific region (these
figures are not available for the 2008 survey)(Bamfield 2007). While these
rates are not unusual for such surveys, it does highlight the caution that
needs to be exercised when looking at these data, particularly when
making comparisons between regions and countries and changes over
time. Any changes in the composition of such relatively small samples
can and will have a dramatic impact on the results, for instance just
four responses cover Iceland in the Global Retail Theft Barometer in 2007,
while the most recent National Retail Security Survey relies upon responses from just 134 companies to represent all of the US (a figure which
was as much as three times higher when the survey was first started in the
early 1990s).

As can be seen when looking at the composite data provided in
Table 4.1, the range is considerable with the study undertaken by the
National Supermarket Research Group in the US in 2002 concluding that
their respondents had an average shrink rate of 2.32 per cent – the highest of all the studies under consideration (National Supermarket Research
Group, 2003). The lowest rate was recorded by a study undertaken by a
German organisation representing the retail sector (Eurohandelinstituts)
in 2003 which concluded that the average rate of shrinkage amongst
respondents in Germany was 1.23 per cent (Horst, 2004). If a rather crude
average is taken of all of these studies, then 1.65 per cent is the overall
rate of loss.

Five of the ten surveys were carried out solely on the Supermarket/
Fast Moving Consumer Goods sector: the National Supermarket Research
Group survey undertaken in the US (2003); the Association of Brazilian
Supermarkets (ABRAS) survey in Brazil (2005); the ECR Europe Shrinkage
Survey covering 18 countries in Europe (Beck, 2004a); the Food Marketing
Institute study covering the US (2007) and the study completed by ECR
Australia in 2002. This sector is arguably more prone to non-malicious
shrinkage through the stocking and selling of food items that are liable to
go out of date or be damaged, which may explain why four of the five
have an above average rate of shrinkage. However, it could also be due to
the fact that some of the other surveys, such as the National Retail Security
Survey in the US purposefully exclude wastage and spoilage from their
estimates which will inevitably mean that the overall level of loss is lower.

The most recent and probably most comprehensive (certainly in terms
of the number of countries covered) is the Global Retail Theft Barometer

which concluded that the average rate of loss amongst the retailers taking part in the 36 countries surveyed was 1.34 per cent (Bamfield, 2008), one of the lowest rates recorded by any shrinkage survey over the past six years. Whilst it is the survey with the largest number of participating countries, it is still not strictly 'global' in its reach as it does not cover the most populace country (China), nor the largest country (Russia), and had only one country from Africa (South Africa), and just three from Latin America (Argentina, Brazil and Mexico).

The survey with the longest pedigree is undoubtedly the annual studies undertaken since 1991 by academics at the University of Florida. These 16 sets of data (a survey was not completed in 1999 and the most recent covers 2007) provide a unique time series showing how the rate of shrinkage has purportedly changed in the US for more than a decade and a half (Figure 4.1).

As can be seen, the first survey undertaken in 1991 calculated that shrinkage was 1.79 per cent of retail turnover. Over the next few years, this figure increased to its peak in 1994 at 1.95 per cent. Since then the figure has dropped and stabilised at around about 1.6 per cent although the most recent survey covering 2007 recorded the lowest ever rate at 1.44 per cent. As with any study of this kind, extreme caution needs to be observed when interpreting changes over time as it is extremely unlikely the same retailers have responded in each of the years surveyed. But it does show how, while shrinkage in the US has dropped somewhat from its peak in 1994, it remains a stubborn problem that has changed relatively little since the first study back in the early 1990s (despite how much more we now know about the problem and the plethora of 'solutions' currently available).

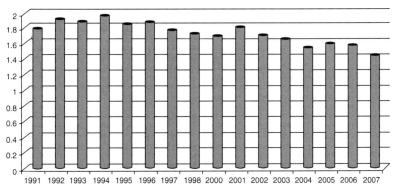

Figure 4.1   Annual National Retail Security Surveys – Overall Rate of Shrinkage

Many of these studies also try and put an overall value on the cost of shrinkage. For instance, the Global Retail Theft Barometer estimates that the total cost of shrinkage in the 36 countries taking part in the survey was $104.5 billion (Bamfield, 2008). The 2004 ECR Europe Shrinkage Survey, which covered FMCG retailers and manufacturers operating in 18 countries, concluded that the overall cost of shrinkage was €24.17 billion (Beck, 2004a). And the most recent National Retail Security Survey undertaken in the US by Hollinger and Adams (2008) surmised that total shrinkage losses amounted in that country to $34.8 billion. However, all of these are partial geographic snapshots of the total cost and none offer an estimate of the possible global cost of retail shrinkage. However, if we use a shrinkage average of 1.65 per cent of retail sales and the most current estimate of global retail sales ($14.07 trillion) offered by Planet Retail (2009), then a total global figure for shrinkage would be $232 billion.

The cost of managing shrinkage

In addition to the cost of actual losses incurred by retailers, there is also the associated cost of responding to the problem. The 2008 Global Theft Retail Barometer estimates that retailers in the 36 countries surveyed spent on average 0.33 per cent of retail sales on shrinkage management, equating to $25.5 billion. There was, however, considerable variation by country and region, with US retailers averaging the highest at 0.44 per cent, and retailers in Asia Pacific the least (0.16%) On average European retailers estimated that they spent 0.34 per cent on responding to shrinkage and retail crime. Hollinger and Adams (2008) produce a slightly higher percentage from their survey of US retailers, suggesting that 0.47 per cent of retail sales are spent on controlling losses and shrinkage. If we look at the last seven years of this survey, then we find that, while there have been some fluctuations in the amount spent over the years, the average is around about 0.5 per cent of retail sales. If we were to use the overall average offered by the Global Retail Theft Barometer (0.33%) and the most recent estimate of global retail sales ($14.07 trillion), then total global annual expenditure on loss prevention could be as much as $46.4 billion (Planet Retail, 2009). If we were to add this to the figure above which surmised that globally shrinkage could be costing nearly $232 billion a year, this would mean that the total cost of global shrinkage could be as much as $278 billion a year – just below the GDP of Denmark and slightly ahead of South Africa – ranking the country of shrinkage 29th in the world (World Bank, 2009)!

The two studies also offer a breakdown on how loss prevention budgets are allocated. The Global Retail Theft Barometer estimates that over one half of all expenditure is on in-house security employees (54.8%), with a further one-third being used to employ third party security staff, such as contract guards and store detectives (32.9%). Most of the remaining spend was taken up by expenditure on technologies and loss prevention equipment (31.6%), estimated by Bamfield to be worth $8 billion a year (2008). Hollinger and Davies draw slightly different conclusions from their recent survey of US retailers, estimating that of the total amount of retail sales spent on loss prevention, 57.1 per cent is used to pay for pay roll (internal loss prevention staff), 24.5 per cent non-capital costs (external security staff) and 18.4 per cent on capital expenses (equipment).

Indirect costs of shrinkage

While a total figure of some $278 billion a year for shrinkage should be eye wateringly large enough to encourage most retailers to recognise this as a major business priority, there are a myriad of indirect costs that could also be attributed to the problem of shrinkage, such as extra product shipment costs to cover those items that have been lost, damaged or delivered to the wrong location, as well as the extra labour costs associated with these activities. It is not our intention to try and identify all of these factors, but instead focus upon just two which we feel offer good examples of the wider impact shrinkage can have on retail operations: the indirect costs associated with defensive merchandising strategies and shelf out of stocks. While much more difficult to quantify than the direct costs of shrinkage itself and the associated expenditure on its management, both these factors can have an impact upon retail profitability.

Defensive merchandising is where retailers attempt to prevent primarily external theft by restricting customer access to goods by placing them behind counters or in locked cabinets. The 2007 Food Marketing Institute report highlighted that approximately one half of respondents suggested that they used defensive merchandising strategies on cigarettes, baby formula and liquor (Food Marketing Institute, 2007). While there are no studies indicating the direct impact on sales, as we described in Chapter 2, the move by retailers away from traditional means of selling products from behind a counter towards self service aisles delivered improved shopper satisfaction, lower costs and increased sales.

The second area is the impact of shrinkage on shelf out of stocks. A 2003 study by Corsten and Gruen estimated the global rate of shelf out of stocks was 8.3 per cent. They went on to conclude that this translates into lost sales for the retail industry equivalent to 3.9 per cent of sales. Using the global estimate for all retail sales of $14.07 trillion (Planet Retail, 2009), this equates to potential losses of $586 billion a year through products not being available on the shelf for customers to purchase.

Like shrinkage, out of stocks have been a stubborn problem faced by retailers, although a number of relatively recent technological advances were anticipated to reduce its impact, including the introduction of the barcode and automatic ordering systems (DeHoratius *et al.*, 2008). The latter in theory allowed retailers to move away from the process of manual ordering of stock by store staff towards a system whereby little store-based interventions were required. As goods are scanned at the checkout, they are then automatically reordered and shipped to the store. However, shrinkage significantly corrupts this process. Goods which are unknowingly removed from the store (stolen either by staff or customers) or become damaged but not recorded as such, lead to the store inventory becoming compromised. The automatic replenishment system does not know that the stock is no longer in the store and so does not reorder. The outcome is that the shelves become empty as a consequence of shrinkage. Corsten and Gruen's study estimated that 34 per cent of out of stocks was due to wrong ordering. If we took a conservative estimate that shrinkage was the underlying root cause of perhaps just one-half of the store ordering problem, then shrinkage would account for 17 per cent of all out of stocks. This would generate an indirect cost of shrinkage to the global retail community of $92 billion a year.

Retail risk and shrinkage

Shrinkage does not impact equally on all types of retailers – some are much more likely to have higher levels of loss than other types of outlets, depending primarily upon the type of products stocked (but also as we will argue later, on the way in which they go about responding to the problem). The surveys by Bamfield (2008) and Hollinger and Adams (2008) offer some recent insights into how the rate of shrinkage varies between different types of retailers, although they do not share the same business classifications. The US study reveals that retailers of autoparts/ accessories, cards/gift/novelties, and crafts and hobbies have significantly higher levels of shrinkage than all other types of retailers surveyed. At the other end of the spectrum, retailers specialising in jewellery/watches, consumer electronics/computers/appliances, and furniture have relatively low levels of loss (Hollinger & Adams, 2008). The Bamfield survey offers a very different picture: vehicle parts/hardware/DIY/building materials, cosmetics/perfume/beauty supply/pharmacy, and apparel/clothing and fashion/accessories are considered to be well above the average rate of shrinkage. Those considered to be well below average are toys and games/ hobby and craft, footwear/shoes/sports goods and sporting goods, liquor, wines, beer/off-licence. It is very difficult to draw any conclusive points from these two surveys, not least because of the different ways in which they classify the businesses responding to their surveys. Certainly auto parts feature in both surveys as suffering high levels of shrinkage, but it is difficult to explain why for instance crafts and hobbies is high in one and low in the other, other than as a consequence of the relatively small sample sizes upon which the data is based.

Goods vulnerable to shrinkage – Hot products

Most of the published literature tends to focus on those products that are perceived to be most vulnerable to malicious shrinkage. For instance, the recent Global Retail Theft Barometer summarises the products that are deemed by respondents to be the most likely to be stolen (Bamfield, 2008) and found that razor blades/shaving products and cosmetics/face creams were at the top of the list, followed by perfumes, alcohol, fresh meat and expensive foodstuffs, infant formula and DVDs and CDs. Further down the list are to be found small electrical items and fashion clothing. The survey notes the relative vulnerability of new product lines and respondents suggested they lost between 2 per cent and 5 per cent of these items to theft.

The survey undertaken by the Food Marketing Institute (2006) offers a slightly different 'top five' stolen items: meat, health and beauty care items, analgesics, baby formula and then razor blades. However, much of this data is problematic as it is simply based upon what respondents *think* are the items most likely to suffer from shrinkage rather than what is actually lost. While these opinions may be based upon personal reflections on data available from within their own organisations, they can also be a result of commonly held views about the items traditionally viewed as prone to shrinkage. However, a study by Beck and Chapman presented data on the vulnerability to shrinkage of one company's range of products, which showed that 8 per cent of SKUs were responsible for 30 per cent of all shrinkage losses, while 20 per cent of products accounted for one half of all losses (Beck & Chapman, 2003).

In his important study which set out to understand what it was that made certain products more likely to be stolen, Clarke developed the deft acronym CRAVED to explain his findings (1999). His suggested that 'hot products' had a number of characteristics that made them much more liable to be stolen; they were: Concealable (easy to hide when being stolen); Removable (easy to remove); Available (easily accessible); Valuable (either personally to the thief or to others who may wish to purchase it); Enjoyable (generally the product is enjoyable to own or consume); and Disposable (a ready market for the stolen item exists). Of these factors, Clarke suggested that the ability to dispose of the stolen goods easily was the critical variable in explaining why some goods are more likely to be stolen than others. While the emphasis upon the ability to dispose of stolen goods adds value in helping to understand why certain products may be more prone to theft by 'professional' shop thieves (the typology of shoplifting will be discussed in detail in the next chapter) whose primary objective is converting stolen goods into cash (often to buy drugs), it is perhaps less important in explaining thefts by more opportunistic thieves who steal for personal consumption. In general terms retailers are more likely to be able to respond to the C, R and A (the extent to which they are easy to steal) then they are the V, E and D (their value or worth). Products can be made less easy to Conceal and Remove and their Availability can be better controlled, but trying to impact upon their Value and Enjoyability goes counter to most product and brand marketing theories, and impacting upon the Disposal of stolen items is probably beyond the remit of most retail companies (although some benefit denial devices such as bottle tags and ink tags as well as unique product marking strategies might be considered as ways to respond to this problem).

Gill *et al.* have gone on to explore in more detail the way in which the value or worth of a product impacts upon its likelihood to be stolen and coined the acronym AT CUT PRICES to try and explain these characteristics (Gill *et al.*, 2004). The 11 factors were considered to be: Affordable (could be purchased with available cash); Transportable (easy to move around); Concealable (easy to hide); Untraceable (have few auditable markings); Tradeable (can be exchanged for other things as well as cash); Profitable and Reputable (well known brand); Imperishable (long life span); Consumable (needs regular replacement); Evaluable (quality can be verified); and Shiftable (good regular market for the items). While this research certainly takes our thinking to a new level of granularity in understanding what it is about certain items that make them more likely to be stolen, perhaps what is most important about this research and Clarke's study is not necessarily the functionality of the acronyms, but more the value of ensuring that retail companies spend time identifying which products are 'hot' within their own organisation. We will return to this topic in Chapters 8 and 9.

Before leaving the subject of hot products, it is important to reflect upon the issue of non-malicious hot products – those items that are highly prone to shrinkage but are not caused by theft. Here the literature is almost non-existent and is a good example of how the malicious component of shrinkage has dominated the loss prevention agenda. A report by Barua, Mani and Whinston (n.d.) provides some basic numbers and estimates that 10 per cent of all perishable goods are rendered unusable before they reach the consumer and that inventory write offs in the global retail industry from spoilage and obsolescence amounts to $120 billion (which is more than the total figure for all shrinkage estimated by Bamfield's Global Retail Theft Barometer). The Food Marketing Institute survey (2007) also offers some insight in to this matter although their sample is relatively small (47 companies representing just 7,260 outlets) and there is little detail about the methodology they adopted. They asked respondents to calculate what percentage of interstore departmental turnover was accounted for by shrinkage. While the overall shrinkage figure for the sample was 1.52 per cent, Bakery Departments had an average rate of 10.39 per cent and Delicatessen Counters averaged 10.36 per cent – the former being 584 per cent above the overall average and the latter 582 per cent. Given that neither loaves of bread nor cocktail sausages regularly appear in the top five stolen items, it can be assumed that these departments are suffering such high losses due to non-theft issues. What is required is a 'CRAVED' or AT CUT PRICES for non-malicious shrinkage hot products. We feel that there are four key factors that help to identify such products: sensitivity to time, expectations of consumers; reprocessing, and vulnerability of packaging (SERV).

Sensitivity to time

This can impact upon products in a range of ways. Firstly there are those products which have a finite date by which they need to be sold – a sell by date which means they become worthless once a certain date has been reached or they need to be reduced in price as this date becomes closer. Examples would be ready-made meals or all fresh foods. Retailers which incorrectly forecast demand for such products can have high levels of shrinkage on such items. This also relates to products such as newspapers and magazines which can quickly become out of date through being superseded by more up to date versions. While most retail organisations will have some form of returns policy with the suppliers of such products which enable them to claim a refund on unsold stock, very often a very specific time window within which they must be returned exists and a failure to have a process in place to meet this deadline can lead to shrinkage.

Secondly, products which are highly seasonable can also be prone to shrinkage, for instance fresh turkeys at Thanksgiving or Christmas time, or ranges of apparel that are dependent upon the time of year, such as bikinis in summer time or coats in winter, or whose attractiveness to consumers is demand limited (for instance particular ranges of fashion apparel or toys). Thirdly, product ranges which are highly dependent upon a particular promotion can also be prone to high levels of shrinkage, for instance event-specific branded items such as those relating to particular major events such as sports (the Olympics, the Super Bowl or the Football World Cup) or celebrity promotions. Once these events have passed, then consumers may be unwilling to purchase such items and the stock will have to be written off or discounted. All of these factors can be heavily influenced by poor stock forecasting and supply chain inefficiencies and can lead to significant levels of loss for retail companies.

Expectations of consumers

The second area relates to products which are deemed unsellable due to the demand that the presentation of the product be as 'perfect' as possible. Any blemishes or any signs of damage on the product will render it worthless to the consumer (Jones, 1997). Examples here include high value spirits such as whiskeys and brandies that are retailed in boxes, some electronic goods such as MP3 players, collectible items such as memorabilia and gift items such as cards. Ensuring that these goods pass through the supply chain in perfect condition is critical if retailers are not to incur shrinkage.

Reprocessing

Within the Supermarket/Hypermarket sector and specialist food outlets, raw materials are often brought in to produce fresh products such as bread and cakes within the store. Similarly, bulk items such as large cuts of meat may be delivered which are then used to meet the needs of individual customers. As with any manufacturing process, waste can be produced – products can be wrongly cooked, badly sliced and so on which will generate shrinkage. Similarly, products which enter retail stores in loose format or for self selection by weight by customers can also be vulnerable to this type of loss. For instance, DIY stores may sell nails by weight, or types of wire by length. Unless this process is carefully monitored and controlled, so that customers and staff are not able to exploit opportunities for mis-weighing or measuring, it can lead to shrinkage.

Vulnerability of packaging or products

Certain products are highly prone to be damaged as they move through the supply chain due to the nature of the product itself or its packaging. Examples would include fresh eggs, fresh fruits and vegetables and cartons or cardboard-based packages of food such as juices, milks and breakfast cereals (referred to as ambient packaging). It is estimated that in the UK alone, 1.6 million tonnes of food is wasted by the retail sector each year, caused in part by produce being damaged in the supply chain (Wrap, 2008). In the US it has been calculated that as much as 35 per cent of losses are suffered in the food chain, with retailing being considered accountable for 5.6 per cent of this amount. Perhaps more alarmingly convenience stores were estimated to waste approximately 26 per cent of all the food produce they received (Jones, 2009).

Hot products – Malicious and non-malicious

While virtually all the published literature on hot products has tended to focus on those items that are most likely to be stolen, the few retail estimates that exist would suggest that the losses from non-malicious hot products is far higher, and yet such items rarely feature in discussions on shrinkage by loss prevention specialists nor the suppliers of 'solutions'. Why is this the case? We would argue that there are at least five reasons. First, loss prevention is still predominately viewed as a security-related function whose job is to catch and deter criminals. External and internal theft is seen to be the main cause of loss despite the fact that nobody really knows what percentage they make up of the overall picture of loss – unknown losses are termed 'unknown' for a reason.

Secondly, the loss prevention function rarely engages with those parts of the business that are responsible and accountable for known losses – they are often justified as the inevitable cost of doing business and not something which requires the attention of the loss prevention department. Thirdly, the huge growth in 'solutions' marketed to 'solve' the external theft problem, particularly by technology providers, ensures that non-malicious shrinkage problems remain out of the spotlight – catching opportunistic shop thieves is seen to be a bigger fish to catch than understanding why there are piles of damaged goods at the back of the store. In addition, the former is much more likely to be 'solved' with yet another high tech fix than the latter (which may simply require a change in store processes and procedures and perhaps better staff management or training). Fourthly there is a link between the availability of certain types of products and known loss (such as ready-made meals and fresh bread) where a retailer would prefer to have too much stock and suffer losses than be out of stock and disappoint the consumer. Pursuing this type of loss too vigorously might be viewed as counter to the broader business ethos of the organisation. Finally, because a significant number of retailers have still not invested in systems that enable them to monitor losses at item level, hot product lists tend to be produced which are premised more on preconceived notions of what products are likely to be vulnerable to shrinkage rather than those which are actually suffering high levels of loss. Hence, razor blades rather than leeks (which one major UK retailer recently identified as its biggest shrinkage item) frequently emerge at the top of the list.

We argue that getting to grips with the hot products in a retail store is a critical way of tackling shrinkage – it enables the loss prevention team to focus on the products most at risk – the vital few rather than the trivial many – which in turn can also lead to a diffusion of benefit as related products and categories can also be impacted by the solutions imposed on the hot products (Carter, *et al.*, 1988; Masuda, 1992). But what is important is that hot product lists are generated from actual data rather than hearsay and guesswork and that shrinkage is viewed as much more than just items which have been stolen. The list must take account of all forms of shrinkage and this in itself may prove to be an eye opener to the loss prevention manager who has traditionally considered malicious shrinkage as their primary area of responsibility. They may well be pleasantly surprised to find that reducing rates of loss on hot products caused by non-malicious shrinkage may well prove to be much easier, quicker and more cost effective than chasing thieves.

Estimating the causes of shrinkage

Numerous surveys have been undertaken trying to gauge the extent to which the four areas of shrinkage are responsible for losses in retail organisations and detailed in Table 4.2 is a summary of this data from nine recent surveys over the past seven years.

As can be seen, there is relatively little consensus amongst the various surveys undertaken on the relative proportion each type of loss makes up of the overall shrinkage figure. Four of the surveys suggest that external theft accounts for the largest proportion off loss, with the study undertaken in New Zealand concluding that the vast majority of shrinkage in that country was due to this factor (65%). However, four of the remaining five studies consider internal theft to be the factor most responsible for losses, with the study undertaken by the National Supermarket Research

Table 4.2   Estimated Causes of Shrinkage from Nine Recent Surveys

Source		External	Internal	Inter-company	Process Failure
			Malicious		**Non-Malicious**
			Per cent		
National Retail Security Survey (US)*	2008	34	44	4	15
Global Retail Theft Barometer	2008	41	36	6	16
Food Marketing Institute (US)	2007	32	39	9	21
ABRAS Supermarket Shrinkage Survey (Brazil)	2005	12	16	8	65
ECR Europe Shrinkage Survey	2004	38	28	7	27
Retail Council of Canada	2003	35	40	7	18
New Zealand Survey of Retail Theft & Security	2003	65	12	3	20
National Supermarket Research Group (US)	2002	20	57	–	–
ECR Australia	2002	35	25	11	29
Average		35	33	8	26

*3% was considered 'unknown' in this survey

Group concluding that the majority of loss (57%) was due to this cause. Only one of the studies surmised that process failure was the dominant factor in accounting for losses – the survey undertaken by ABRAS, the Brazilian Supermarket Association, which concluded that process failures accounted for a startling 65 per cent of all the losses for this part of the Brazilian retail sector. The two studies undertaken by ECR Australia and ECR Europe produced the next highest percentages relating to process failure (29% and 27% respectively), but still no where near the estimate from Brazil. There was little evidence from any of the surveys that inter-company fraud was considered a major explanatory factor, with the highest proportion being offered by the ECR Australia study (11%).

Understanding the significant variance in these studies is not easy, but there are a number of factors which can shed some light on these discrepancies. First, the surveys are undertaken at different times, with the earliest being completed in 2002 and the most recent in 2008.

Secondly, they vary in terms of their geographic coverage, with some focused on one country while others have a much broader range such as the Global Retail Theft Barometer (36 countries). Thirdly, they vary considerably in the types of retailers that are included and excluded. For instance, the ECR (Europe and Australia) surveys are focused exclusively on the Fast Moving Consumer Goods Sector, while the National Retail Security Survey in the US and the Global Retail Theft Barometer cover a much broader range of retail respondents. Fourthly, the definition of shrinkage used in each of the surveys is not the same and as detailed above, this can have a dramatic effect upon what respondents decide to include and exclude in their estimates which in turn will affect how they apportion losses in the business (for instance, if stock going out of date or wastage is not included within process failures then this will be viewed as much less of a problem).

Fifthly and perhaps most importantly, because the majority of losses within retail are potentially unknown (Beck, 2004a) respondents are having to estimate what proportion each of the factors make up of the overall cost of shrinkage. This is often reflected in the wording used in these surveys. For instance, the Global Retail Theft Barometer asks respondents: 'Please *estimate* what percentage of 2007–2008 shrinkage in your stores is most likely to have been caused by: Employee Theft, Customer Theft, Administrative Error and Supplier Fraud' (Centre for Retail Research, 2008) (emphasis added). Similarly the ECR Europe survey asked respondents: '... what percentage would you *estimate* was due to process failures, internal theft, external theft, and inter-company fraud?' (Beck, 2004a) (emphasis added). Respondents are essentially being asked to make an informed guess. Given this, the percentages outlined in Table 4 can only been seen as a measurement of how respondents currently feel about each of the factors they are requested to make estimations about – they are socially constructed and more than likely a distorted picture of the problem based upon personal prejudice (Klemke, 1992). Therefore, using these surveys to make any sense of the extent to which different types of malicious and non-malicious causes are responsible for shrinkage (and in turn deciding what area should be prioritised in terms of loss prevention expenditure) is ultimately a deeply problematic process and liable to a considerable degree of potential error. This is not to say that such surveys have no value whatsoever – far from it – they undoubtedly give us insights to a problem that has traditionally remained difficult to comprehend, but we need to be fully aware of their limitations, especially when they are being used to compare and contrast between different countries and between various years.

Getting to grips with shrinkage

This chapter has set out to shed light on the scale and extent of the problem of shrinkage. This is not easy, not least because of the problems associated with defining the term shrinkage – it has been in use for over a hundred years and yet we still do not have an industry agreed standard as to what it actually means. Across the globe different retailers use it to describe a wide range of different losses. In addition, they vary enormously in the way that they calculate the cost of shrinkage. Any modern retailer trying to benchmark their loss prevention performance based purely upon published evidence is relying upon comparisons that are highly prone to error and more often than not based more upon opinion than fact. For instance, the most recent editions of the NRSS survey undertaken by the University of Florida and Global Retail Theft Barometer produce overall shrinkage estimates for the US of 1.44 per cent and 1.48 per cent respectively. Give that the latter includes losses through wastage and spoilage while the former does not, one would have expected a much greater differential between the two (Hollinger & Adams, 2008; Bamfield, 2008).

What the various surveys undertaken to try and understand the scale and extent of the problem do share in common is their ability to starkly highlight the enormous cost of shrinkage to the retail sector. We estimate that the annual cost of shrinkage globally could be as much as $232 billion, with a further $46.4 billion being spent on responding to the problem. Taken together, shrinkage could be costing retailers (and ultimately consumers) $278 billion a year, a figure which takes no account of the possible additional consequential losses generated by shrinkage-induced factors such as shelf out of stocks and defensive merchandising.

In addition, developing detailed understanding of how these shrinkage costs relate to particular products is an important part of *New Loss Prevention*, enabling companies to focus on the vital few rather than the trivial many. But in order to achieve this, both malicious and non-malicious losses need to be measured and understood together to ensure that the items actually suffering the most loss are properly prioritised and targeted.

In the next chapter we go on to look in detail at each of the types of shrinkage highlighted earlier, focusing first on those defined as malicious shrinkage: external theft, internal theft and inter-company fraud, and then moving on to consider non-malicious shrinkage: process failures.

5
Understanding Shrinkage

This next chapter looks in detail at the four types of loss that are most frequently used to describe shrinkage. These are subdivided into two groups which are those that can be viewed as malicious shrinkage: external theft, internal theft and inter-company fraud, and non-malicious shrinkage: process failures. The retail context within which these types of losses occur is considered together with the scale and extent of the problem, and where possible and appropriate, information on the types of people involved and their motivations.

Malicious shrinkage

External theft – The 'bogeyman' of shrinkage?

Of the various types of malicious shrinkage suffered by retailers, perhaps the one that has received the most attention and focus is external theft or shoplifting as it is often referred to – 'an act of theft from a retailer committed during the hours the store is open to the public by a person who is or appears to be a legitimate customer' (Sennewald & Christman, 1992: 7), or as Kraut rather mischievously put it '… the acquisition of goods at minimum cost' (quoted in Baumer & Rosenbaum, 1984: 57). In many respects it has dominated the loss prevention agenda since the early developments in mass merchandising at the end of the 19th century although accounts of people stealing from merchants has a very long history indeed with records of incidents dating back to Elizabethan England (Cameron, 1964; Abelson, 1989; Klemke, 1992). This section will review what we know to date about the broad contours of external theft (or as one retailer rather drily described it, non-paying store visitors), starting first of all looking at what is known about the scale and extent of the problem.

Scale and cost of the problem

As mentioned earlier in the previous chapter, trying to gauge the extent of the various causes of shrinkage is extremely difficult. The broad ranging shrinkage surveys offer little consensus on the proportion of shrinkage accountable to external theft although a rather imprecise average would suggest about 35 per cent (see Table 4.2 in the previous chapter). A considerable number of academic and practitioner-based studies have been undertaken to try and understand more fully the extent of the problem of external theft (for various reviews see Murphy, 1986; Klemke, 1992; Hayes & Cardone, 2006) although virtually all have come up against the same methodological problems that undermine their validity and make it almost impossible to know the true extent of the problem.

The survey of retailers in the US undertaken by Hollinger and Adams (2008) suggests that the cost of shoplifting amounted to $12 billion, while the Global Retail Theft Barometer estimated that it was costing $43 billion in the 36 countries surveyed. However, both figures are based upon extrapolations from estimates of the scale of the problem made by retailers themselves, which as discussed earlier, raise concerns about the extent to which they represent what is really happening within retailing. In a survey of retailers and manufacturers undertaken by the Home Office in the UK in 2002 it was found that 47 per cent of retailers claimed to have been a victim of at least one incident of shoplifting in the past 12 months, which was a 4 per cent reduction on the total reported in a similar survey undertaken in 1993 (Mirrlees-Black & Ross, 1995; Shury *et al.*, 2005). Official crime statistics on the problem shed little light, not least because of the huge amount of under reporting that takes place by retailers (Hollinger & Davies, 2006; Shury *et al.*, 2005). Between 1997 and 2007 official statistics on shop theft/shoplifting in the UK show a modest 7.6 per cent increase, with the figure declining in the last few years (Home Office, 2009).

More innovative methodologies have been applied to try and gauge the extent of the problem of shoplifting, including 'systematic observational' studies where a random selection of customers entering a retail store are discretely followed and observed to see if they steal anything, and 'systematic counting' studies where each item in a retail store is identified with coloured stickers notifying its type and location, and then audited on a daily basis (Buckle *et al.*, 1992). One of the first of these types of study was undertaken by Astor in 1971. He concluded that 6.6 per cent of customers were liable to steal, although details of the methods employed to ascertain this figure are sketchy. Buckle and Farrington reported in 1984 on a study they completed using the same methodology and they concluded that 1.6 per cent of those followed stole something from the store. Baumer and Rosenbaum (1984) concluded from their study that 3.6 per cent of those followed went on to steal something although they were only certain at the 2.7 per cent level. However, when they factored in 'observer error' they concluded that the most likely figure was 7.8 per cent. More recently, Dabney *et al.* (2004) undertook a year long study of a single drug store in the US where they used CCTV cameras to follow a sample of shoppers as they shopped in the store. They estimated that 8.5 per cent of the customers they decided to electronically follow in the store eventually went on to steal something, although their sampling method was not randomised and therefore this result cannot be generalised to estimate theft rates in the wider population.

A profile of offending

Because of the difficulty in accurately gauging the extent and cost of external theft it is also problematic trying to understand the types of people most likely to steal. One of the biggest debates surrounding this issue is the extent to which shop theft is undertaken by amateur thieves (sometimes referred to as opportunistic thieves) stealing for personal use compared with highly motivated professional thieves whose primary purpose is to sell on the goods that they steal. A number of authors have developed typologies to try and categorise the various types of thieves operating in the retail environment. Table 5.1 details some of these typologies.

One of the earliest studies of shoplifting was undertaken by Cameron (1964) and she used the terms 'Booster' and the 'Snitch' to differentiate between the types of shoplifter she observed. A Booster was a professional

Table 5.1   Various Published Shoplifting Typologies

Shoplifting Typologies			
Cameron	Moore	Farrel and Ferrara	Hayes
Booster	Semi-Professional	First Class	True Professional
Snitch	Amateur	Second Class	Hardcore Professional
	Episodic	Third Class	Casual Professional
	Occasional	Expert	Primary Household Shopper
	Impulse	Pathological	Impulsive Shoplifter
		Impulse	Juvenile Shoplifter
		Youthful	Pathological Shoplifter
		Indigent	

thief who stole items for resale while a Snitch was somebody who stole items for personal use. Moore (1984) went on to expand this bifurcation and suggested there were five main types of thief: semi professional (steals for resale, targets high value items and uses a high degree of technical skill); Amateur (shoplifts on a regular basis for financial gain); Episodic (steals because of psychological problems); Occasional (steals infrequently due to financial difficulties or peer pressure); and Impulse (steals low cost items for personal use with no planning). Farrell and Ferrara developed a similar typology although used First, Second and Third Class to differentiate between the different types of offenders (1985). First Class referred to professional thieves who stole for resale and used highly skilled methods; Second Class also used skilled methods but stole primarily for personal use; and Third Class are amateur thieves who use little skill and steal for personal use. Within the category of Third Class the authors broke this down further to try and differentiate between a range of different types of amateur thieves including impulsive, youthful and pathological.

Finally, and most recently, Hayes provides perhaps one of the most detailed and considered typologies (Hayes & Cardone, 2006). He initially agrees with most of the previous typologies that differentiate at the macro level between Professional (steal for resale) and Amateur (steal for personal use) thieves but he goes on to offer a range of sub categories which offer further detail on this initial dual classification based upon degree of planning, sophistication, skill, success, financial scope and frequency. He considers that there are three types of professional thief: the True Pro who prefers to work in teams to steal for resale and will avoid violence in favour of guile and sophistication; Hardcore Pro who may well be involved in other forms of crime and is not averse to using violence and brazen methods of stealing; and Casual Pro who may use some of the methods of the previous two groups, but is not dependent upon stealing to subsist. Within the category of Amateur, Hayes breaks this down into four categories: Primary Household Shopper (steals occasionally or habitually items they cannot afford as part of their normal household budget such as cosmetics and gifts); Impulsive Shoplifter (deemed to be the largest group of shoplifters and steals due to greed, stress, impatience or embarrassment); Juvenile Shoplifter (young people who steal for a range of reasons including peer pressure, perceived need and thrill seeking); and Pathological Shoplifters (those who have a pathology, are on medication or are kleptomaniacs).

Hayes is correct in concluding that none of these categories are necessarily mutually exclusive and that offenders may move between the different categories, but beyond the distinction between Professional and Amateur most of these typologies have little practical relevance for retail practitioners – it is unlikely that most retailers will be able to either identify particular sub groups or develop prevention strategies to respond to them (some specialist retailers with very specific consumer profiles, such as predominantly young people may be able to do this). Where the more straightforward Professional/Amateur differentiation does offer value is in the design and development of preventative methods to respond to them. Research suggests that Amateur thieves are much more likely to be put off by the overt presence of security devices such as security/sales personnel, CCTV cameras and monitors, EAS tags, Safer Cases and security notices than professional thieves (Butler, 1994; Beck & Willis, 1998; Gill, 1998, 2007; Gill, Bilby & Turbin, 1999; Hayes, 1999; Tonglet, 1998). The latter are much more cynical when evaluating most of these types of preventative device and will rarely be deterred by their presence (perhaps except for vigilant retail and security personnel). The key question is how many shoplifters can be categorised as professional compared with amateur – if the former group are predominant then this could have major implications for retail security policies and practices.

This is a question that has vexed practitioners and researchers for more than 50 years and will continue to do so for the foreseeable future. The difficulty lies in the fact that perhaps as few as 1 per cent of shop thieves ever get caught (West & Farrington, 1977) which makes any estimates based upon offender statistics highly unreliable. Cameron back in the early 1960s suggested that professionals accounted for 10 per cent of all shop thieves and just 6 per cent of those ever apprehended (Cameron, 1964), while studies by Jobin and Serdahely came to similar conclusions (quoted in Baumer & Rosenbaum, 1984). All those studies are more than 30 years old and so may have little relevance to the modern retail environment. They are also premised upon potentially flawed data from apprehended shoplifters (professional thieves may simply never get caught) or studies with limited methodologies. However, the 2008 NRSS survey offers much more up to date information showing that respondents considered the overwhelmingly majority of shoplifting incidents were committed by amateurs (75.7%) despite the apparent growing concern about the threat from Organised Retail Crime in the US.

Indeed, the recent emphasis in the US on Organised Retail Crime (ORC) might suggest that a different offender profile is now becoming more prevalent in that country with estimates from the industry suggesting it may cost as much as $35 billion a year (Hayes & Cardone, 2006). There is, however, no research to date which can validate this number and some commentators now recognise that it is probably a made up number created to try and arouse greater interest in the subject and help the industry's case to get new legislation passed to create a new offence of ORC (Richardson & Palmer, 2009). A simple comparison with the data from the last NRSS study (2008) suggests that this figure seems extraordinarily high. The NRSS study concluded that total losses from shrinkage amounted to $34.8 billion, of which $15 billion was apportioned to external theft (Hollinger & Adams, 2008). Respondents themselves then went on to suggest that only 24 per cent of this external loss figure was likely to be due to ORC (about $3.6 billion or about a tenth of what has been claimed previously). Either the NRSS study is wildly inaccurate, both in terms of the total cost of shrinkage and/or the amount apportioned to external theft, or the case for ORC is being hugely overstated. This is not to say that incidents of ORC do not occur as numerous articles in the US media have highlighted cases, as have loss prevention practitioners, and US politicians seem to be willing to pass new legislation. But it may be another example of the industry eagerly seeking out a new version of the 'bogeyman' to blame for their continuing high rates of loss rather than focusing upon internal problems. What is important is that the loss prevention industry is not seen to be making numbers up to suit their particular agenda – one of the hallmarks of a true profession is the integrity of the evidence base upon which it makes any assertions.

External theft in context

Considerable amounts of research have been undertaken trying to understand more fully the methods, motivations and means of preventing external theft, although few recent studies take us beyond the assumptions made in the 1960s, 70s and 80s. It is a considerable problem faced by retailers, although the extent is still not fully known. It is carried out by a vast array of different types of people with numerous motivations although we still do not know whether it is predominantly the amateur or professional thief who accounts for the majority of losses (it may be that amateur thieves account for the most incidents but professional thieves account for the greatest value stolen, but we simply do not know with any certainty).

What is clear, however, is that it continues to dominate the loss prevention agenda. It is the subject that most practitioners feel happiest talking about and engaging with. It is certainly the subject that solution providers spend the majority of their time and development initiatives upon – constantly searching for the next panacea to sell. We think this has been driven by at least three reasons. First, it is much easier for everyone employed in an organisation, from the innocent to the deviant, to blame the 'outsider' for unaccounted losses. The spectre of hoards of merciless wily thieves robbing retailers of profits is often far more palatable and believable than the prospect that it is the staff that they employ that are taking the goods or that the organisation itself is woefully inefficient and prone to damaging, misplacing or writing off the goods they had intended to sell.

Secondly, prioritising catching the 'bad guys' appeals greatly to the types of people who have traditionally been employed to work in loss prevention departments – former police officers and military personnel – where an emphasis upon detection and measuring performance based upon the number of people arrested is often valued greater than ensuring retail excellence in the way in which goods are moved, managed, measured and monitored throughout the supply chain. Thirdly, developing responses to external theft has spawned an enormous global industry focused particularly upon the development of ever more advanced forms of technological intervention offering the shrink-prone retailer beguiling panaceas to the problems they face. This is a powerful lobby group keen to encourage the prioritisation of external theft and always ready to spend the budget of a loss prevention director on yet another 'solution' waiting to finding a suitable problem.

One of the key messages of *New Loss Prevention* is to recognise that while shop theft is undoubtedly a problem that most retailers face, it is too easy to assume that unknown losses are due mainly to this problem – by their very nature they are unknown and simply blaming them on the 'bogeyman' of shrinkage can mean that the real causes of the problem are ignored and losses simply continue. What we would like to argue is that external theft should be viewed within the broader shrinkage landscape – it undoubtedly should be on the agenda, but it should be seen to share that agenda with the other causes of shrinkage – internal theft, process failures and inter-company fraud. As stated earlier, unknown loss is described as 'unknown' for a reason, and yet there is a strong tendency within the industry to assume that external theft is the biggest culprit.

There needs to be a greater willingness to undertake root cause analysis of why external theft occurs within the retail environment and to more fully understand the role store processes, procedures and routines can play in providing the opportunities for theft – what we term operational failures. As one senior loss prevention executive succinctly put it, 'you cannot apprehend your way out of shrinkage' (Beck, 2007a: 29), while Curtis in his pioneering and highly progressive book entitled *Modern Retail Security* published in 1960, came to a similar conclusion: 'If you only work on detecting thieves, the real causes of your trouble are not located and corrected' (Curtis, 1960: 790). Getting to grips with the opportunity enhancing elements of store systems and processes should be the first step in tackling the problem of external theft – until that happens, not only will the bogeyman keep getting the blame for most shrinkage losses, but people will continue to expand an inordinate amount of time and money trying to catch him/her.

Internal theft – The enemy within?

Scale and cost of the problem

It can be argued that internal theft is the proverbial 500lb Gorilla in the corner of the retail store – most see it, but few like to discuss it and even fewer are willing to take it on. That said, there is a considerable amount of research that has been undertaken trying to get to grips with the nature, scale and extent and means by which it can be controlled and prevented. Back in the early part of the last century Edwin Sutherland's pioneering work brought the subject of 'white collar' crime to the fore (1949) – criminality undertaken by persons of 'social status' as part of their daily work. More recently Clinard and Quinney (1973) offered a more useful categorisation of what white collar meant and suggested two subcategories: occupational and corporate crime. The latter is most relevant to the retail sector and they considered it to be individuals or groups of individuals carrying out criminal acts as part of their legitimate work for personal gain. In contrast, corporate crime was viewed as criminal acts carried out by executive officers/senior officials in the name of benefitting the company. A key difference was that occupational white collar crime victimised the host company whereas corporate crime was seen to benefit the company. Since then, more nuanced definitions of employee theft have been offered and perhaps the most useful for the retail sector is that developed by Hollinger and Clark in 1983. They defined it as 'the unauthorised taking, control, or transfer of money and/or property of the formal work organisation perpetrated by an employee during the course of occupational activity which is related to his or her employment' (1983: 1).

Hollinger and Clark also developed an important distinction between two types of employee theft, namely property deviance and production deviance (1983). Property deviance refers specifically to incidents where staff steal or purposefully damage the assets of their employer, while production deviance relates to incidents were staff essentially steal 'time' such as by working slowly, absenteeism, claiming pay for hours not worked, and so on. Most of the current literature relating to the retail sector focuses on the former although useful studies have been undertaken on the latter (see for instance Ruggiero & Steinberg, 1982; Sieh; 1987; Slora, 1989; Marcus & Schuler, 2004). Within this book we will be focusing only upon property deviance although we do recognise that production deviance can also generate significant losses for the retail sector.

As with external theft, trying to get to grips with the scale and extent of the problem is not easy. There is a wide range of literature which points to it being a significant problem to the entire business community, and one which has been prevalent for a considerable amount of time. In the US it has been estimated that employee theft accounts for between 10–15 per cent of the cost of consumer goods (Hollinger & Clarke, 1983) and that it plays a major part in the bankruptcies of between 30 and 50 per cent of all companies going into insolvency (Greenberg, 1997 quoted in Hollinger & Davis, 2006). More broadly Hollinger and Davis (2006) quote the 2004 *Report to the Nation* which estimates that a 'typical organisation loses 6 per cent of its annual revenue to occupational fraud which translates into $660 billion in annual fraud losses' (2006: 206). It is also an issue which has been of considerable concern to retailers for many years. Curtis writing over 36 years ago notes: 'internal theft in retail operations has reached a crisis stage', going on to opine that it was a bigger problem than 'all the nations [the US] burglaries, car thefts, and bank holdups combined' (1973: 1).

Within the retail sector, precise numbers on the scale of the problem are generally difficult to attain, not least because official statistics are severely compromised by the very low rate of reporting of incidents by retailers. Most companies prefer to apply their own sanctions to offenders, such as dismissal or demotion rather than processing them through the formal channels of the criminal justice system. This is frequently done because companies perceive it to be easier and cheaper, and because it reduces the possibility of bad publicity (which company wants to highlight how ineffective their internal controls are?). As a result, official statistics are of little value in understanding the scale and extent of the problem of internal theft in the retail sector. Moreover, incidents of staff dishonesty collected and collated by retailers themselves provide only a partial snapshot of the problem, not least because it can only ever be based upon those actually caught. Bamfield's analysis of two years worth of data on recorded incidents of staff theft by four major UK retailers estimated that these incidents only accounted for 4.4 per cent of total losses thought to be caused by employees in these companies (Bamfield, 2006a).

However, other sources of information are available, including the various shrinkage surveys undertaken by academics, consultants and representative bodies (see Tables 3.2 and 4.1 earlier). As discussed early the veracity of this data is highly questionable, not least because respondents are asked to estimate how much of their loss is caused by various categories of shrinkage. The longstanding NRSS survey undertaken by the University of Florida offers the best indication of changes over time in how seriously US retailers have viewed the problem of internal theft. From the first study back in 1991 until the most recent data published in 2008, retailers have estimated that internal theft accounts for 40 per cent or more of all shrinkage, with the most recent study estimating that it is responsible for 44 per cent of all losses (Hollinger & Adams, 2008), making it the largest single cause of shrinkage (external theft is the next largest component and was estimated to account for 34%). In financial terms this amounts to just over $15 billion a year lost by the retail sector in the US to staff theft.

The Global Retail Theft Barometer carried out by Bamfield (2008) concludes that internal theft is estimated to account for 36.5 per cent of all losses in the 36 countries surveyed, costing $38 billion a year, putting it behind external theft as the key cause of shrinkage. However, his comparable data for the US broadly concurs with the NRSS findings (internal theft representing 46.4 per cent of all shrinkage losses) concluding that employee theft is the single biggest cause of shrinkage in that country. Estimates from a number of other countries surveyed by the Global Retail Theft Barometer also show relatively high levels of loss being apportioned to internal theft, with Canada, (44.9%) and Mexico (43.8%) being the two nearest to the US estimate. For retailers in Europe the average was considered to be 30.7 per cent, in Asia Pacific 22.7 per cent, in Africa 35.7 per cent, and Latin America 42 per cent.

Trying to understand why American, Canadian and indeed Mexican retailers perceive the problem to be so much more significant than many of the other countries taking part in this survey is difficult. It could be that employee theft is simply more prevalent in these countries compared with other countries (due to differing cultural, social and economic factors). Or it could be that retailers in these countries have access to better quality data which provides them with a more accurate picture of the problem (or vice versa). Or it could be that the fixation with external theft as the dominant cause of shrinkage is much more prevalent outside of these countries. It is obviously not possible to draw any accurate conclusions without further research, but the significant difference in attitude amongst respondents concerning the size of the problem of internal theft is profound.

A profile of offending

Much research has been undertaken trying to understand why staff steal from organisations and a number of conclusions can be drawn. The first is that staff may be under some form of financial pressure to steal; they may have built up personal debt, may have a drug or gambling addiction or may simply have developed a life style that is beyond their current income's capability to meet (Duffin *et al.*, 2006). They therefore steal from their employer to meet these external financial pressures. Another explanation, and one that has received considerable academic attention, is that dishonest employees have low morale through some perceived inequity – they feel that they are being ripped off by the company and hence seek 'compensation' (Altheide *et al.*, 1978). Hollinger and Clark (1982) found from their survey of retail employees that those who were purposefully seeking other employment, were given insufficiently challenging tasks, thought that their employer did not care about them, or felt exploited, were much more likely to engage in acts of dishonesty. Equally Ditton (1977) found that dishonest employees stole to make up for what they saw as low wages, while Greenberg (1997) concluded that staff stole to even the score and redress perceived inequity with their employers. In his seminal work on dock workers, Mars draws a similar conclusion that staff stole to make up for what they saw as exploitative working conditions (1974, 1982; 2000).

A third area relates to issues concerning the organisational culture within which dishonesty takes place – the impact that the social and cultural environment workers operate within can have upon their propensity to steal. Here research has shown that 'learned behaviour' can be a key factor; in other words the attitudes and actions of co-workers can directly influence the likelihood of an individual becoming dishonest in the workplace (Curtis, 1979; Hollinger & Clark, 1983; Kamp & Brooks, 1991; Kresevich, 2007). In addition, offenders can develop 'neutralisation' techniques to justify their wrongdoing and overcome any feelings of guilt they may harbour (Sykes & Matza, 1957). This is often reflected in phrases that offenders may use, such as: 'they can afford it', 'it's a victimless crime', and 'I deserve it'. As Hollinger and Davis succinctly put it, these 'guilt neutralising vocabularies' were often found to be used by staff to excuse their dishonest behaviour (especially by older employees) (Hollinger & Davis, 2006: 217). Greenberg has carried out much work in this field trying to understand the motivations for behaving dishonestly in the workplace and highlights how those staff who have achieved a 'conventional level of moral development' and are aware of the negative consequences of their actions upon the business and their fellow workers, are less likely to be dishonest (Greenberg, 2002: 985). He quotes a useful metaphor first used by Treviño and Nelson to understand how best to deter staff dishonesty: 'put good apples in good barrels' (Greenberg, 2002: 1001).

Perhaps the most important explanation for understanding why some staff steal from their employees relates to the degree of opportunity their role provides them to get away with deviant behaviour (Beck, 2006a; Duffin *et al.*, 2006). Hollinger and Davis suggest that the extent to which staff are likely to try and profit from the opportunities that are presented to them as they go about their prescribed tasks is dependent upon the perceived value of the products they may be interacting with and the extent of cash handling they perform (2006). When one considers most retail environments, many of the factors that facilitate staff offending are very much to the fore. Perceived value of products is an important concept here in that some retail environments will stock many products that while they have an intrinsic value (customers will pay money to buy them) they are not considered of sufficient 'perceived value' as to make them highly prone to staff theft. This relates specifically to our earlier discussion on hot products and what makes some items more likely to be stolen than others. For instance, many fresh food products are not generally prone to malicious shrinkage (you do not often hear stories of staff being dismissed for trying to steal food items, although they may be disciplined for 'grazing' – eating stock while at work), but certain brands of health and beauty products and small electrical items are considered much more likely to be stolen.

Undoubtedly what external thieves consider to be 'hot items' are probably very similar to those that staff thieves consider to have 'perceived value'. However, staff also frequently have access to the hottest item of all – cash (Beck, 2006a). In order for retailing to work, staff must be put in a position whereby they can accept, exchange and process cash – it is the lifeblood of the retail operation. So the opportunity for theft in the retail environment is potentially enormous – staff are continually surrounded by, and frequently required to interact with, extremely desirable products. In addition, many of them are required to handle on a regular basis large amount of cash. And all of this can happen within a relatively uncontrolled and often semi-autonomous environment. It is hardly surprising then that Hollinger and Davis posed the not unreasonable question: 'given that so much opportunity exists, why isn't there even more theft given the numerous opportunities for taking things in the retail store?' (Hollinger & Davis, 2006: 211). One answer could be that there is and retailers are simply unable to identify its true extent amongst all the unknown loss that accumulates in the shrinkage pile (or perhaps retailers simply prefer to apportion it to external theft as it is politically far more expedient).

Nagin *et al.* (2002) came up with a useful phrase for these types of offenders – 'rational cheaters' – those who steal because the opportunities exist and the anticipated benefits of crime exceed the likely costs. Moreover, Bamfield found in his analysis of recorded incidents of employee theft in four large UK retailers that perhaps as much as 90.6 per cent of the value of all staff theft incidents go undiscovered (Bamfield, 2006a).

While eliminating all opportunity from the retail environment would be both difficult and ultimately counter productive (retailers would probably not sell very much) understanding the role that company processes and procedures play in creating opportunities for dishonest activities is an important component of *New Loss Prevention* and is a topic we will return to in Chapter 7. In many respects this is reinforced by the literature on deterring internal theft which looks at the mechanisms that are most likely to stop a member of staff stealing from their employer.

Deterrence is made up of three key elements. The first is the extent to which an offender 'believes' they are likely to be caught – the perceived certainty of detection. The second is the harshness of the punishment they think they will receive if they are caught – the perceived severity of punishment and the third relates to celerity – the speed with which they will be punished. What is important with each of these factors is that it is the perception of the offender that matters and not the reality of whether they will be caught or punished. So the theory goes that the 'rational cheater' will consider the likelihood of being caught and the consequence of being caught before they will undertake a dishonest act. Both of these factors need to work together to create the maximum deterrent effect. For instance, if the risk and consequence of being caught are both perceived to be very low, then the offence is more likely to happen. However, if the risk is perceived as low but the consequence high then the event may still happen, particularly for certain types of staff (young/part time/temporary staff) (Speed, 2003). Ideally, potential offenders need to consider that the risk of apprehension is very high and that if they are caught then they will be severely and quickly punished (such as reported to the police and charged with a criminal offence). The reality of most retail environments, and the existing evidence on how few staff are ever caught supports this view, would suggest that the actual risk and consequence for retail thieves are both very low. Most internal thieves are probably never caught and those that are, are often either demoted or dismissed, knowing fully well that they can probably walk down the high street and get another job with one of their former employer's competitors the next day (Duffin *et al.*, 2006).

Retailers have recognised these challenges and have employed a range of ways to try and increase the risk of perceived capture and punishment, such as organisational controls, pre employment screening, training programmes, investigation strategies and ensuring that offenders are, where ever possible, prosecuted through the criminal justice system. None will work in isolation but what is of particular interest to us is the role that company processes and procedures can play in providing the opportunities for offenders to perceive that their risk of being caught and punished remain very low.

Before we move on to conclude this particular section, it is important to consider the issue of collusive theft between members of staff and customers. This is a topic which straddles the boundaries between staff theft and customer theft. We would argue that as a subject it should reside within the field of staff dishonesty as it would not be possible without the active involvement of an employee. Relatively little research has been undertaken on this subject although a study by Bamfield suggested that retailers thought as much as 40 per cent of customer theft was linked to staff collusion (1998). While this may seem an extremely high figure, the reality of modern retailing would suggest that the opportunities available for this type of behaviour to take place are many and varied. In a more recent study, Duffin *et al.* interviewed former members of staff who had been dismissed for a range of reasons relating to theft and non-compliance, and found that one-third had colluded with family, friends or colleagues to commit staff dishonesty (2006).

There are a number of ways in which collusive theft can take place. Perhaps the most prevalent is 'sweethearting' where a member of staff working at a checkout will either not scan items for friends, members of their family or colleagues, or enter a product code for a cheaper item than is actually being purchased (Curtis, 1973; Martinez, 2004). Other types of collusion include: refund fraud, where an accomplice receives a fraudulent payment for goods that have not actually been returned; false markdown, where the price of an item is artificially reduced; and staff discounts, where a member of staff allows friends and family to use an employee discount card to obtain lower prices.

All of these methods, but especially the first type – sweethearting – can be notoriously difficult to monitor and detect. For example, it can be near to impossible (through human observation at least) to notice whether a check out operator has decided not to scan a single item against a back drop of perhaps dozens of tills and many thousands of items being scanned every few minutes. Certainly compared with autonomous acts of customer or staff theft then collusive offending is much less risky. For example, a collusive staff member cannot be found with the stolen items or cash about their person, while the collusive customer is far more likely to be viewed with minimal suspicion as they appear to be acting 'normally'. In addition, even if suspicion is raised, the member of staff can simply claim that they made an honest mistake (Bamfield, 1998). Taken together then, the estimate proposed by Bamfield's research on the scale of the problem of collusive thefts may be far more realistic than first envisaged. More encouragingly, new technologies are emerging that claim to be able to identify sweethearting as it takes place and other forms of collusive behaviour are open to ameliorative responses, not least because they frequently leave an auditable trail.

Internal theft in context

Internal theft in the retail sector is a profoundly difficult subject to get to grips with – its causes are many and varied and its importance and impact is often over shadowed by the omnipotence of external theft. A simple reflection upon the way in which most retail organisations operate, and indeed the ever growing pressures they are under to cut costs and streamline processes and procedures, would suggest that employee thieves are in the best position to take advantage of the myriad opportunities presented to them by the tasks they are asked to undertake every day. Indeed, Curtis has suggested that there may be more than 4,000 methods for employees to steal from a retailer (Curtis, 1973). The role of opportunity in understanding internal theft is critical as is the potential impact of risk and consequence upon the likelihood of dissuading them from taking advantage of these opportunities (or helping others to take advantage). How organisations minimise opportunities through increasing perceived risk and consequence is fundamental to developing an effective loss prevention strategy. We believe that the way in which store processes and procedures are developed, monitored and reviewed is a key part of this. Understanding how dishonest employees take advantage of the opportunities presented by poorly designed and poorly supervised processes will enable loss prevention practitioners to begin to identify the root causes of a significant part of their shrinkage problem. As Curtis reflected back in 1960: 'Error control is important because failure to operate systems properly will lead to embezzlement, defalcations [fraud] and other forms of theft. If you have a good error control program you improve your store operations, reduce losses and decrease opportunities for employee dishonesty' (1960: 588). As we will detail in Chapter 7, retail companies need to carry out a detailed analysis of the way in which current processes and procedures can potentially facilitate deviant behaviour by store staff – after all, the staff are the ones who use (and sometimes abuse) these systems everyday.

Inter-company fraud – Process driven loss?

Scale and cost of the problem

Relatively little is known about the scale and extent of inter-company fraud beyond that which appears in the various shrinkage surveys undertaken over the past years. Available evidence would suggest that it is a lesser and decreasing part of the overall shrinkage problem faced by retail organisations and their suppliers. An averaging of the various surveys undertaken over the past seven years suggest that the cost of inter-company fraud accounts for about 8 per cent of all losses (see Table 4.2 in Chapter 4), with the recent Global Retail Theft Barometer concluding it accounts for 6 per cent and the NRSS just 4 per cent (Bamfield, 2008; Hollinger & Adams, 2008). The highest estimates come mainly from the surveys covering the FMCG sector, with the study completed in 2002 by ECR Australia providing the highest estimate at 11 per cent. But unlike the other categories of shrinkage covered in these surveys (internal and external theft and process failures) there is unanimous agreement that it is the least of the problems faced by retailers.

There seem to be three main types of inter-company fraud that occur most often where the retailer is the victim. The first is when a supplier does not deliver the correct quantity of stock as stipulated in the original order – for instance the retailer is expecting ten boxes of stock, but only receives eight boxes. A common method of achieving this is to have 'hollow' spots in pallets of goods, so that while it may look like a full pallet is being delivered, boxes in the middle of the stack may be missing. Another variant of this can be when a vendor deliberately under delivers products in terms of their anticipated weight. For example, a retailer may be expecting ten boxes of fresh meat, with each box containing 50 kilos, but eventually receives ten boxes only containing 30 kilos of meat. In this instance, the vendor provides the right quantity of boxes, but the contents are not as the original order stipulated.

A second form of inter-company fraud is when a supplier does not deliver the expected type of goods but instead substitutes inferior products and passes them off as those originally ordered. For example, a retailer may be expecting a delivery of premium meat, but instead receives much poorer quality meat instead.

A third area of fraud can be when retailers decide to return goods to the vendor as part of an original agreement. In this case the vendor receiving the returned goods deliberately pays back a lower credit than the value of the goods being returned. For example, a retailer may arrange for 20 boxes of stock to be returned, but is only credited with the value of 15 boxes.

Some authors (Purpora, 1993; Martinez, 2004; Kimiecik & Thomas, 2006) suggest a fourth area which is when representatives of suppliers steal goods from retailers as they are delivering stock (either at the back of the store, or when carrying out replenishment work within the store). This can be either from the goods they are delivering or simply other stock which is present within the store (such as other goods that have recently been delivered and are easily accessible within the receiving area, or product placed on shelves near to where they are replenishing their own products). In our view, this is not inter-company fraud but simply a type of external theft – inter-company fraud is when a supplier deliberately sets out to make a gain from their customers by using one of the three methods detailed above.

In contrast to the types of inter-company fraud detailed above, where the retailer is the victim of the fraud, there are some examples of where retailers can be the perpetrator and the supplier is the victim (Young, 2004). In these cases, the primary methods are: a retailer will falsely claim not to have received the amount of goods delivered by a supplier; claim a proportion of the products were damaged on arrival (when they were not); or claim to have returned a quantity of stock, when in fact they had not. In such circumstances the retailer will demand a fraudulent credit for the seemingly missing, damaged or returned stock from the supplier.

All types of inter-company fraud rely upon a very simple premise – the complexity and scale of modern retailing together with the continuing pressure to reduce costs – provides the ideal context within which deviant behaviour can take place. For example, increasingly retail stores do not check all the goods that arrive at the back of the store – there is a presumption that the quantity stated on the delivery note is correct. Similarly, the administrative process for returning goods to a supplier may be sufficiently convoluted as to make it highly unlikely that discrepancies between quantities returned and credits provided will be readily identified, particularly when there may be thousands of such transactions taking place each week.

Inter-company fraud in context

Inter-company fraud is an offence that relies almost exclusively upon an absence of, or break down in, retail processes and procedures – it preys upon weaknesses in the system that provide opportunities for dishonesty to go unnoticed. Staff may not check the quantity of goods arriving or may not check that the products are those which were originally ordered. Undoubtedly, receiving areas in retail stores are busy spaces and the drive within modern retailing is to minimise costs wherever possible, particularly relating to staff costs. A quick way to achieve this is to reduce the amount of laborious counting of incoming stock at the back of the store, particularly when most stock may be arriving from the retailer's own distribution centre. While future developments in technology, such as Radio Frequency Identification (RFID), which promises to automate much of the checking and verification of goods arriving at a store, may well consign most inter-company fraud to the history books (Beck, 2002a, 2006b), it still offers an excellent example of how retail processes and procedures can provide the ideal opportunity for deviant behaviour to take place.

Process failure – The acceptable face of shrinkage?

Scale and cost of the problem

If published information on the scale and extent of internal and external theft and inter-company fraud is often piecemeal, partial and largely opaque, then that available on process failure or administrative error is virtually non-existent. A review of many of the published texts on shrinkage management and retail loss prevention (Edwards, 1974; Jones, 1997; Purpora, 1993; Hayes, 2007; Kimiecik & Thomas, 2006; Sennewald & Christman, 2008) highlights clearly how this area of loss has been largely ignored – none have any notable sections focusing on this issue (the terms administrative error or process failure do not appear in the content pages nor indexes of any of these texts). Understanding why this is the case is not easy to understand although the primary reason is probably the ongoing prioritisation of malicious shrinkage by practitioners – the securitisation of the function and the belief that thief catching and deterring is primarily what they do. It is perhaps also a problem that has been seen to be the responsibility of other parts of the business, notably audit, store operations or finance and hence not something that the loss prevention department should or has to deal with (Bernstein, 1963).

The various shrinkage surveys undertaken over the past few years provide some numbers on the scale and extent of the problem although as with the other types of shrinkage, there is little consensus (see Table 4.2 in Chapter 4). A rough overall average suggests that about 26 per cent or one-quarter of all shrinkage losses are caused by process failure ranking it as the third major cause behind internal and external theft. The survey undertaken by the Brazilian Supermarket Association (ABRAS) in 2005 has generated the largest estimate from any country survey to date, suggesting that process failures were responsible for 65 per cent of all losses suffered by supermarkets in that country. The NRSS survey offers the lowest estimation, just 15 per cent, with the Global Retail Theft Barometer just slightly above this figure (16%).

More anecdotally, Baumer and Rosenbaum concluded from their research that perhaps only 10 per cent of shrinkage was due to 'non-theft losses' (1984) although much more recently one US retailer (Lowes) has suggested that 80 per cent of their losses can be attributed to employees, of which 40 per cent they estimate is due to theft and the remaining 40 per cent is due to 'paper shrink' (administrative error) (Hennessee, 2003). The latter is certainly a revealing figure and is the second highest published estimate uncovered to date. More recently, personal communication with one of the largest US retailers (who wished not to be named) revealed that they now estimate process failures cause as much as two thirds of all their losses (a figure which has only recently come to light through more detailed analysis of their shrinkage data).

In theory, retailers should be able to get a relatively accurate metric on a number of the factors that contribute to process failures as recording practices often exist, such as when stock is written off, designated as waste or when it is reduced in price, although it can be problematic ensuring these processes are strictly followed by store staff. Once again, however, the problem is undoubtedly compounded by variations in the definition of shrinkage used by retailers – some simply do not consider losses from damages or products past their sale by date to be part of their shrinkage figure because it is, in part at least, known and readily apportionable to specific causes. Some of the terms used to describe it are perhaps indicative of this attitude – 'paper shrink', 'wooden dollars' and 'clerical error' to name but a few.

What exactly is process failure? In simple terms it is the sum of all the things that go wrong as products make their journey from delivery to the retailer to their final exit at the front door of stores in the hands of a customer, excluding theft by staff and customers (Fisher *et al.*, 2000). The list of causes is potentially very long. The modern retail environment, as we detailed in Chapter 2, is often extremely complex; many companies will have hundreds of geographically dispersed outlets, thousands of employees (some of whom will have questionable levels of commitment and motivation), tens of thousands of SKUs (many of which will only be subtly different such as variants in flavour or pack size), multiple deliveries per week (some from the company's own distribution centres, others by suppliers and third party logistics providers), and a myriad of IT systems designed to monitor and record rapidly changing inventories. Given this, it is perhaps perfectly understandable that mistakes are made on a daily basis.

It is not the purpose of this book to highlight all the possible causes of process failure as the list is too long to allow a full analysis here, but it is instructive to look at just some of the main areas to give an indication of the types of issues that make up this problem (for a more detailed list of process failures, see Chapter 3). Three types of process failure can be identified: losses caused by process variance (e.g. auditing errors, checkout errors, losses incurred through the movement of goods in the supply chain and data errors), product losses (e.g. goods that are damaged, wastage and spoilage); and losses caused by value variance (e.g. price reductions, pricing errors and missed claims).

Process variance losses   Potentially costly errors can be made when new products are initially entered on to a retailer's system – item set up problems. This can occur when wrong quantities of product are associated with a particular Uniform Product Code (UPC). For example, one retailer provides an example where a garden patio set, which was made up of four chairs, was incorrectly entered on their system so that the recorded price related to one chair rather than the set of four (Hennessee, 2003). Identifying this single error reduced shrinkage on patio furniture by 55 per cent in this retailer. Problems can also occur when changes to the store master file are done incorrectly, such as changes to quantities or prices of particular products. In addition, confusing and contradictory information on packaging can also create process failures, such as when a manufacturer puts more than one bar code on a product's packaging, such as multi-packs where each item may have a bar code as well as the overarching packaging. Checkout staff could then inadvertently scan the wrong bar code (for a single item rather than the multi-pack) and losses will ensue.

Maintaining accurate inventories is one of the greatest challenges facing retailers and errors can and do cause major losses both in terms of shrinkage and lost sales. Estimates vary on the extent of inventory error; DeHoratius and Raman (2008) found in their study that 65 per cent of inventory records in one retailer were inaccurate, while Fisher *et al.* (2000) note an inventory review undertaken by a book retailer which found that in 19 per cent of the instances that their computer system said a book was on hand, it could not be found in the store. They also quote a similar statistic from retailers that have made store level inventory data available to customers over the Internet so they can check availability before coming to the store. They find that roughly 20 per cent of the time that the computer says an item is in stock, it cannot be found hours later when the customer comes to the store to buy it. These problems can be caused by data errors as stated above, errors in the delivery of goods to stores (wrong quantities, products etc), errors in the receiving of goods at stores (wrong data entered on to the inventory), errors at the checkout (for instance staff using generic or 'dump' codes to reduce customer waiting times when bar codes will not scan properly), and errors when stock taking takes place. The last problem is particularly acute and is a subject that generates considerable debate amongst loss prevention practitioners.

Some believe that regular stock takes can introduce more error into the system than originally existed (Turbin, 1998), while others argue that achieving accurate inventory, particularly through regular cycle counting, is the only way to guarantee sufficiently accurate and up to date data that will enable shrinkage to be identified (Yake, n.d.). This is a subject we will return to later in this book as we are more aligned with the latter view than the former. Either way, inventory inaccuracy can cause major operational problems in terms of out of stocks and stock reordering, both of which can ultimately lead to more dissatisfied customers. But it can also be used by dishonest staff as a convenient cloak of anonymity, obscuring their deviant behaviour and making it easier for them to point the finger of guilt elsewhere (such as at external thieves).

Product losses   Products moving through retail supply chains can be highly prone to damage or being soiled, both of which can lead to shrinkage. Customers are highly unlikely to want to buy products that are not in a good condition and retailers have to regularly 'write off' stock that is no longer considered to be in a saleable condition. This can happen at many points within the supply chain – as the goods are picked at the warehouse, as they are loaded on to delivery trucks, as they are transported to stores, as they are unloaded in the store and put away, and when they are finally moved to the shelf. At each point poor packaging, incorrect handling and stacking and exposure to the elements can all lead to products being sufficiently damaged and soiled to cause them either to be reduced in price or simply thrown away – both of which lead to shrinkage.

For those retailers selling perishable goods there is the added problem of products that have a finite date by which they must be sold otherwise they become worthless, or have to be reduced in price to try and encourage customers to buy them. Fresh foods such as fruit and vegetables, meat and fish and ready-made meals fall into this category as do certain newspapers and periodicals. A stated earlier, a report by Barua *et al.* (n.d.) has estimated that 10 per cent of all perishable goods are rendered unusable before they reach the consumer and that inventory write offs in the global retail industry from spoilage and obsolescence amounts to $120 billion.

Value variance losses This category of process failure covers those causes of loss that refer to changes in the value of the product which mean that the anticipated return is not realised. This includes price reductions where the original price of a product is reduced in order that the product is more likely to be sold. Examples would include: ready-made meals close to their expiry date; end of line clothing; and partially damaged boxes of washing powder. In addition, this would include losses caused by errors in the way in which goods are priced and sold in the business. Examples would include: goods coded incorrectly on the store inventory system; staff incorrectly pricing product in the back room areas or on the shelf; a mismatch between agreed and actual selling price; or a member of staff entering the wrong price at the till.

Process failures in context

A number of loss prevention practitioners have argued that some of the types of losses from process failures, such as products being delivered to the wrong store, are merely 'wooden dollars' and is therefore not a problem that requires much of their attention. The argument goes that if stock is 'missing' from the inventory in one store due to shipping or counting errors then it will ultimately appear either in the store sometime in the future or somewhere else in the system – either in the DC or in another store – and therefore overall the business has not lost out as the stock can still be sold. We would argue that this is an unacceptable way to view the problem for three reasons. First, any inaccuracies in store inventories reduces the likelihood of loss practitioners being able to clearly identify the true causes of shrinkage – the fog generated by compromised book stock data makes it less likely that the true causes of shrinkage will be identified quickly (Yake, n.d.). Secondly, unaccounted for stock can present ideal opportunities for deviant staff – if the company does not know where the stock is, how will they know when it goes missing? Thirdly, if the wrong goods end up in the wrong place, then this can lead to the need for additional stock and transportation to correct the error, which can in turn increase the likelihood of products being damaged or going out of date.

We would like to argue that process failures should be a key part of what loss prevention practitioners focus upon, not only because it could account for as much as 40 per cent of losses, but also because it severely impacts upon the validity of the shrinkage data which is used to set priorities. Without good quality data loss prevention managers will continue to base their decisions largely upon guesswork, personal prejudice and gut instinct. In addition, 'fixing' many process failures can often be much easier and quicker than dealing with other types of shrinkage such as external and internal thieves, primarily because it is often about ensuring that staff throughout the supply chain maintain and observe company procedures and processes. It does not necessarily require significant investment in new technologies – the solutions are often much more straightforward in the form of better training, supervision and control. What it does require, however, is not only a change of mindset within loss prevention practitioners, but also a different set of skills which are more focused upon retail management than thief catching. Monitoring master file accuracy and item set up codes is certainly not as exciting as chasing organised retail crime networks, but in terms of reducing the overall cost of shrinkage to the business, it could be far more beneficial. It also requires loss prevention managers to operate across functions within the business such as buying, store operations, auditing and finance as well as with product manufacturers (such as negotiating better packaging or improved delivery processes and procedures).

Loss prevention practitioners need to become 'agents of change' within the business rooting out the causes of administrative shrinkage and co-ordinating a collective and more systemic response. For instance one retailer has established a Manager of Merchandise Shrink Control whose job is to focus exclusively on what they call 'paper shrink' (Hennessee, 2003). We believe that it is time for process failure to be firmly on the agenda of loss prevention practitioners and not something that is seen at best as merely an adjunct to what they do or as something which has little or no cost to the business.

Understanding shrinkage

Getting to grips with the true causes of shrinkage is vital if finite loss prevention resources are to be used most effectively. To date, the issue of external theft has dominated the loss prevention agenda. In this chapter we have referred to it as the 'bogeyman' of shrinkage not to downplay its role in causing shrinkage, but to highlight how it has to date often been used as a convenient scapegoat to blame for the majority of unknown losses within the business. As we have argued earlier, it is often much easier to blame the outsider for retail losses rather than looking within at those employed by the business, a tendency encouraged by a veracious 'solutions' industry keen to sell yet more technological panaceas. The research on internal theft suggests that it is at least if not more of a problem than external theft and if that is combined with the largely ignored area of process failures, then perhaps as much as 70 to 80 per cent of the shrinkage problem is located within retail businesses. Given this, the ongoing obsession with chasing and deterring shop thieves should be viewed as a poor use of loss prevention resources.

Undoubtedly, the impact of shrinkage on the retail sector is vast – globally equivalent to the GDP of many major countries. But its impact is often more profound than just on the bottom line profitability of retail businesses. It also impacts upon manufacturers of retail goods as well. They and the retailers lose sales when goods are not available on shelves due to out of stocks or when retailers use defensive merchandising to protect products they view as shrinkage prone. Ultimately, it is the customer who pays the highest cost through increased prices to cover shrinkage losses, through products not being available on the shelves and through less choice.

The next chapter will move on to look at how loss prevention has been tackled in the past and how this has to a certain extent undermined existing efforts to reduce the overall impact of shrinkage on the retail sector.

6
Traditional Approaches to Loss Prevention

As detailed earlier in this book, shrinkage is a problem that has an enormous impact upon the profitability of retail organisations and their suppliers, and also negatively affects the consumer through increased prices and reduced availability and selection. It is also a problem that has arguably been with retailers since the very earliest days of trading goods although the move to mass merchandising and open display of products, sometimes referred to as the emergence of the culture of consumption, undoubtedly added fuel to the shrinkage fire. The history of retail loss prevention stretches back over 140 years with accounts of the use of store detectives and security operatives readily available from the early years of the previous century (Abelson, 1989). At this time 'protection departments' as they were often called were cloaked in secrecy, partly to ensure that the retailer's facade of a welcoming and open shopping environment was not sullied by awareness of their need to employ staff who viewed customers (and staff) as a threat. This culture of secrecy can still be seen to a certain extent today, with the publication of loss data continually viewed by many as undesirable and likely to undermine confidence in the business. Back in the early part of the 20th century the use of serving police officers in larger US departmental store retailers to act as investigators and store detectives began to become more common, with the likes of Macey's establishing a protection department in 1902 (Abelson, 1989) employing such staff.

At this time the growing threat was seen to come from shoplifters as retailers increasingly felt that all customers could no longer be trusted and the staff could not be wholly relied upon to protect the store's interests. It is worth reflecting that this was a time when mass consumerism was becoming established and retailers were developing many of the now taken for granted approaches to encouraging customers to part with their hard earned cash through the development of ever more innovative, attractive and appealing (tempting) shopping environments. It is also a time when many of the approaches to loss prevention that we see today began to be established, not least in terms of reducing opportunity, increasing the risk of apprehension and attempting to engage store staff in the loss prevention process. For instance, the turn of the 19th century began to see a rise in defensive merchandising through the use of glass show cabinets – 'goods can be displayed without risk from the nimble fingers of the shoplifter' (Abelson, 1989: 78). In addition, there was the introduction of relatively simple risk amplification equipment such as mirrors to enable staff to keep an eye on customers when their back was turned and the growing use of electric lighting to reduce the opportunities afforded by dimly lit shopping spaces. At the same time some of the more enlightened retailers began to appreciate that the growing army of retail staff employed in some of the larger retailers were at best ambivalent about the problem of shrinkage. This was perhaps not surprising, and indeed sounds very familiar to the challenges faced by many retailers today. Store staff were poorly paid and educated and no doubt painfully aware of their own inability to share in the seemingly highly self indulgent and blatantly materialistic world in which they worked. Some of the early social welfare programmes established by retailers were consciously developed not only to try and improve staff morale (which was thought might help with sales) but also to increase staff vigilance of losses. Outings and staff discounts all embody attempts to improve the esprit de corps of workers trying to make 'the store' into 'our store' in the hope that affiliation with the business might help to mitigate losses (Abelson, 1989). In addition, some retailers such as Marshall Field in the US tried incentivisation schemes such as a $5 reward for the successful detection of shoplifters. The early part of the 20th century also saw the introduction of the 'test shopper' whose task was to ensure that staff were maximising any sales opportunity, providing good customer service, and were following store processes and procedures so that potential losses were minimised. Such techniques and the growing legion of store detectives were the key components of early loss prevention strategies employed by retailers at the beginning of the 20th century.

What is perhaps quite remarkable, and hence why we have dwelled upon this period in the history of retailing and loss prevention, is that much of what was established over 100 years ago is still present in much of the thinking of loss prevention in the 21st century. While the retail

environment is much more complicated, multi-layered and technologically advanced, the underlying ethos of the early mass merchant
retailers is very much present – shop theft is a key threat and we need
to employ security personnel, opportunity reduction and risk enhance-
ment technologies, and hopefully engage our greatest asset, store staff,
in dealing with the problem.

What we would like to do is reflect upon what we see as some of the
limitations to many of the approaches adopted by retail loss prevention
departments over the past 20 years or so. This is certainly not to say that
all retail loss prevention departments are alike or all are incapable of effectively managing the problem of shrinkage – there are plenty of examples
of excellent practice out there (see for instance Beck, 2007a). But we think
there are a number of key factors that have led to shrinkage remaining
such a stubborn problem for most retailers to get to grips with and it is,
we believe, enlightening to reflect upon them at this stage.

A regrettable yet inevitable function

For many organisations the issue of shrinkage and its management has
traditionally been viewed as a regrettable yet inevitable part of operating
in the retail sector – something which must be endured as part of the
process of making profits from selling goods to consumers. Certainly staff
need to be employed to deal with the problem, but they are viewed very
much as an unfortunate cost to the business, which wherever possible,
should be kept to a minimum. They are also frequently seen as the
retailer's police force, held in reserve and only called upon when things
go horribly wrong, such as the kidnapping of a store manager or threats
to contaminate stock. This representation of loss prevention as a burden
on the business and a function that plays little or no role in helping to
generate profit inevitably means that its status within the business, and
its capability to secure support for its activities, can be severely compromised. This status as 'cost' centre rather than 'profit' centre – a have to
have rather than want to have retail mentality – directly impacts on how
the rest of the business views not only those tasked to deal with shrinkage, but also how they view the problem itself. It can lead to it being marginalised within the business and not seen as being as important as other
retail functions and activities. Indeed, it is not unusual to hear of the loss
prevention department being rather disingenuously described as the
'profit prevention' department by other functions within retail businesses. Changing this mind set within the business is an important part
of *New Loss Prevention*. Communicating to the rest of the business the

value effective shrinkage management can bring is an important first step in not only ensuring their compliance, but ultimately their support and commitment.

Moreover, the fact that explicit shrinkage data is rarely if ever reported to shareholders through company reports adds further to the perception that it has only a peripheral role to play within retail businesses. Indeed it would be interesting to see how different the situation might be were retailers to be judged by external analysts as much on their shrinkage performance as they were on their sales results!

Crisis driven shrinkage management

While it has often been seen as inevitable yet regrettable, traditional loss prevention is also frequently guilty of adopting a crisis-driven approach to dealing with shrinkage problems as they emerge in retail businesses. For example, a company audit may suddenly reveal that losses from shrinkage have grown considerably in the last year. The response from traditional loss prevention will be to assume that it is the usual suspect – external theft – and move quickly to secure funding for the most recent technological panacea they have come across to deal with this problem. More than likely, they will then not monitor or evaluate the performance of the intervention, and when the next shrinkage crisis emerges, they will begin this cycle again.

Breaking this crisis-driven reactive approach to managing shrinkage involves adopting a much more systemic and systematic methodology, one which seeks to understand, through proper measurement and analysis, the root causes of the problem. Only when they are fully understood are any decisions then made about introducing interventions aimed at reducing the problem. And once an intervention is introduced, it is then carefully monitored and evaluated to better understand the positive impact it is having (or not as the case may be) so that this learning can be utilised in future business decisions. We will look in more detail at how a more systemic and systematic approach can help businesses break this crisis-driven cycle in Chapter 8.

Living in a data desert

As the old adage goes if it cannot be measured it cannot be managed and a lack of high quality data has plagued the loss prevention industry ever since it was first created. This is regularly reflected in the annual surveys that are carried out around the world where the majority of the causes of stock loss can only be estimated by respondents. This is not a new problem and accounts back in the early part of the 1900s graphically illustrate the extent to which loss prevention practitioners were very much operating in the dark in terms of the scale and extent of the losses caused by shrinkage. For instance, Abelson quotes from documents produced by the US retailer Macys in 1915 where the losses from shrinkage were described as 'unfathomable' (Abelson, 1989: 112). Some 45 years later Curtis is seen to be ruefully reflecting upon the difficulties of getting accurate data on the loss of goods through the supply chain (1960). And more recently Hayes (2003: 8) can be found concluding that '[the] lack of rigorously obtained data on loss prevention management remains a problem ...'. Why has obtaining accurate data on shrinkage been, and in many respects continues to be, such a problem? The answer lies partly in the complexity of the retail environment and the ways in which retailers account for their stock. Modern retailing is a phenomenally complex and dynamic environment with a myriad of opportunities for shrinkage to occur – was the right stock delivered at the right time to the right place at the right price? Was it damaged en route? Did it go out of date or have to be reduced in price? Was it incorrectly returned to the supplier? Did a member of staff steal it or perhaps help a customer to steal it? Did a shopper steal it? Did somebody break in after the store was closed and steal it? All of these causes and more can account for shrinkage and yet trying to measure these events is potentially difficult, particularly when it is not viewed as one of the core activities of the business.

For the most part, the majority of retailers rely upon audit data as the source of their shrinkage information. How this audit data is collected varies enormously and can have a significant impact upon the quality of the shrinkage information which is subsequently extracted from it. For instance, stock audits can be carried out by either internal people (principally store staff) or externally contracted audit teams. They can also vary by how often the audits are carried out, for instance, some companies may only carry out an audit once a year, while others might have a more frequent timetable, such as every three or six months. In addition, the number of stores and the number of products audited may vary – some companies might choose only a sample of stores to audit, while others may have an auditing programme which counts only particular subsets of products at different times in the year (cycle counting)

Each can cause problems in generating accurate shrinkage data. The periodic stock audits can create long time lags between a shrinkage event occurring and it eventually being recorded. For instance, a product could go missing in January and it may not be recorded until an audit is carried out as much as a year later. After such a length of time it is almost impossible to know what caused the shrinkage to occur. In addition, counting all the stock in a store accurately (particularly a large store that may have more than a million items to be counted) has proved to be a task highly prone to error (Turbin, 1998; DeHoratius & Raman, 2008). Item level adjustments in the stores can also cause problems in the accuracy of shrinkage data. This is when stores update their inventory files as they identify stock outs (stock not available on the shelves or in the back of the store) so that the automated reordering system is made aware to send more stock. Staff may adjust the stock inventory without accurately checking whether the store does not actually have any stock available, for instance it could be in a different location in the store or in the backroom area. This can lead to incorrect adjustments and hence incorrect shrinkage data (which are compiled from this data). Cycle counts can suffer from the same problem – staff not checking thoroughly enough whether all the stock has been located within the store when they are completing the count (this is especially the case in large supermarkets and hypermarkets where a product may be being displayed at numerous locations within the store).

Given these varying approaches to generating audit data and their inherent challenges, the quality of data available to the loss prevention practitioner on shrinkage within their businesses can be poor and lead to significant problems in identifying the true causes of shrinkage. For instance, the inevitable time lag inherent in most current auditing strategies means that the causes of many losses remain unknown. As detailed in Chapter 4, for some retailers as much as 51 per cent of their losses are unknown (Beck, 2004a) and if we use the earlier estimate for the total cost of global shrinkage ($232 billion), then this could total as much as $118 billion of retail losses are unknown to the sector. This paucity of data on the extent of the problem of shrinkage undoubtedly plays a pivotal part in producing poor product protection. Not knowing means not understanding, which means that any response will be inevitably piecemeal, partial and poorly defined. As an ECR report on shrinkage highlighted:

> In theory, the concept of stock loss reduction is simple. It can be described in terms of the three following steps: make stock highly visible so that loss is immediately noticed; quickly identify the causes of the loss; and implement preventative solutions to resolve the cause of the loss and prevent reoccurrence (Beck *et al.*, 2001: 15).

Where the industry continues to struggle is obtaining good quality data to make the first step possible, particularly information at item level. Indeed, it is interesting to compare the way in which retailers collect data on shrinkage compared with the way in which they collect information about cash within their businesses. Most companies would consider it extremely bad practice to only count the cash in their tills once every ten weeks, or perhaps only once a year! Clearly it is much easier to count a single item (cash) than multiple items of stock, but the disparity in priority is striking and reflects upon the way in which relative 'value' is measured and recognised in retail businesses.

Good decisions and effective threat assessments rely upon having high quality, reliable information on the problems faced by the business. Within loss prevention, this continues to be the exception rather than the norm which in turn is dramatically inhibiting the decision-making capabilities of those tasked to deal with it.

Loss prevention as security

Another characteristic of traditional approaches to shrinkage management is the narrowness of scope loss prevention departments have often been given or have cultivated for themselves. This has arisen from the early traditions of loss prevention that saw it primarily as a security function set up to deal with the growing problem of theft. Indeed, this was often reflected in the name given to it – usually the Security Department. This role was primarily concerned with the protection of the business from external threats, primarily by outsiders such as the risk of theft and burglary, violence and robbery. Such departments were responsible for the physical security of buildings such as the installation and use of alarms, locks and bolts and the deployment of security personnel such as guards and store detectives. But it also covered the protection of key staff as well, such as the senior managers within the business. In addition, this 'securitised' notion of loss prevention is reflected in an emphasis upon investigations of possible crimes and the interrogation of likely offenders. A survey of loss prevention managers by Hayes highlighted this particular issue. He found that when asked how they spent their time, the most common response was 'responding to current issues' such as large employee theft incidents or violence in particular stores, compared with 'long-term loss prevention planning which was the second least chosen area (Hayes, 2003: 13).

This narrowness of scope is also seen in the type of shrinkage that such departments prioritise – principally unknown losses. This leads to other areas of shrinkage management being undertaken by other functions within the business such as audit and store operations, including shrinkage caused by process failures (waste, damage, problems with returns, stock going out of date, price reductions etc).

While this representation of loss prevention as 'security' is less prevalent in this century than the last, it can still be found in many retailers operating around the world, where those employed to do this task see themselves more as the company's police force than a complimentary part of the retail management framework. As such, performance is often measured in 'body counts', such as the number of staff and customers arrested and convicted, and the amount of cash and goods recovered, than by the contribution made to business profitability and sales. Undoubtedly some of the functions outlined above are a necessary part of ensuring that a business is properly secured, but the key is developing a loss prevention function which considers this to be just one part of a broader responsibility for delivering a 'loss less sell more' culture.

Policing retailing

Following on from the previous point, retail loss prevention has a long tradition of looking to the police, military and other security services as a source of recruits, particularly at senior levels. Indeed, a successful career in one of these services was often all that was needed to secure a job in retail loss prevention (and for some retailers it still is) (Curtis, 1971). At first glance, this would seem a logical recruitment strategy, particularly if a business subscribes to the 'securitised' notion of loss prevention described above – former police officers will likely have significant experience of dealing with crime and carrying out investigations and interviewing suspects – the bread and butter of much of their former work. However, some have questioned the suitability of such experience within the modern loss prevention function, where the emphasis is (or at least should be) much more upon delivering retail excellence than it is upon catching thieves.

Whilst not wishing to tar all former police officers and military personnel with the same brush (we have met many who are extremely good at what they do), they have often come from a culture that is very alien to that found in retailing (such as allowing some crime to happen because it is cheaper than trying to prevent it) and one which is steeped in adopting a highly reactive and crime oriented approach to what they do (something which was expected of them in their previous roles). Good loss prevention management requires a very different set of skills grounded in a keen appreciation of the fundamental precepts of retailing – as one senior retail member of the ECR Europe Shrinkage Group succinctly put it – 'it is much easier to train a retailer to be a loss prevention manager than it is to train a former police officer to become a retailer'. As has often been said, good loss prevention is not rocket science, but it does require a keen understanding of the retail business and how its operations can enable and inhibit loss within the business. This is not to suggest that any former police or military personnel should not be employed within a retail loss prevention function – they certainly should as they can bring some valuable skills to the team – but a preponderance of this type of personnel (particularly in senior positions) can lead to a loss prevention function that becomes more concerned with catching thieves than it does with helping the business to deliver retailing excellence. As Maslow's much quoted phrase neatly summarises, it is tempting when your only tool is a hammer, to treat everything as a nail (Maslow, 1969).

Working in isolation

Another trait of what might be described as 'old loss prevention' is a tendency to be isolated within the business and seen as the only function tasked with dealing with shrinkage. Research both by Beck (2004a) and Hayes (2003) has highlighted how most loss prevention managers view store operations as their primary partners within the business, with other functions such as buying, human resources, marketing and finance as having a marginal role to play in helping with the problem of shrinkage. As we will document later, *New Loss Prevention* requires those responsible for managing shrinkage to be 'agents of change', orchestrating a cross functional approach to deal effectively with the problem. Unless this is the case, then solutions will be more focused on dealing with the symptoms of the problem than the root causes and as such will have a limited impact. Collaboration outside the business is also an attribute rarely seen in the old forms of loss prevention, particularly with the manufacturers who provide the goods to the retailer. This more systemic approach seeks to understand how the root causes of shrinkage may be tackled much further down the supply chain such as in the way in which goods are packaged and transported. As an ECR Europe report found, 'shrinkage is a problem that transcends ... company boundaries – it is something that requires genuine partnership and co-operation if it is to be managed efficiently and effectively' (Beck *et al.*, 2001: 6).

Adopting an 'isolationist' approach to loss prevention can lead not only to the wrong solutions being sought and applied, but can also act as a disincentive to those currently employed in other functions to see a future role in loss prevention as a meaningful way to progress their retailing careers – who would want to work in a function that is viewed as a marginal back water within the overall business structure?

Myopic management

If old style loss prevention can be viewed as isolationist, then it also has a tendency to suffer from myopia as well – with the problem primarily being seen to occur at the end of the supply chain; in the retail stores. This is in part a function of the prioritisation of shop theft as the primary cause of stock loss (see below). Certainly the store is the point at which customers are allowed to interact with the products and where many of the current technology 'solutions' are most easily applied, but as an ECR Europe survey of loss prevention managers found, up to one third of loss takes place before the goods have reached the retail outlet, highlighting the need to look at losses of goods in transit and while being stored in distribution centres (Beck, 2004a). Certainly the stores are a very vulnerable part of the supply chain, but they are very much *a part* of the chain and stock loss practitioners need to look beyond the retail outlet and recognise that good loss prevention is about considering how losses occur throughout the entire supply chain. Indeed, the stores could be the victim of being the first point of product loss visibility – shrinkage which occurred prior to this location is 'washed' through the system and only gets recognised at this stage because it is the first time stock is the subject of more formalised counting and accounting procedures.

It would seem, therefore, that a possible cure to this loss prevention myopia is adopting a much more systemic and systematic approach to understanding the problem of shrinkage within the business – identifying the true location of the loss through good retail data capture systems and developing operational excellence.

Constantly searching for the 'bogeyman' of shrinkage

As detailed in the previous chapter, external theft has been an ongoing priority for many loss prevention practitioners, often to the detriment of other causes of shrinkage that become marginalised and forgotten in its wake. Undoubtedly the impact of shop theft on the retail community is considerable and much research has been undertaken trying to get to grips with the scale and extent of the problem as well as identifying those most likely to engage in it and what might be used to detect and deter them. However, as we have argued early, it overly dominates the old loss prevention agenda and the search for the 'bogeyman' of shrinkage is often undertaken in such a way as to relegate other key causes of shrinkage to the periphery. Partly this can be explained by some of the factors outlined above – the preponderance of former police officers and the 'securitisation' of the function can lead to the catching of external thieves becoming the primary role of loss prevention. But it is also a function of relative ease – the targeting of shop thieves can be viewed as the path of least resistance – both politically and operationally. As detailed earlier, targeting internal theft is fraught with difficulties not least in the way in which the company may be viewed by external groups if it is seen to be unearthing large amounts of fraud and theft committed by those who have been previously selected, entrusted and presumably controlled by retail management. It is also a potentially difficult crime to uncover as staff have significant amounts of opportunity almost constantly available to them as well as detailed knowledge of the company's processes and procedures that will enable them to cover their tracks or ensure that losses are presumed to be the work of outsiders.

In addition, losses from process failures can often be excused as mere 'wooden dollars' where the company has not really lost anything, and the missing stock will eventually show up somewhere else in the supply chain and its value will still be realised. As we argued earlier, process failure losses are often viewed as the 'acceptable face of shrinkage' or simply an inevitable (and regrettable) cost of doing business – more the preserve of accountants and audits than loss prevention practitioners. And so external theft is viewed as the easiest and most natural problem for loss prevention teams to address, usually egged on by a supplier industry that has an endless conveyor belt of new 'solutions' ready to fix the problem.

Yet it is the problem that loss prevention practitioners arguably has the least control over. It is committed by an enormous array of people who: are motivated by a myriad of complex and interwoven reasons; are not employed by the business; often have unfettered access to a wide range of desirable and easily stealable goods within an environment that is predominantly understaffed; operate within societies that sometimes have rather ambiguous attitudes towards the morality and seriousness of the offences they carry out; and in the unlikely event that they are ever caught, are likely to be dealt with by a criminal justice system which is often portrayed as more interested in decriminalisation rather than handing down more punitive sanctions for the crimes they have committed. The odds are severely stacked against the loss prevention practitioner who decides to prioritise shop theft as the main focus of their work. In contrast, both internal theft and process failures operate strictly within the bounds of the business itself – a potentially controllable space where activities can be monitored, behaviours affected and sanctions imposed. In addition, root causes can be more easily identified and ameliorative responses developed that are fit for purpose and meet the overall objectives of the business.

Arguably, old loss prevention's obsession with chasing down the bogeyman of shrinkage can only end in a fruitless and unending quest to control the uncontrollable. This is not to say that responding to external theft should not be part of what loss prevention should do; it is undoubtedly a concern that needs addressing, but its dominance of the agenda can undermine a more rounded and realistic approach to reducing the problem of shrinkage in retailing.

Seeking the technological 'fix'

We live in a world increasingly awash with technology with recent estimates suggesting that there are now over one billion personal computers in use (Gartner, 2008) and as many as 6.68 billion Internet users (InternetWorldStats, 2008). Technology is becoming embedded in all parts of our lives (quite literally with the proposed developments in RFID technologies) and is often portrayed as the cornerstone of modernity (Misa, 2004). While debates continue about the extent of the impact new technologies have upon our society, there is undoubtedly a widely held belief that the last 70 years has seen the birth of the 'scientific age' and that human advancement can best be achieved through the 'appliance of science'. This has been most marked in the fields of communication, medicine and travel, but it has also been seen in the world of loss prevention.

The quest for ways in which technologies can help in the fight against shrinkage have a relatively long history. As detailed earlier, the turn of the 20th century saw retailers beginning to use discretely located mirrors to enable staff to keep an eye on suspicious customers when their backs were turned (Abelson, 1989). By the 1950s and 1960s loss prevention practitioners were starting to use a host of technologies to assist them in their work, including: communications devices such as radios and listening devices; observation devices such as rudimentary CCTV, cameras and two way mirrors; protection devices such as alarms; detection devices such as fingerprinting equipment; and probing devices such as lie detectors (Curtis, 1960). Perhaps more prosaically, this period also saw one author hypothesising that the use of ionisation machines may play a role in reducing shrinkage as the distribution of negative ions in the shopping space would be likely to reduce internal and external theft (Curtis, 1960). The 1970s saw the first uses of Electronic Article Surveillance (EAS) devices, initially through the attachment of hard tags to goods viewed as being at risk from external theft (Bamfield, 1994; Dilonardo, 1997). From this point onwards, EAS technologies have evolved considerably and have become a key part of the shrinkage reduction strategy of many retailers (Handford, 1994). EAS tags now come in many shapes and sizes, with some being applied at the point of manufacture (source tagging) while others can contain a dye substance that will irreparably damage the tagged product if offenders try to remove them (ink tags) (Dilonardo & Clarke, 1996).

The 1980s and 1990s saw the more widespread use of CCTV technologies both within the store environment and more broadly across shopping environments, with perhaps the UK leading the way in introducing hundreds of thousands of cameras surveilling public spaces including town centres and shopping centres (Loveday & Gill, 2003; Lyon, 2007; McCahill, 2002; Norris & Armstrong, 1999). More recently still we see developments in the use of Radio Frequency Identification technologies (RFID) as a means to combat retail shrinkage, with plans a foot to uniquely tag all products manufactured in the future so that they can be monitored and tracked remotely, creating a level of product transparency that would offer loss prevention practitioners an unprecedented window on their shrinkage problem (Brock, 2001; Hodges & Harrison, 2003; Parliamentary Office of Science and Technology, 2004; Beck, 2006b).

This brief and incomplete potted history of technological developments in the world of loss prevention highlights a number of key issues that have influenced the way in which the industry has progressed. Firstly, loss prevention practitioners have been enthusiastic advocates of new technologies – they are keen to find the technological fix that will solve their shrinkage problems, particularly external theft. The idea that a single technological silver bullet is available to slay the shrinkage dragon is one which seems to appeal to the loss prevention community. It is also a message that the multi-billion dollar loss prevention supplier industry is keen to reinforce. Beck and Willis in the early 1990s, as part of a broader study, carried out a relatively unsophisticated review of the advertising used by security companies targeting the retail sector in a range of UK-based publications (Beck & Willis, 1995). These were companies primarily selling Closed Circuit Television (CCTV) and Electronic Article Surveillance (EAS) and the language was almost universally that of absolute solutions solving a plethora of problems relating to crime and shrinkage. The use of the words 'solution' 'answer' and 'proven' was frequent and widespread. It is not difficult to see how such messages will resonate with a loss prevention practitioner who is struggling to reduce losses from shrinkage, particularly when under pressure from senior management and lacking the necessary data to understand what might be really causing the problem.

Secondly, many technologies introduced to try and deal with external theft have a limited period of time when they have an effect – the equivalent of a loss prevention half life. Offenders quickly become familiar with the technology and begin to develop methods to circumvent its effectiveness. For instance, there are now a host of ways in which EAS tags can be defeated by the wily shop thief, such as using an aluminium lined bag (the magic bag trick) to block the signal between the tag and the antenna pedestals located at store exits, bending the tags and shielding the tag through holding it close to the human body (Caime & Ghone, 1996; Gill, 2007). Similarly, identification by CCTV has proven to be easily defeated, not least by simply wearing a hat! Moreover, this 'half life' of course means that there is a constant need to develop new technologies that attempt to address the deficiencies of the previous versions – the equivalent of an arms race in which ever more sophisticated and ingenious solutions are required to counter the guile of the ever evolving wily thief.

Thirdly, security technologies can have a negative impact upon levels of staff vigilance as employees no longer consider themselves to have a role in store security because they perceive the technology is now taking care of this function (Beck & Willis, 1992). Technologies can also be undermined by poor store compliance – confidence in EAS has been seriously undermined by often high levels of false alarms caused by faulty or poorly installed technology and staff forgetting to either remove or deactivate the tag at the point of sale. This in turns has led to the rise of the 'crying wolf syndrome' where staff assume that any alarm is probably false because it has been on so many previous occasions. This degree of staff apathy can then be exploited by the committed shop thief who may be cheerfully waved through the detection gates by a member of staff as the alarm is activated!

Fourthly, there is relatively little published evidence on the effectiveness of many of the most common technologies employed by loss prevention practitioners (Beck, 2008), with EAS being the one subject to most attention (see for instance Dilonardo, 1997). The studies that do exist are usually wholly funded by the technology providers themselves and few would stand up to the rigours of any form of independent assessment of the methodologies use to generate their findings. To often they are carried out by the self interested and the untrained (Pawson & Tilley, 1997). Even the number of studies covering the most popular technology – EAS – that can be considered reliable is small, with the findings being rather mixed and inconclusive on its impact on shrinkage. Technology providers have also been shy in commissioning independent research that looks at the way in which their products actually work in the retail environment, particularly when it comes to those for whom the system is originally designed – offenders themselves. Probably little wonder as the few available studies based upon this type of methodology show that offenders have rarely anything but contempt for devices such as EAS and CCTV and consider them as a minor irritation to their thieving activity (Gill & Loveday, 2003; Gill, 2007). Indeed, if CCTV or EAS were a drug, we would be absolutely appalled at the way it has been introduced and widely used without any rigorous prior testing of its likely impact on the patient.

Loss prevention practitioners are not alone in adopting a 'technocentric' approach to responding to the challenges that they face – many other parts of the economy have positively blossomed as new technologies have been introduced, such as communications and medicine. But old loss prevention is perhaps guilty of leaning a little too heavily on this particular crutch, especially when it is not clear that the crutch actually works in the first place. It is of course deeply appealing to think that complex issues such as external theft and staff theft can be solved simply by the application of a technology, but the reality is very different. On many occasions they are introduced based upon gut instinct rather than rigorous assessment, and then merely react to the symptoms of the problem rather than addressing the underlying causes. In some cases they can actually exacerbate the situation such as making staff less inclined to take loss prevention seriously (Beck & Willis, 1992). Above all, technologies need to be seen as merely adding another option to the loss prevention tool box, but only when it has been thoroughly tested and its supposed impact verified within a given context. If it is not, then the 'appliance of science' will continue to fail to deliver effective solutions to the problem of stock loss.

Old loss prevention – Turning the corner

While our intention in this chapter has not been to undermine the efforts of a loss prevention community that has often responded admirably to a working environment that has become ever more complex as retailing has evolved into a global phenomenon increasingly responsible for the economic well being of many post-industrial countries. As we have mentioned elsewhere, the complexity of modern retailing is extraordinary and some could argue that keeping rates of shrinkage relatively static over the past 30–40 years is a success in itself. But there are key issues which we believe have seriously undermined the ability of loss prevention practitioners to deliver even more effective shrinkage management. Getting to grips with the measurement of the problem is a fundamental part and this knowledge gap has often left loss prevention managers fumbling in the dark, often alone. It has meant that problem that is most visible and most acceptable tends to get the most attention – external shop theft. It is also exemplified by an understandable desire to seek a quick technological fix to the problem.

As detailed at the start of this book, our approach to loss prevention seeks to address these issues through developing an approach which is much more grounded in adopting a systemic and systematic method to understanding the shrinkage problems faced by retailers, premised upon rigorous and robust data. It seeks to use a collaborative framework where loss prevention practitioners act as agents of change orchestrating a cross functional strategy to respond to the problem. Above all, it prioritises the identification of operational failures as the root causes of shrinkage. In the next chapter we will outline this approach much further.

7
Operational Failure as a Driver of Shrinkage

The previous chapters have sought to outline the context of shrinkage and its management in retailing, focusing particularly upon the impact of changes within the overall retailing landscape, the scale, nature and extent of the problem and some of the barriers currently facing loss prevention practitioners. This next chapter seeks to outline the broad contours of what we see as *New Loss Prevention* and its underlying theory. Central to our approach is understanding the role of operational failures as a root cause of shrinkage and how these need to be fully understood before any remedial actions can be taken to deal with the problem. As detailed previously many of our concerns about the existing ways in which loss prevention practitioners have gone about responding to shrinkage have been centred on an inability to move beyond seeking solutions which are targeted more at the symptoms of the problems than the root causes. This can often be seen in ad hoc and piecemeal interventions designed to deal with external theft and the marginalisation of significant shrinkage generators such as internal theft and process failures.

Underpinning our argument is the way in which we see operational failures as the primary mechanism for creating the opportunities for malicious shrinkage and the circumstances within which non-malicious shrinkage can occur. We will start off by first considering what we mean by the term operational failure and then go to explore the role of opportunity in understanding criminal behaviour and more generally the theory of situational crime prevention which we feel has a vital role to play in setting the broader context for our thesis. It is worth reiterating at this point that we recognise that operational failures are not the root cause of all the shrinkage suffered by retailers, but we do feel that to date their role has been marginalised and that they account for a far greater proportion of shrinkage than is currently recognised.

Understanding operational failures

The starting point is to understand what we mean by the term 'operational failure'. We adopt a relatively broad definition which sees operational failures as any fault in the design, implementation, operation, monitoring and control, and review of processes and procedures used within the retail environment. Operational failures can occur at any point in the supply chain from point of manufacture through to the eventual sale of goods to the customer (and beyond in respect of product returns). These failures can then lead to, in some situations, circumstances or opportunities for malicious and non-malicious shrinkage to occur. In order to understand the nature of operational failures, it is perhaps useful to look at a number of examples.

A company may have a procedure in place whereby all high value goods are to be stored in a secure cage at the back of the store. This procedure, however, is not followed because the only member of staff with the key is on holiday, and so high value stock is left outside the secure cage. Some of this stock is then stolen by a member of staff. The outcome of this is a case of internal theft, but the root cause of the problem is that the company has an inadequate procedure in place for dealing with situations where the key holder for the secure cage is on holiday. A dishonest member of staff has used the *opportunity* presented by this operational failure to steal stock.

Let us look at another example. A forklift truck driver working in a distribution centre crashes into a pallet of stock causing much of it to be written off and subsequently destroyed. The reason why the crash occurred was because the driver of the forklift was driving too quickly, and the reason he was doing this was because his pay is calculated on the number of pallets he moves in a day. Therefore the company's policy of performance-related pay for forklift truck drivers has (partly) created the *circumstances* under which the shrinkage has occurred.

Let us look at another example of how operational failures can be the root cause of shrinkage and how changes made by one part of the business can have an unintended impact. A retail company has brought in a new procedure where at the end of a shift working on a checkout, a till operator no longer has to reconcile the amount of money taken with the recorded sales. This was done in the interests of saving time in the cashiers office (and money as less cash audit staff are now required). This change in procedure is then exploited by staff working early shifts who steal cash in the knowledge that many other members of staff will have used that till subsequent to their offending. In this case the change to the auditing procedure creates the opportunity for the cash to be stolen with low levels of risk. This is also an example of where changes to operations by one part of the business can have indirect but palpable consequences for managing shrinkage. In the financial world this is often described as 'moral hazard', where decisions taken at one level for a particular reason (in this case to save staff costs) have an impact in another area, but consequences do not directly impact upon those who took the original decision (Kaplin & Norton, 1996). So in this case, it could be that store operations see a saving in staff costs, but the loss prevention department sees an increase in shrinkage. For the former, shrinkage is not a metric used to judge their performance and so they have little interest in the negative outcome of more shrinkage. For the loss prevention department, the impact is profound, but unless the root cause is identified, then they could make decisions to try and respond to the problem which are unnecessary, such as installing cameras above all the checkouts and installing software to monitor transactions by each operator.

Let us look at a final example. A particular (date sensitive) product is consistently considered to be out of stock at the shelf, despite the store regularly reordering the product through manual adjustments to the automatic ordering system. Persistent external theft is viewed as the root cause of the out of stocks. A more detailed analysis reveals that the store has plenty of the items in the back of the store (in fact too many because of the constant reordering of further stock and much of the product has to then be written off) – the problem is that the staff are not able to easily identify the stock in the back room areas. This is due to the nature of the outer packaging of the product which makes it difficult to differentiate from other similar items. It is revealed that the design of the outer packaging, which consists of only a bar code has been primarily designed for ease of handling in the manufacturer and retailer distribution network. Once again, attempts to reduce the shrinkage on this item could have been focused upon trying to deal with a perceived external theft issue, such as applying EAS tags, installing CCTV or even implementing defensive merchandising techniques such as placing the item behind the counter. However, root cause analysis reveals that an operational failure – in this case poorly thought through external packaging of the product making it difficult for store staff to quickly identify the product – is actually the problem. The solution then is not necessarily more security, but instead more thought on how the packaging can be redesigned to enable store staff to quickly recognise the product amongst the many others in the backroom area.

While these are four markedly different examples, they all highlight the importance of undertaking root cause analysis to understand the role of operational failures in either creating the circumstances under which shrinkage can occur, or the opportunities for offenders to commit malicious acts against the business. Operational failures (in all their guises) need to be the starting point at which the root causes of shrinkage are examined. Too often previous attempts to tackle shrinkage have merely dealt with the symptoms of their failure for instance in the last two examples described above. Undertaking a detailed analysis of how the business processes relating to a particular product impact upon its likelihood to suffer from shrinkage is the key premise of *New Loss Prevention*. In the next part of this chapter we will review how this supposition is supported by existing theories, in particular those coming from the world of criminology which seek to explain the link between situation and opportunity.

Opportunity through operational failure

Situational crime prevention

The role of opportunity in explaining criminal behaviour has a long and established position within criminological thinking, most noticeably in the work of Clarke and others on Situational Crime Prevention (Clarke, 1980; Clarke & Mayhew, 1980). This theory seeks to explain how changes to the environment and how it is managed can reduce the opportunities for crime to occur. It is therefore more focused upon the setting for crime rather than the attributes of those committing the offence. In this respect, if differs from most established criminological theories which are more concerned with understanding why certain individuals or groups are more likely to become involved in deviant behaviour, focusing particularly upon psychological or social influences such as upbringing, class, poverty, social exclusion and so on. Tilley, arguing in favour of situational crime prevention notes that such distal factors, so far as they are understood, are far harder to alter than proximal ones (such as the circumstances in which crimes take place (Tilley, 1997).

Situational prevention comprises opportunity-reducing measures that: 'are directed at highly specific forms of crime; involve the management, design or manipulation of the immediate environment in as systematic and permanent way as possible; and make crime more difficult and risky, or less rewarding and excusable as judged by a wide range of offenders' (Clarke, 1997: 4). The idea of the role of situation in determining (in part) the likelihood of offending behaviour is not new and can be traced back to the work of Bentham in the 19th century, but more recent theorising has increased the significance of situation in providing explanatory power and has led directly to the development of a number of other related theories which will be discussed below, namely Rational Choice Perspective and Routine Activity (Cornish & Clarke, 1986). It also shares similar principles with the work of Newman and others who looked at the opportunities for designing out crime in residential environments (the idea of defensible space) and more generally the developments in Crime Prevention Through Environmental Design (CPTED) (Jeffery, 1977; Newman, 1996). This work looked specifically at the ways in which the built environment could be adapted to reduce the opportunities for offending to take place, such as improving street lighting and limiting the points of access for non-residents.

A number of writers have elaborated on the importance of the situation in acting as a key driver of offender decision-making – Felson and Clarke refer to them as 'invitations to crime' – where situational prevention can reduce the number of such 'invitations' and hence make it more difficult for those who do offend to escape responsibility (Felson & Clarke, 1997). Similarly, Cornish and Clarke (1986) describe them as 'choice-structuring' factors referring to the way in which offenders will make decisions based upon the opportunities presented by the situation they are presently in. Building on this, Cusson (1993) refers to situational deterrence which reflects upon the way in which offenders are far more concerned about the chances of getting caught than they are about the subsequent punishment, and so it is more important to try and increase the risk of apprehension through manipulating the situation in which offenders operate.

Two linked theories are important to consider when trying to understand how operational failures can provide the opportunities for dishonest activity to take place in the retail environment: Rational Choice Perspectives on crime and Routine Activities theory.

Rational choice perspectives

This theory is premised upon the idea that potential offenders make a calculation about what are the likely benefits of committing the act, and whether it is worth it given the degree of effort required, the perceived likelihood of apprehension and subsequent severity of punishment. It assumes that behaviour is goal oriented (see below) and the situation makes the accomplishment of the task possible. 'The assumption is that the actor (more or less committed, depending on his or her motivation) will take the path of least resistance (a rational choice, or series of rational choices) in order to accomplish the criminal goal; if the paths to that goal are made too difficult, he or she will desist, or "give up"' (Becker, 1968; Newman, 1997: 9). As detailed early in relation to staff dishonesty, Nagin *et al.* (2002) came up with a useful phrase for offenders – 'rational cheaters' – those who steal because the opportunities exist and the anticipated benefits of crime exceed the likely costs.

Specifically defining rationale choice is, however, not a straightforward task, even though the overarching concept has been widely discussed, not least because it is difficult to conclude that all humans perceive rationality in the same way. For this reason many writers (such as Clarke, 1997; Simon, 1978) prefer the terms 'limited' or 'bounded' rationality as it portrays the sense that not all actors will have access to complete information or be fully aware of their circumstances and hence may act in a way which for others would be considered irrational. In addition, there may be dispositional factors (such as upbringing, education, poverty etc) which can play a part in framing a person's perception of rationality.

Routine activities theory

First developed by Cohen and Felson (1979) this theory suggests that in order for an offence to take place, you need to have the coming together of three key factors: a likely offender; a suitable target; and the absence of a capable guardian. In line with other theoretical work on situational crime prevention, it is less interested in the motivations of the offender and is more concerned with the way in which these three factors converge in time and space. An example within the retail environment would be a member of staff handling valuable stock unsupervised or unmonitored – the employee is the likely offender, the goods are the suitable target and the lack of any supervision or monitoring is the absence of a capable guardian (note that a guardian need not necessarily be a person, it could be a form of security device). More recent work has suggested two further elements could/should be added to the original model: the inclusion of an 'intimate handler' or somebody who knows the offender well enough to afford a substantial brake on the latter's activities (Felson, 1986); and 'crime facilitators' such as automobiles or guns or perhaps access keys or cards, or even a 'mark down' gun.

What is important about this theory is that it views the offender as only one of the elements in a criminal event – their action is dependent upon a number of other factors, many of which are not controllable by the offender.

Opportunity makes the thief

What these theories propose is that all humans have a potential propensity to be dishonest. Understanding why humans are likely to commit crime goes into the realms of philosophical debates concerning the overarching purpose of human actions and is certainly beyond the scope of this book, but it is important to understand the motivation for human behaviour and the overarching desire to benefit oneself. This takes place according to any given actors needs, values, moral disposition and emotional preferences. While we are not advocates of a Machiavellian outlook on human nature which essentially takes an 'anything goes' approach to securing personal benefits, we are also not aligned with that of say Adam Smith and others who see the natural moral orientation of human life as essentially benevolent.

What seems more likely is that some people's causal liabilities are more easily triggered than others (Tilley, 1997). Most people will have some level of preparedness for some rule infraction at some time in their lives. Tilley suggests that there is a crime readiness continuum stretching from those who have a very low (but not non-existent) likelihood of committing a crime through to those who are highly criminogenic. He proposes that those at the lower end of the continuum are much more easily deflected away from misbehaving by relatively simple measures such as shaming or assumed risk, while those at the other end require much more involved measures such as incapacitation (for instance prison) or high levels of monitoring (Tilley, 1997). The key point to Tilley is that society cannot be divided into motivated or non-motivated offenders but more into a range of groups with varying levels of readiness to commit crime (which in part is created by distal factors such as upbringing, education, poverty, socialisation and so on), and who may or may not be triggered to offend depending upon the situation and opportunities presented to them.

Wortley also uses the term 'readying' to explain how situations can act upon a person's likelihood to take advantage of opportunities that arise (1997). He argues that they can occur prior to cost-benefit analysis (bounded rationality) and may significantly affect that analysis, but do not necessarily determine the behavioural outcome. He goes on to suggest that there is a need to recognise the role *readying processes* can have in the decision-making of offenders. Moreover, Wortley sees opportunity reduction theories as being underpinned by extensive psychological literature dealing with fundamental questions about the nature of human behaviour and the propensity to commit criminal acts. Common sense suggests that there is a great deal of variability in the way that we act – we are not always confident nor timid, polite nor rude, or honest nor dishonest. Rather, behaviour often depends upon where people are, who they are with and what they are doing. Very often most people can recall situations where they have acted in a way which at a later date might be considered to be 'out of character' A view of potential offenders which sees their criminal propensities as fundamentally affected by situational forces better conveys a dependency upon the environment that we have all experienced at one time or another (Wortley, 1997).

Responsibility and opportunity

It is also important to recognise that while the blame for committing the act rests squarely with the offender – some advocates of situational crime prevention relate the responsibility for creating the opportunity in the first place with all contributors to the situation, whether proximate or distant – be it the product designer, the security technology developer, the store manager or work colleagues (Newman, 1997). This has implications for the social control of crime and the allocation of responsibility. If a causal analysis of why a particular product is more likely to be stolen reveals that it is due mainly to the design of the packaging and a refusal by the manufacturer to change it, then it would not seem unreasonable to allocate some of the blame accordingly. This is most certainly not to say that the offender is no longer responsible for their behaviour, but that some of that responsibility should be spread so that others take necessary precautions to reduce their likelihood of being victimised (see our earlier discussion on the rise of self selection shopping in Chapter 2).

Operational failure and malicious shrinkage

The theories described above underpin our thinking relating to the role operational failures have in creating shrinkage in the retail environment. In terms of malicious shrinkage they provide the situation in which a range of actors, be they members of staff or customers, are given the opportunity to commit offences. All people have some probability of committing crime depending on the circumstances in which they find themselves. We do not draw hard distinctions necessarily between criminals and others but that a continuum exists whereby some are more or less likely to take advantage of the opportunities presented to them dependent upon the way in which they rationally portray the situation.

This moves away from dispositional theories that suggest that the tendency to offend is essentially fixed although we do recognise that some distal factors such as upbringing, personal economic circumstances and so on are undoubtedly likely to have a role in formulating their bounded rationality. But few offenders are so driven by need or desire that they have to maintain a certain level of offending whatever the cost. For many the elimination of easy opportunities for crime may actually be sufficient to deflect them from offending. What is certainly true in the retail environment is that it is usually much 'easier to change situations rather than souls' (Cusson, 1992, quoted by Sève, 1997: 190). People can and do make choices, but they are rarely able to choose the choices open to them (Felson, 1994). The context is crucial for the choices people make, the results of which are observed in their behaviour (Tilley, 1997).

Another key component of the theories relating to situational crime prevention which we feel is a fundamental part of *New Loss Prevention*, is the importance of focusing on specific forms of offending (or in our case shrinkage). Developing effective solutions (or in our case operational excellence) requires a detailed understanding of the context and circumstances in which the offence took place – it is necessary to delve into the micro levels of understanding if appropriate and lasting solutions are to be created. For example, trying to develop solutions to deal with the problem of domestic burglary requires a detailed analysis of the various types of burglary that occur, for instance domestic burglary compared with commercial burglary. And even within each of these sub categories, further specificity is required, for instance domestic burglary where only jewellery is stolen compared with incidents where only electrical items are stolen. An example from the world of retail loss prevention would be breaking down incidents of theft by type of product category, and then analysing particular items within a category. If the analysis remains only at the category level, then potential solutions are likely to be ineffective as we have insufficiently nuanced information to make the right decisions. In many respects this has been a key problem with retail loss prevention and something which we touched upon in the previous chapter – unless sufficiently granulated data is collected and analysed, proposed solutions are more than likely going to be ineffective and poorly targeted.

Some have argued that the retail environment is 'pregnant' with opportunities for members of staff and the public to steal (Pease, 1997); as detailed early, Hollinger and Davis have reflected on the plethora of opportunities members of staff have to steal within the retail space and posed the not unreasonable question: 'given that so much opportunity exists, why isn't there even more theft given the numerous opportunities for taking things in the retail store?' (Hollinger & Davis, 2006: 211). As we hypothesised earlier, it could be that there is and retailers are simply unable to identify its true extent amongst all the unknown loss that accumulates in the shrinkage pile (or perhaps retailers simply prefer to apportion it to external theft as it is politically far more expedient). Whilst in part this is almost certainly true, it could also be that successful retailers (in terms of having low shrinkage) have minimised the degree of operational failures within their business which in turn has reduced the perceived opportunities for staff to take advantage. The current controls, checks and balances and processes and procedures mean that most staff draw a (bounded) rational conclusion that given the risks and consequences and amount of effort required compared to the potential rewards, it is simply not worth offending.

Operational failure and non-malicious shrinkage

While minimising opportunity through the effective design, implementation, monitoring and control and continual review of company processes and procedures can have a significant impact upon malicious forms of shrinkage, we also would like to argue that non-malicious forms of shrinkage are equally impacted by operational failures, but without the causal linkage generated through opportunity or 'readying'. In some situations the operational failure itself can lead directly to various forms of shrinkage, such as poor stock rotation processes leading to products being either marked down or written off, or they can generate the circumstances under which shrinkage may occur, such as excess stock being stored outside and subsequently getting damaged by unexpectedly bad weather.

As with malicious shrinkage, the key is to understand the underlying or root causes of the shrinkage problem through a detailed review of the operational processes and procedures relating specifically to the products suffering from shrinkage. In the next chapter we will outline in more detail how through the use of the Shrinkage Road Map, and in particular through the use of tools such as Process Mapping, and Failure Mode and Effect Analysis (FMEA), the links between operational failures and shrinkage can be quickly and easily identified.

Focusing on operational failures first

Detailed in Figure 7.1 is a representation of how we view the linkages between retail shrinkage and operational failures within the retail environment. We fully recognise that there are some types of shrinkage that cannot be directly impacted upon through the manipulation of business processes and procedures, such as accidental damage of goods by customers (such as a bottle of wine being dropped whilst a customer is looking at it), planned shrinkage by retailers or their suppliers (such as the deliberate overstocking of goods to maintain shelf presence or to ensure continued high levels of quality such as with fresh bread products) or highly organised and determined shop thieves who will overcome most forms of store security (by brute force or a degree of planning). But we feel that each of these play only a relatively small part in explaining the majority of shrinkage suffered by retailers. Most would agree that the first two types rarely feature towards the top of the shrinkage concern list for most retailers, while the latter, although more debatable (certainly with respect to the ongoing concerns about the impact of organised retail crime in the US), is still a relatively (thankfully) rare event for most forms of retailing.

We suggest that the vast majority of shrinkage can be effectively tackled through the elimination (or at least minimisation) of operational failures within retail businesses. The starting point for most businesses should be tackling the 'quick wins' that can be achieved through ensuring operational excellence. Once they have been achieved, and mecha-

Figure 7.1   How Operational Failures Drive Shrinkage

nisms have been put in place to monitor compliance and review suitability, loss prevention should then move on to the more thorny and problematic forms of shrinkage created by persistent and committed thieves. Dealing with this problem may undoubtedly require much more than addressing operational failures (although there are certainly benefits to be gained from reviewing their impact), but careful cost benefit analyses needs to be undertaken to ensure that any proposed 'solutions' do not end up costing more than the original problem. In some respects, this is as much a challenge for the providers of loss prevention technologies as it is retailers themselves. Too often we have seen 'solutions' searching for 'problems' with little prospect of success because the overall cost of implementation far outweighs the financial benefits accrued by the retailer. As the old adage goes, solutions need to be 'fit for purpose' and in the harsh economic realities of the retail world, this means costing less than the original problem they were introduced to solve.

Operational failure as a driver of shrinkage

Earlier in this book we argued that shrinkage continues to be a significant threat to the retail sector and that most current approaches are at best keeping a lid on the problem. This has in part been caused by an overly narrow and often confused analysis of the true causes of shrinkage, focused especially upon external theft. This has led to many so called 'solutions' being developed which deal more with the symptoms of the problem than the root causes. In this chapter we have tried to argue that loss prevention practitioners need to recognise the key role operational failures play in causing of shrinkage. We have adopted a broad ranging definition for operational failures viewing them as any fault in the design, implementation, operation, monitoring and control, and review of processes and procedures used within the retail environment. This can be at any point in the supply chain from point of manufacture through to the eventual sale of goods to the customer (and beyond in respect of product returns).

Using the theoretical framework provided by situational crime prevention we argue that operational failures provide the opportunities for much of the shrinkage caused by malicious shrinkage and is the root cause of virtually all forms of non-malicious shrinkage. Focusing on an opportunity/circumstance-driven interpretation of retail loss enables loss prevention practitioners to begin to identify the root causes of the problem, which in turn can then facilitate the development of solutions which are 'fit for purpose' and likely to be more long lasting and appropriate for the dynamics of a modern retail environment. We are certainly not suggesting that all forms of shrinkage can be resolved by adopting this approach (highly determined thieves will always find a way to circumvent even the most robust and high tech barriers placed before them, particularly in an environment such as retailing), but we do suggest that most forms of loss can be addressed in this way, and it should certainly be the starting point for ameliorative actions before moving on to the more challenging aspects of the shrinkage conundrum.

Most would agree that the retail environment is a space which is laden with temptation and opportunity – indeed it could be argued that the phenomenal global success of retailing in the last 50 years or so has in part been premised on these two variables. But they both bring with them risk – there is often a very thin line between positive encouragement to shop and spend, and to steal. We would argue that it is the responsibility of the retail community to ensure that both the working environment for employees and the shopping space for customers, is not overly laden with overt opportunities to cross this line.

There is undoubtedly a delicate balance to be struck between selling and security (Beck & Willis, 1998) – to maximise sales and minimise losses – but getting this balance right is undoubtedly difficult and requires retailers to recognise their responsibility as generators of opportunity through the way they design and run their businesses. We suggest that this can be achieved through a detailed understanding of how operational failures play a role in creating these opportunities and also recognising that through their manipulation, provide a means to minimise them. In the next chapter, we move on to look at how operational failures can begin to be identified within retail organisations, making use of the Shrinkage Road Map.

8
Identifying Operational Failures

Given our overarching premise that operational failures are the root cause of most forms of shrinkage, the next step is to describe an approach, which has been developed over a number of years by the ECR Europe Shrinkage Group for identifying these failures. This work, which began back in 1999 sprung from the Group's desire to develop a new way to begin to address the challenges of shrinkage within the retail sector. In the subsequent years, the Group has road tested this approach in over 40 companies and across more than 100 supply chains. It is thought to have produced savings in excess of 600 million for those companies that have used it. The approach is called the *Shrinkage Road Map*, and it is made up of a series of steps that enable loss prevention practitioners to more accurately identify the root causes of the problems they face and then develop 'fit for purpose' solutions to deal with these problems (Beck, Chapman & Peacock, 2002, 2003). What is unique about this method is that it was designed by a wide range of different groups including retail loss prevention practitioners, representatives from both manufacturers and logistics, and academics specialising in supply chain management and criminology. By bringing together such a multi-disciplinary group, a much more holistic, systemic and collaborative framework was achieved, which we believe can only add to the value of the Shrinkage Road Map (Beck *et al.*, 2003). As detailed below, underlying this approach are five key principles.

Key principles

The first is the requirement to adopt a systemic approach to identifying and analysing stock loss problems from a supply chain perspective. Supply chains consist of a large number of diverse activities, each concerned with different aspects of the handling of products and exchange of information. These various activities combine to form a series of processes and procedures (and potential areas for operational failures to occur). These processes and procedures consist of diverse, inter-linked tasks and hence analysing them enables the plethora of possible operational failures within the entire supply chain to be identified.

The second is adopting a systematic approach to understanding the problems of shrinkage. Supply chains are inherently complex and there-fore to understand the vulnerabilities they present any investigation needs to break down the overall activity into a series of manageable com-ponent parts. In addition, one of the most common mistakes made by those investigating operational failures is a presumption that existing processes and procedures are being followed by those tasked to carry out the work. An understanding of the vulnerabilities posed by operational failures cannot be achieved through an analysis of presumed practices – being systematic therefore, also requires the development of first hand knowledge of what actually happens at each of the steps in the activity rather than what is supposed to happen as products move through the supply chain.

The third is developing an approach which is focused on identifying the key areas of risk within the business, something which has been described as the 'hot concept' (Beck & Chapman, 2003). This seeks to identify the 'hot' products, places, processes and people within retail organisations and making them the focus of initial ameliorative actions. By doing this, the loss prevention function ensures that its limited resources are not spread too thinly and that their attention is focused on the vital few rather than the trivial many.

The fourth principle underpinning the Shrinkage Road Map is the need for accurate and timely shrinkage data. As detailed earlier in this book (Chapter 6), a common failing of traditional approaches to dealing with shrinkage has been a lack of transparency in understanding the root causes of the problem. This in turn has led to knee jerk reactions and the implementation of 'solutions' premised on little or no reliable in-formation. The Shrinkage Road Map encourages the collection and ana-lysis of as much data as possible relating to the shrinkage problem under consideration prior to any decision-making relating to possible solutions.

The final principle underpinning the Shrinkage Road Map is the impor-tance of developing a collaborative approach. We will come back to this in the next chapter where we look at how retail organisations can achieve operational excellence and develop an overarching loss prevention model for keeping shrinkage low, but identifying the root causes of operational failures will often mean looking at the problem outside the confines of a particular retail department or indeed a given company. Much of the success achieved with the Shrinkage Road Map has been through the bringing together of all parties who have some responsibility for the movement of goods through their entire life cycle (from the moment of manufacture right through to the time when the customer leaves the store with the product) and therefore can have an impact not only upon the propensity for shrinkage to occur but also how it might be alleviated.

The Shrinkage Road Map

The Shrinkage Road Map is intended to act as a manual or guide, describing the overall activities that need to be undertaken in order to reduce shrinkage through the identification of the root causes of specific problems. This guide consists of a general approach made up of the steps a company needs to follow, together with techniques and tools to help undertake each phase and to deal with problems that may be encountered (Beck *et al.*, 2003). The general approach that forms the heart of the guide is shown in Figure 8.1. As can be seen, this structure is both simple and systematic and provides the means for planning and undertaking stock loss reduction projects while guiding users towards continuous improvement through the cycle.

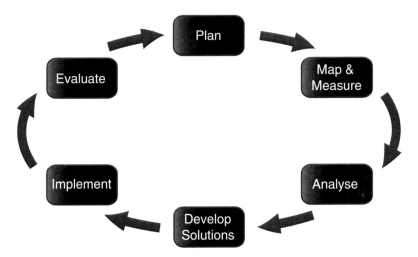

Figure 8.1   The Shrinkage Road Map

The Shrinkage Road Map is designed to enable both problem diagnosis and solution implementation. The structure consists of a sequence of steps where through well-planned investigations, the operational failures that can present opportunities for malicious and non-malicious loss are exposed. These vulnerabilities are then prioritised and subsequently analysed to reveal the underlying root causes. The multidisciplinary project team can then work together to develop appropriate solutions. These solutions are, where appropriate, tested in trials where their effectiveness is assessed. Where a solution is found to be successful it is then implemented widely and business practices standardised around it.

This approach to shrinkage reduction recognises that given the uniqueness of each business environment and product category where losses occur, the prescription of a single, 'right' strategy for reducing shrinkage is inappropriate. Instead, whilst a basic structure is provided, the approach is intended to be tailored to match prevailing circumstances in order for it to be effective. Knowledge regarding the scope for variation around this approach, what does and does not work and the reasons why, come with learning through experience. Indeed, shrinkage like other complex problems within organisations are best addressed by analysing them in their context in order to arrive at appropriate solutions – simply trying to import learning from other contexts is likely to prove to be unsuccessful because the important impact of context is lost (Pawson & Tilley, 1997; Grint, 2005). It is therefore important to recognise that reducing shrinkage is a long-term and on-going learning process. Success comes from using a systematic approach to building the capability to identify and understand the root causes of shrinkage and reinforce practices that reduce loss.

As detailed earlier, this approach provides a means for involving not only a range of retail employees from different functions, but also those who may be external to the company such as logistics providers, manufacturers and loss prevention technology providers. By adopting this inclusive approach, it means not only that a broader range of experiences can be called upon, but also commitment to implement any agreed solutions may be more forthcoming. To help undertake the steps in the Shrinkage Road Map, a number of techniques and tools are utilised. These were chosen to aid not only communication and understanding but also ascertain the root causes of operational failures. Within this review of the Shrinkage Road Map we highlight some of these tools and techniques but others can also be used by those making use of it to better fit the prevailing local circumstances.

As shown in Figure 8.1 the Shrinkage Road Map consists of six sequential steps that join to form a circle of diagnosis and implementation. These steps are described below in more detail, along with a number of techniques and tools that can be used to help accomplish the objectives of each step and overcome problems that may be encountered. However, there is a preliminary step which needs to be reached before a Shrinkage Road Map project can start, one which we describe as the 'wake up' call to the problem of shrinkage in the business.

Step 0: Recognise that stock loss shrinks profit and sales

As we have noted earlier, current attempts to address shrinkage are characterised by a heavy reliance upon reactive strategies that are only triggered when a particular problem becomes intolerable. Such knee jerk and insular reactions not only fail to resolve the root causes of loss, but they can also have a detrimental effect upon the profitability of a company. Hence, the Shrinkage Road Map has a preliminary step which can be characterised as a 'wake up call' to those within the business. This prerequisite step seeks to ensure that the business recognises that existing approaches are not working and also contextualises the problem of shrinkage along side other corporate objectives. This step needs to show how shrinkage is acting as a drain upon the profitability of the organisation. Indeed, by articulating the size of the problem relative to other business objectives, shrinkage has a better chance of being appropriately prioritised. Often, this is best achieved when the benefit of a new approach can be expressed as a positive, for example, 'if we can reduce shrinkage and increase sales by x per cent, we can grow overall profits by x per cent'. This statement of the financial benefit can help secure senior management support for the project which in turn can ensure that others who need to be involved recognise its importance and hence provide the necessary resources required to make it happen. Unless this is the case, then implementing the Shrinkage Road Map will prove highly problematic and those required to engage with the process will not show the necessary commitment and securing the appropriate resources will prove difficult if not impossible.

Once a clear understanding of the scale of the benefit to the organisation of prioritising a particular shrinkage problem has been established, and the necessary support has been garnered from other functions and organisations that need to be involved, then a Shrinkage Road Map project can begin.

Step 1: Develop a project plan

The first step in the Shrinkage Road Map is planning. Planning is based upon setting clear, realistic, attainable objectives with criteria for knowing when these objectives are met. This requires the shrinkage team to have answers to the following questions:

- Which products are to be the focus of the project (this needs to be highly focused and not based upon generalised categories of goods)?
- What are the goals of the stock loss reduction activity (such as clearly defined and measurable impacts upon shrinkage, sales and or out of stocks)?
- How far along the supply chain will the investigations take place (such as from point of manufacture to the retail distribution centre or from the point of delivery to the store and eventual sale to a customer)?
- Who needs to be involved in the project and how will they react to it (this will vary depending upon the range of the supply chain being considered)?
- When is the date by which some benefits must be identifiable (the project may have to take account of seasonality and expectations within the business)?
- What are the constraints to undertaking the Shrinkage Road Map (such as seasonality, possible ambivalence or hostility from particular parts of the organisation about the work of the group)?

The answers to these questions guide the project team's activities towards achieving their goals. Starting the project in this way is especially important in cross-functional/inter-company projects where the effectiveness and efficiency with which project resources are used dramatically improves with up-front investment in planning.

Step 2: Map key processes and measure problem

The second step focuses upon a rigorous diagnosis of the problem based upon the range of the supply chain selected and the products under consideration. It also needs to consider all the operational processes and procedures which play a part in the products' life cycle. As detailed in the previous chapter, *New Loss Prevention* seeks to identify the operational failures that can create the opportunities for malicious shrinkage and lead directly to non-malicious shrinkage. This step, therefore, is a crucial part of the Shrinkage Road Map. It seeks to develop a very detailed map of a given product's physical movement through a retail supply chain and the information flow associated with it. The aim is to identify how at each point the product and its associated information interacts with various people, processes or procedures, and whether potential failures associated with this flow create the opportunity for shrinkage. The most effective way to do this is through the use of Process Mapping.

Process mapping

Documenting the movement of particular products through a supply chain helps individual people view their work from a process perspective. Often, existing ways of working have never been described or even viewed as processes – they can often simply be viewed as 'the way we do things'. Process mapping is a technique used to detail business processes that focuses on the important elements that influence behaviour, allowing the business to be viewed at a glance (Soliman, 1998). In addition, mapping and measuring a process establishes the performance base line that enables the effectiveness of any potential solutions to be measured.

Process mapping can be carried out at a number of different levels, with some focusing more at the macro level, such as the movement of products between different locations, such as from a manufacturer's site to a distribution centre and then on to a store; the meso level, such as the movement of goods within a particular location, such as from the back of a store to the front of the store; and at the micro level, such as the precise movements and processes associated with a product as it moves within a given part of a location, such as a receiving area within a store.

The data for creating a process map is best collated by physically following products as they pass along the supply chain. This involves visiting each site that the product passes through and documenting the steps involved in its journey such as receiving, storage, dispatch and so on. It is important to stress the importance of physically following the product. As detailed earlier there can be an enormous difference between what is suppose to happen and what actually does take place as the product moves along the supply chain. Indeed, many obvious operational failures can be identified at this stage, such as goods which are supposed to be secured in a locked cage actually being left unattended for many days in the back of the store because staff cannot either be bothered to move them or there is insufficient space in the secure cage.

In addition, process mapping also entails not only following the physical journey the product takes but also the flow of information associated with it – its electronic path through the business. As detailed in

Chapter 5, many forms of process failure shrinkage can be caused by employees incorrectly processing data relating to particular products, which in turn can provide opportunities for malicious shrinkage (for instance staff may realise that some products have not been entered on store inventory and so can be stolen with few consequences), or non-malicious shrinkage (such as the wrong price being associated with a given product and hence customers pay less than what they are suppose to leading to reduced profits for the business).

A key part of process mapping is talking to the people who have responsibility for the product as it moves through different parts of the supply chain. Much can be learnt about the vulnerabilities a product faces by speaking to those who deal with it on a day-to-day basis. They are also those who have direct responsibility for implementing and following the processes and procedures that have been designed to ensure the product eventually reaches the consumer at the right time, at the right price and in the right condition. Prudent questioning about the applicability of, and adherence with, existing processes and procedures can be highly illuminating when trying to determine the operational failures that can be the root causes of shrinkage for any given product.

Generally speaking, the more detailed a process map can be, the more useful it becomes and is an important component when analysing the overall threats a given product faces as it moves through a supply chain.

Measuring the problem

As we identified in earlier chapters, a paucity of data continues to be the Achilles heal of modern loss prevention, with perhaps as much as 51 per cent of all causes of loss remaining unknown (Beck, 2004a). This clearly undermines any attempts to get a coherent understanding of the causes of shrinkage. Guesswork then inevitably becomes the order of the day which in turn becomes tainted by prejudice and self interest. But as IT systems develop, the quantity (but nor necessarily the quality) of shrinkage data has improved. Increasingly, good retailers are now able to generate shrinkage data at item level, which offers a much greater degree of clarity about the overall landscape of shrinkage within any given location. In order to understand how operational failures may be impacting upon the shrinkage of any given product, data needs to be collected as much as possible along the entire supply chain. As noted earlier, very often losses incurred in the supply chain prior to the store may only be identified at the very end of the journey – the losses are washed along and only identified when store audits take place. The presumption then is that the losses must have occurred in the store rather than prior to its arrival.

The Shrinkage Road Map, therefore requires detailed measurement of where, when and how losses occur for the product under consideration, and this must be done at as many points along the supply chain as is feasibly possible. This may require the collection of new data, but it could simply mean the collation of existing data which is normally used for a different purpose. Either way, as much clarity as possible is required about the circumstances in which any losses take place.

Step 3: Analyse risk, identify causes and prioritise actions

Once the process map is complete and all available data has been collected, the next stage is to analyse the process itself together with the data collected to determine and prioritise the many possible operational failures that could create the opportunity for shrink. With these 'drivers' of shrinkage prioritised, the possible root causes of these failures can then begin to be understood. A useful tool for undertaking this is Failure Modes and Effects Analysis (FMEA) – a method which has long been used in the design of motor vehicles, machinery and weapons manufacture. This tool is particularly good at identifying the various ways that processes and procedures may fail, as well as determining the effect of different failure modes (Stamatis, 1995). In particular, FMEA enables you to score the potential risk of different failure modes based upon the severity of the loss should a failure happen, the likelihood of a failure occurring and the ability to detect that a failure has occurred. Once these scores are made they can then be multiplied together to provide an overall risk score for each of the potential failure modes. This enables the most vulnerable failures to be identified and then these become the focus of the next stage of the Shrinkage Road Map – the selection of potential solutions.

Using the example presented in Chapter 7 earlier, where high risk goods were not put away in a secure cage at the back of the store because the key holder was on holiday, the FMEA tool would be used to gauge the impact of this event on the business based upon severity, likelihood and detectability. Severity would be based upon the quantity of goods being left unsecured (the more products there are, the higher the score). Occurrence would be scored upon the frequency with which this event happened – the more often the key holder is absent, the higher the score. Finally, the likelihood of detection would be scored based upon the speed with which the business would become aware of any potential loss. For instance, if daily counts take place of this product, then any loss would be very quickly identified. However, if the stock is only ever counted once a year, then the loss would be highly unlikely to be noticed quickly. These three scores would then be multiplied together to give this particular failure mode a risk score. The project team would repeat this process for all the other potential failure modes for the product under investigation (there can be as many as 100 failure modes for any given process under inspection).

Once all the failure modes have been completed, the project team can utilise two further techniques to begin to understand the root causes of the highest scoring operational failures: Cause and effect analysis and Five Whys.

Cause and effect analysis

Cause and effect analysis benefits from a long and successful history of application in the investigation of quality problems and is fairly simple to understand and use (Juran & Gryna, 1988). Having identified specific symptoms of poor performance, or in this case particular high risk operational failures, the cause and effect diagram is an effective way of capturing possible contributing causes to it.

This technique is especially useful when employed to structure the outcome of a brainstorming session with a project team, when they contribute their findings, experience and understanding (Ishikawa, 1990). The main spines of the diagram are given broad headings (these are fairly arbitrary and can be selected by the project team) around which causes to the symptom of a problem are grouped. To focus effort, the major causes of problems need to be identified from amongst the trivial many. Where possible, this should be achieved statistically through the collection of data highlighted in the previous stage of the Shrinkage Road Map. If all the data is not available, then it is possible to get the project group members to identify many of the most significant problems from their experience. This approach follows the Pareto Principle that the 'vital few' causes are responsible for the bulk of problems (Juran & Gryna, 1993).

Five Whys

Once initial ideas have identified the main causes of the shrinkage problem for a given product, another technique – the Five Whys – can be used to explore the deeper underlying root causes (Bicheno, 1998). This technique explores the underlying causes of losses as fully as possible by repeating the question, 'why?' five times as this has been found to be the number of times it takes before the root cause of the problem is identified

(Ishikawa, 1990). For example, and to use an example detailed earlier in this chapter:
    Initial problem: Stock is left outside the secure cage:

Why? Because the key holder is on holiday and did not give the key to another member of staff.

Why? Because they assumed there was another key.

Why? Because this is what existing store operating procedure stated, but unfortunately this was not now being followed.

Why? Because the store manager had not reviewed operating procedures for over 12 months.

Why? Because the store manager was under considerable pressure to focus on sales.

Through the use of this deceptively simple technique, the root causes of problems can be quickly identified.

Through the use of FMEA and a number of other tools and techniques, it is possible to identify the key failure modes associated with any given process and identify what the underlying root causes may be. This approach, however, is critically dependent upon the previous step – developing a comprehensive process map of the products movement and information flow through the supply chain – without it the various modes of failure will not be identified. It is also dependent upon the quality and diversity of the people brought together in the project team. By having representatives from different parts of a retail business and indeed those from outside the organisation, fresh insights and alternative interpretations of likely causes can be developed. This third step in the Shrinkage Road Map is as much about brainstorming ideas and experiences as it is about collating information and drawing conclusions. Once this step has been completed, then the project team can move on to the next part of the Shrinkage Road Map, which is concerned with developing solutions and prioritising actions.

Step 4: Develop solutions and prioritise actions

One of our criticisms of 'old loss prevention' is that it often starts its stock loss reduction efforts at this stage – implementing solutions. The multi-billion dollar 'solution' provider industry is not short of ever new and increasingly technologically advanced options to tempt the loss prevention practitioner that has a pressing shrinkage problem. There are many 'solutions' searching for problems in the competitive world of loss prevention and it is easy to see how practitioners can quickly become transfixed by the often beguiling promises of providers offering the panacea to reduce shrinkage and protect their bonus.

However, implementing 'solutions' without first undertaking the steps of planning, mapping and measuring and then analysing the potential operational failures associated with the processes and procedures of a given product, we feel, will inevitably lead to failure. Unless root cause analysis has been carried out, then there is a real danger that any proposed solutions could be merely dealing with the symptoms rather than the underlying causes of the problem.

The majority of solutions are usually extremely context-specific and it is not the purpose of this book to detail all those that are available to the loss prevention practitioner. However, for many problems there could well be a number of potential solutions and therefore, the Shrinkage Road Map approach suggests using a Solution Matrix to determine the applicability of any given range of potential solution (see Figure 8.2).

Most solutions can be gauged against two key variables: the ease with which it can be implemented in a given retail environment, ranging from very slow and hard to accomplish through to being very fast and easy to implement; and the improvement potential it can deliver, ranging from low through to high (this could be expressed in monetary terms or perhaps in a percentage reduction in shrinkage) The improvement potential also takes into account the anticipated cost of the solution. Given these two variables, potential solutions can then be placed upon the matrix based upon how they score. So for instance, in the example below, proposed solutions 1 and 2 are viewed as having a high improvement potential, but are considered to be slow and hard to implement. Solution

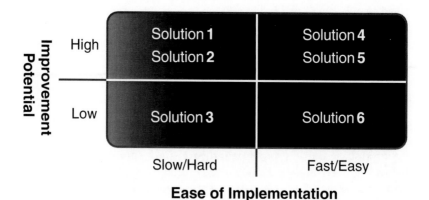

Figure 8.2   The Shrinkage Road Map Solution Matrix

3 has a low improvement potential and is also slow and hard to implement. Solutions 4 and 5 are viewed to offer a high improvement value and be fast and easy to implement. Finally, Solution 6 is regarded as fast and easy to implement but yields a low improvement value. Using this simply matrix it is possible to quickly conclude that Solutions 4 and 5 are potentially the most suitable while Solution 3 would seem to be the least desirable option.

Step 5: Implement solutions

In a similar manner to the approach used to plan the original Shrinkage Road Map, the implementation of any proposed solution requires project planning. Critical to successful implementation is the identification of a primary sponsor who will be responsible for delivering the benefits of the project. To achieve success the sponsor, usually a senior manager, needs to ensure that the project team constructs a clear and robust business case. This business case defines what is to be delivered, the benefits this will bring and the resources required (Beck, 2008).

The creation of an implementation plan is necessary to map the best use of resources to achieve the desired objectives within time and cost limitations. Here the tools of project management will prove useful, whether applied to small or large-scale projects. Where a project team undertakes planned change for the first time, the plan should consider not just the task but also the learning necessary to deliver it. At a top level, a project plan is constructed by following a sequence of steps, as described below:

- Identify the overview tasks needed to complete the project.
- Show the interrelationships between tasks and the sequence in which they can be undertaken.
- Estimate the types and amount of effort needed to complete these tasks.
- Calculate the resource profile over time to complete the project.
- Identify potential risks to successful project delivery.
- Mitigate risks or plan contingency.
- Iterate the plan to match it against resource availability.
- Secure resource.
- Put in place procedures for evaluation.

Evaluating the effectiveness of the stock loss reduction effort provides information that guides the direction of the next cycle of loss reduction – evaluating the implementation.

Step 6: Evaluate implementation

The stock loss reduction project ends with an effective solution in place. However, this is not the end of stock loss reduction as a whole. From the organisation's perspective, evaluation of one project is important in order to determine the success of the solution and guide future projects. The review is therefore the last step of one project and perhaps the first step of the next.

The ability to sustain significant improvements in stock loss over long periods of time rests on the capability to learn from experience and to ensure that companies access the wide range of developing tools at their disposal. Therefore this review of the implementation must be objective. All too often reviews are undertaken with the aim of justifying the work that has been done and fail to provide an honest appraisal of what solution worked and why. As Pawson and Tilley (1997) remarked, they can often be carried out by the self interested and the untrained leading to results that can be at best unreliable and at worse misleading. Accordingly, the evaluation should be rigorous, robust and led by somebody who can provide an objective review, independent of equipment providers and those who may have commissioned the project in the first instance. They need a clear mandate to assess the performance of the implemented solution and compare this against the level of performance originally planned. This assessment should consider how the implementation of solutions was justified, for example by the use of a cost/benefit analysis (see Beck, 2008 for a review of how this can be carried out). This information provides the feedback that allows the stock loss reduction team to objectively consider the effectiveness of the approach the project team took to reducing stock loss and the specific solutions they implemented.

In addition, the aim of this feedback phase is to identify whether any further action is required before the current project can be signed off and to gain a better appreciation of successful approaches and solutions that might be applied during future projects. It should be noted, however, that the evaluation process may need to be ongoing as the performance of an initiative can change as its 'environment' alters. For instance offenders may gradually find ways of defeating the newly adopted approach or changes in product range or levels of staffing might reduce its effectiveness. Therefore, periodic reviews of newly adopted measures may need to be carried out in order to gauge their effectiveness over time and to evaluate whether any corrective measures need to be taken.

Road map case study

Since its development, the Shrinkage Road Map has been used by countless organisations around the world consistently delivering excellent results. Detailed below is a case study of how it has been used and the results obtained by the two organisations that used it: Tesco in Hungary and Gillette (Beck *et al.*, 2003). The background was that Tesco, who at the time had only recently entered this market, were experiencing extremely high levels of loss on the Mach 3 range of Gillette products. The problem was so severe that Tesco, which was already utilising a range of defensive merchandising techniques to try and reduce losses on these products, issued an ultimatum that they would be delisted within 14 days if the shrinkage issue could not be resolved. Consequently, a project team made up of both Tesco and Gillette staff, decided to try out the Shrinkage Road Map as a means to address the problem. The investigation into the problem revealed that the losses were highly focused in just a few stores and the outcome of the process mapping exercise revealed 150 areas of risk within the supply chain. Once these were prioritised, the project team developed an intervention based upon ten steps grouped into three areas: secure the 'hot product' supply chain; secure in store handling; and define ownership and control loss. A trial was undertaken in three stores to measure the performance of the proposed intervention and the results were extremely impressive: looking only at the items which were the focus of the Shrinkage Road Map, shrinkage was reduced by 74 per cent and sales increased by 288 per cent. Such impressive results subsequently led to the '10 step' programme being rolled out to the other stores in the Tesco Hungarian estate.

Whilst only one example of the way in which the Shrinkage Road Map has been used, this case study highlights the key steps that make up the overall process. The project had a clear call to action: the products were about to be delisted. The project team was collaborative in nature, both Tesco and Gillette were closely involved. They carefully analysed the root causes of the problem, and found major areas of risk within the supply chain. They developed an intervention, which was subsequently tested and evaluated. Then based upon the results, they rolled out the solution to other locations suffering from a similar problem.

Identifying operational failures

The Shrinkage Road Map described above was developed by ECR Europe's Shrinkage Group in an attempt to begin to impose a greater degree of rigour upon the stock loss reduction process through the use of a more systemic and systematic methodology. It is not intended to be a prescriptive solution to the problem of shrinkage but merely a tool to be used to better organise stock loss reduction efforts and help practitioners to think through and develop a more strategic approach. It was also designed to provide a better way of identifying the root causes of shrinkage, focusing particularly upon (but not exclusively) those caused by operational failures.

As we detailed in the previous chapter, understanding the role that operational failures play in creating the opportunities and circumstances within which shrinkage occurs underpins our approach and in the next chapter, we move on to introduce the key themes that make up *New Loss Prevention* and how when they are brought together they create an overarching strategy for effectively dealing with stock loss in the retail sector.

9
Introducing New Loss Prevention

In the previous two chapters we outlined the underlying premise of *New Loss Prevention* – the importance of recognising the role operational failures can have in creating the opportunities and circumstances for shrinkage to occur and how they can be identified through the use of the Shrinkage Road Map. In this next chapter we put this thinking into a broader framework offering an overarching model for delivering effective shrinkage management. This framework seeks to put operational failures within a broader context of the retail organisation and how a series of elements need to be in place in order for shrinkage to be targeted in a rigorous, robust and sustainable manner.

It seeks to put in place a combination of deep seated strategic factors together with a range of organisational and operational approaches designed to enable shrinkage to be managed and controlled effectively and efficiently. It is purposefully conceived as a pyramid because all the elements that make up the pyramid need to be in place in order for it to be sustainable – take out or marginalise any particular factor(s) or block(s) and the whole edifice will come crashing down. Not only does it represent a sense of the interrelationship between different components that are necessary to deliver effective shrinkage management, but it also symbolises how those who ultimately have to deal with the problem on a day-to-day basis (store teams), reside at the top of the pyramid. Unless the underlying building blocks are in place, such as strong foundations (what we see as the strategic factors), then they will be unable, and more than likely, unwilling to take on this role.

As detailed at the start of this book, much of the thinking for this model came from research carried out on a number of retail companies in the US that were, at the time of conducting the research, considered to be performing well. This research has been combined with additional work carried out under the auspices of the ECR Europe Shrinkage Group, which has conducted a large number of action research projects focused on a range of loss prevention problems (including the development and extensive testing of the Shrinkage Road Map outlined in the previous chapter). Detailed below are the results of this work synthesised into the Loss Prevention Pyramid. In order to elaborate more fully each of the components of the Pyramid, we will selectively use some of the quotes from the original research undertaken by Beck (2007a). As with the original research, the quotations will remain anonymous, both in terms of the person making the comment and the organisation they represent.

As can be seen in Figure 9.1, the Loss Prevention Pyramid is made up of 11 component parts which are grouped together under three headings: strategic; organisational; and operational:

Strategic factors

- Senior Management Commitment
- Organisational Ownership
- Embedded Loss Prevention

Organisational factors

- Loss Prevention Leadership
- Data Management

Figure 9.1 The Loss Prevention Pyramid

- Operational Excellence
- Prioritising People
- Collaboration
- Innovation and Experimentation
- Communicating Shrinkage

Operational factors

- Store Management Responsibility

Strategic factors

At the root of the Pyramid are three strategic factors that can be viewed as the foundation stones upon which all the other elements rest. Without these key stones none of the other component parts can be developed, delivered or sustained – they are the bedrock of the model. These factors are: Senior Management Commitment; Embedded Loss Prevention; and Organisational Ownership.

Senior management commitment

At a retail security conference held in London in 2005 a CEO of a major retail clothing company in the UK made a presentation which not only highlighted the importance of taking shrinkage seriously, but noted it was essentially the last free money on the table – growing profits through increasing the number of outlets, or streamlining business functions such as reducing stock holding, were not as beneficial to the organisation as getting to grips with shrinkage. In itself, this was not a new or particularly innovative idea. What was different was that it was a CEO of an organisation making the case. A perennial problem for many loss prevention specialists has been the difficulty of getting the rest of the organisation to take the issue seriously – shrinkage is often perceived as a peripheral part of the overall business not warranting the attention given to other functions such as marketing, sales or distribution. But, without the support and attention of all parts of the organisation, developing solutions to the problem of shrinkage will remain piecemeal, partial and problematic. The key question is how do you get the business to take shrinkage seriously? The consensus answer is that you need senior management (board level) to first of all buy into the importance of the problem to the business, secondly to ensure that the loss prevention function is empowered (through resource and access) to deal with the problem effectively, and thirdly that the rest of the business is 'persuaded' that it should be an ongoing item on their agenda.

In the research undertaken by Beck on the top performing US retail companies, the commitment of the Board to the problem of loss prevention was profound, clear, sustained and genuine: 'we have an awful lot of senior executive support – without it, we couldn't have done what we did'; 'the support from the Board is tremendous – they recognised early on that sorting out shrink could make a real difference to the business'. However, what was also very interesting was that for four of the five companies analysed in this research an event or tipping point had occurred in their recent history that put shrinkage on to the agenda of senior management – a defining moment such as a new high in losses, the need to radically change some form of technology or the acquisition of a new business that tipped the shrinkage balance too far into the red:

> I remember our tipping point very well, 25th March 1995 ... budget review with the Board ... shrink had been running at 0.5% but then went to 1.2% ... it was announced to the Board and then things began to happen....

> Yes there was a tipping point. It was around a technology investment ... a tagging technology. Required a philosophical change in mindset of the leadership team. Had to put money into the technology and make sure that the staff were well trained to use it.

Similar events had occurred in two of the other case studies – the shrinkage figure had 'exploded' when one of the companies had taken over a rival company that had a poor record on loss prevention management combined with a work force that was low on morale and high on procedural deviance. For the other, rapid expansion of the business and an historical organisational segmentation had led to shrinkage growing massively within the business:

> We were so bad as a company ... leadership needed to come from the top ... without that buy-in things will not happen.

So the appearance of a 'crisis' or tipping point was undoubtedly a key moment in enabling/persuading/forcing a loss prevention team to go to the Board (or be summoned by them) and make a case for shrinkage to become a key business priority:

> Shrinkage became a top priority from 1995 until 1998. By that point it had become ingrained in the culture.

As can be seen from the quotes above, many of these companies were not performing well in terms of managing shrinkage – losses were growing and for some they were now considered to be out of control and adversely impacting upon the profitability of the business. However, two things were also clearly important for the case-study companies in this process. First, the head of loss prevention had a well defined and usually innovative plan to take to the Board – the tipping point created a one-time opportunity to propose a new strategic approach for the business on shrinkage (including changes in the financial support for the loss prevention department). This should not be underestimated – getting the right message across to the Board was clearly pivotal in enabling these companies to make a step change in how the problem of shrinkage was to be addressed in the business. Secondly, in all cases the Board was capable of understanding not only the importance of addressing the problem of shrinkage, but also the value it could bring to the bottom line. Generating this understanding was problematic for some of the case-study companies and in order to achieve this they resorted to either, using external and respected consultants to help in the assessment and planning process, or made use of extensive benchmarking exercises with other companies in the market to help make their case.

So without senior management commitment the prospect of delivering any form of effective and sustainable shrinkage management strategy is remote. In order to get this, the loss prevention team need to show how shrinkage impacts upon the business, both in terms of the impact upon the shopper (such as through higher prices and or lack of availability) and the business itself (such as through reduced profits and shareholder value). For example, research by Beck *et al.* (2003) has shown that for the average retailer operating in the Fast Moving Consumer Goods Sector (FMCG) in Europe, the elimination of shrinkage could grow profits by as much as 62 per cent. Even a more modest target of reducing shrinkage by 50 per cent would still lead to a growth in profits of around 30 per cent – a remarkable statistic and one that any other part of the business would find utterly impossible to deliver. As we mentioned in the previous chapter when introducing the Shrinkage Road Map, by highlighting the economic potential of targeting shrinkage, the loss prevention team can get senior management commitment. This in turn can then be used as leverage with the rest of the business to generate urgency and compliance. It can also sanction the apportionment of additional resources to enable the loss prevention team to begin to put in place the other component parts of the Pyramid.

Organisational ownership

The second foundation stone of the Loss Prevention Pyramid is developing Organisational Ownership. As detailed in Chapter 6, traditionally the functions of security, loss prevention, shrinkage management and other crime-related activities such as guarding are seen as the sole preserve of one department – security or loss prevention. Other parts of the business were rarely involved or indeed interested because such activities are viewed as simply an inevitable yet regrettable part of doing business and not something they could or should play a part in managing. In many respects this can be compounded by the attitude of the loss prevention team who can reinforce this ghettoised approach to dealing with shrinkage in a retail company – 'this is our responsibility (fiefdom) and others need not get involved'. Research for ECR Europe by Beck and Bilby (2001) has shown how little other departments within a retail business engage with the problem. Outside the functions of Loss Prevention and Store Operations, this research showed that groups such as Marketing, Store Planning and Design, Buying, IT and Human Resources were rarely involved with dealing with shrinkage.

The case-study companies studied by Beck showed how they had not only ensured that shrinkage was not just the responsibility of one department (their loss prevention function), but also that the rest of the business genuinely recognised that they had a role to play in its management. How this was achieved varied between the companies under investigation, and all were quick to note that it was and remains a difficult task. One respondent highlighted the way in which it happened in their organisation:

> For the first 6 months [after the tipping point] we tried 49 different programmes – most failed. We realised that we cannot do it ourselves – it's about retail owning shrink, it's about logistics owning shrink, it's about the organisation saying shrink is important. So we went to the business and asked for help. It worked and shrink has now become part of the culture of the business.

In this example senior staff quickly realised that simply implementing new shrink 'solutions' would be wholly ineffective unless the parts of the business that interacted with the 'solutions' understood why it was being introduced, how it would affect the rest of the business, and most importantly, who had responsibility for ensuring compliance. In another example, the importance of showing how shrinkage reduction and the loss prevention team can add value was critical in creating organisational ownership of the problem:

> We are big on integration and partnership within the business – how can I help get other parts of the business working better? How can we do things that will drive the success of the other business units?

This respondent went on to describe how they had engaged a particular part of the business with the problem of shrinkage:

> [We] work closely with merchandising/buying – they have a huge amount of data. We took merchandisers round stores to show them the challenges that store staff face in merchandising particular products.

What is interesting about this comment is not only the fact that they were able to get merchandisers/buyers to visit the stores to think specifically about shrinkage issues, but it also shows that the relationship can benefit both parties – loss prevention get hold of valuable data while merchandising/buying begin to recognise the consequences of some of their decision-making.

So making sure that all parts of the business have a sense that they too are responsible for shrinkage management is a fundamental part of creating the environment in which losses can be minimised. Indeed, as one respondent put it: 'it is difficult to think of any part of the business that shouldn't be thinking shrink'. What is also important, and is highlighted by some of the quotations above, is that the loss prevention team need to see themselves as much as 'enablers' as 'doers' – they need to act as 'agents of change' within the business, facilitating the process. One way to think about this is to use the analogy of an orchestra where loss prevention is both the band manager and conductor. You provide a safe venue for the musicians to play, you give them instruments that work properly and you give them a script to follow. After that they have to produce the music although as the conductor you keep an eye (or ear!) upon them to make sure that all of them stick to the script and deliver what the audience want. You could not and would not want to play the music yourself but you make sure you have controls in place to ensure that the musicians deliver. Not wanting to stretch this analogy any further, but effective shrinkage management is making sure that everybody in the business is singing (or playing) from the same song sheet and they all recognise their role in creating a successful outcome.

Embedding loss prevention

While senior executive support and getting all parts of the business to think shrinkage are undoubtedly vital, both can arguably be seen and interpreted as merely window dressing – 'yes, it [shrinkage] is important but we have other things to focus on as well that are more pressing'. This is where the third foundation stone of the Loss Prevention Pyramid becomes really very important – ensuring that loss prevention is *embedded* in the organisational structure and culture. It becomes very difficult to ignore shrinkage when it has become part of everyday duties, tasks, thinking and strategic development. Once again, Beck's case-study companies highlighted the absolute importance of making sure shrinkage management was ingrained in the business:

> We created SOPs [Standard Operating Procedures] for *all* departments and made modifications to the bonus plan – each store has a share of the savings in shrink at that location. (emphasis added)

> Shrinkage is incorporated into the overall philosophy of the business ... mirror up to the company's direction – fast growing innovative company that is willing to try out new things – we are apart of that.

> Getting a seat at the table is the difference between the retailers that want to win on shrink and the retailers that don't care. You've got to get a seat at the table. For instance, I interview any VP coming into the business.

Each of these examples offers an interesting insight, for instance the first highlights the way in which the loss prevention team went through the entire business creating SOPs for how each part should be thinking and dealing with shrinkage in their environment and sphere of influence. It also showed how the embedding and ownership process had been reinforced through incentivisation – reduce shrinkage and you will personally benefit. The issue of incentivisation cropped up in all of the case studies although its use varied considerably. In one, all store staff were bonused on sales and losses: '... it personalises the problem with the staff – losses will impact directly on their bonus'.

For others only the store managers and the loss prevention teams received a bonus based upon their performance relating to shrinkage management. The issue of whether staff should receive a bonus for achieving targets relating to their performance on shrinkage is a hotly debated topic, not least because without accurate measurement of the problem, apportioning responsibility can be problematic. But excellent research by DeHoratius and Raman (2007) has shown how store managers can be effectively incentivised through a combination of both sales and shrinkage targets.

Many of the respondents in Beck's research noted how they had ensured that shrinkage was an agenda item in most meetings and the third quote above highlights how it was felt important that loss prevention was represented at, and able to influence, key decision-making meetings. Indeed, having the opportunity to influence was a recurring theme: 'We are invited along to meetings we never knew existed before! Store planning and design, new product launches, you name it we get a chance to have our say.'

For another respondent, keeping it embedded and on the agenda was initially a real challenge but they had eventually succeeded:

> It was always a battle with other departments to keep it on the agenda; sometimes it was given lip service. In [name of retailer], they have crossed that threshold where everybody really is buying into it. They have made the connection.

One of the fundamental problems of maintaining low shrinkage is keeping the business focused and motivated to deal with the problem. It is all too easy for the business to think that it has 'done' shrinkage and that other priorities can now be developed and resources reallocated. In addition, issues of devolved shrinkage control can be problematic to manage when they rub up against other priorities in the business. For example, a decision to reduce costs in distribution centres by employing greater numbers of temporary staff could lead to more shrinkage in retail stores as picking error rates may increase as a consequence. Similarly, significant discounts offered to a commercial buyer for purchasing high quantities of a particular product, which are subsequently pushed out to stores, could lead to higher levels of shrinkage (stores may not have the space to hold the product properly leading to increased levels of damage and theft).

We are not naive as to suppose that shrinkage will always be viewed as one of the most important and deserving elements within the retail environment. 21st century retailing is an increasingly vicious economic space where reinvention and innovation are key components of any businesses success. But the extent to which dealing with shrinkage can be embedded within the very fabric of the business (both culturally and in terms of processes and procedures) can mitigate against this, especially when it is taken into account with respect to other organisational decisions that may have an indirect impact upon it. Indeed, for some companies, ongoing prioritisation is achieved through the subject of shrinkage management remaining as a main line item on the agenda of senior management, or the establishment of a shrinkage committee chaired by the CEO which meets on a quarterly basis to review the company's current approach to managing the problem.

Strategic factors: the bedrock of success

All three of the elements described in this section can be seen as part of the foundations of a successful loss prevention strategy: senior executive support to ensure the business prioritises the problem and the loss prevention department gets the resource and capability to influence; all parts of the organisation feel that they own the problem; and finally, loss prevention is embedded in the practices, procedures, processes, culture and strategic planning of the entire business. All three are intrinsically linked and vital to creating the organisational climate within which shrinkage management can be successfully fostered. As detailed above, all of the case-study companies analysed by Beck had worked hard to put these elements in place, but that is not to suggest it is easy. In many respects these are the hardest parts of the Loss Prevention Pyramid to put in place and get right. They can be difficult because loss prevention is competing against other parts of the business that also want the attention of senior management and the rest of the business to comply with, and to take accountability for, their initiatives and responsibilities. In this respect this is where the resolve of senior management is crucial – they are the ones that can influence the cultural climate of the business and the way in shrinkage management is subsequently prioritised and acted upon. But once these foundation stones are firmly put in place, the rest of the Pyramid can then begin to be assembled.

Organisational factors

This section now focuses on the next layer of factors that need to be established to create the Loss Prevention Pyramid. They are a series of factors that can be directly influenced by the loss prevention department and affect not only the way the business operates in general but also more specifically the way in which the shrinkage management team functions and interfaces with the rest of the organisation. They are: Loss Prevention Leadership; Data Management; Operational Excellence; Prioritising People; Collaboration; Innovation and Experimentation; and Communicating Shrinkage.

Loss prevention leadership

The first element in the sequence of organisational factors that make up the Loss Prevention Pyramid is Loss Prevention Leadership. Much has been written about the concept of leadership and what this means – some suggest leaders are born and not made, while others hold the entirely opposite view (See Bamfield, 2006b; Bryman, 1999; George & Jones, 2006). The purpose of this section is not to begin to enter this debate, but merely to reflect upon the qualities, attitude and importance of the role of the characters who provided leadership within the loss prevention teams examined by Beck. This is based upon personal interviews with each of them and with interviews with the staff who reported directly to them. Many of the characteristics present can be categorised under the heading of transformational leadership (Avoilo & Yammarino, 2002) and included:

- The ability to develop and communicate a vision that others can follow.
- The ability to manage people individually and understand the contribution they can make and therefore maximise the use of their particular skills and qualities.
- Ensure that staff are trained to challenge the status quo.
- Show genuine interest in their team.
- Recognise the importance of setting stretch goals to maximise team performance.
- Communicate clearly with each member of the team about how they contribute to overall business goals.
- Create a climate of trust that is perceived to operate in both directions (from the organisation and from the individual).

A number of other personal and professional attributes were also very apparent in those that were interviewed by Beck. First, all had a genuine *passion* for dealing with the problem of shrinkage; it was something that was undoubtedly important to them and came across in the way in which they discussed the challenges they face and their desire to succeed.

Secondly, they exuded *energy* that was palpable in the way they talked about the problem of shrinkage and something which could be seen in the staff that reported to them. Thirdly, there was a high degree of *commitment* to the organisation and their loss prevention team. This was reflected in many ways, not least in ensuring that shrinkage was recognised by the Board and the rest of the business as important, but also that their team got the support and rewards for meeting targets and delivering results. Fourthly, there was a real sense that the loss prevention leaders were offering *direction* and *vision* to the business and their team. Creating strategic plans and yearly targets are undoubtedly the overt expression of these qualities, but it was more than this, it was a sense of trailblazing a path that others would want to follow and help create. In this sense they were extremely good at creating *focus* and *direction* for the organisation on shrinkage. Fifthly, they all came across as *team builders* who were willing to listen to the ideas and concerns of their staff, but also willing to fight on their behalf with the rest of the business to ensure that shrinkage remained on the agenda and was, where possible, given the appropriate prioritisation. Finally, there was a real sense that each of the heads of loss prevention had a considerable amount of *experience* of the problem of shrinkage. Their backgrounds and career trajectories were all relatively different, but each had accumulated an impressive degree of understanding.

Much of this was summarised by two of the respondents:

> I never want to be a follower, I want to be a trailblazer and refuse to be second place on anything – technology, tactics, thought leadership, anything ....

> It's about making bold commitments, engaging others about what is possible, and creating challenges, while giving people permission to step forward and contribute.

Whether these attributes and qualities can be made or not is not the subject of discussion here. What is important is that the people who were responsible for leading these organisations on shrinkage had some if not all of them. They provided direction that generated commitment from their immediate staff while at the same time acted as a respected conduit with senior executives in the company.

Data management

As we highlighted in Chapter 6, traditionally loss prevention departments have been seen as data deserts, bereft of information and relying upon anecdote and gut instinct to drive the shrinkage agenda (Beck, 2002b). Where other parts of retail businesses such as marketing, buying and store layout have for a long time been driven by the imperative to make decisions based upon detailed analysis of all available information, loss prevention departments have been operating with the bare minimum of data, which has often been incomplete, usually significantly out of date and for the most part incapable of measuring the real problems faced by the organisation.

In the five case-study companies analysed by Beck, the absolute importance of collecting and analysing a wide range of data was recognised and prioritised: 'The company philosophy is to rely heavily on data and shrink mirrors this and taps into all the existing data systems'. How this was done varied between the companies with some relying solely upon the broader organisational data sources to inform their work, while others did this and also had additional bespoke systems designed for their particular needs:

> We try to build all our reporting into the POS [Point of Sale] … [we] don't have a separate loss prevention database … [we] cannot warrant a data mining package because the existing systems provide the data we need. [We] link into inventory and cycle counts – can measure shrink down to SKU [Stock Keeping Unit].

> We have two sources of data – EPOS [Electronic Point of Sale] data to help us identify outliers and a store-based database where staff can enter incidents of shrinkage. LP staff also download incidents into the database – enables us to identify hot spots in real time.

One of the companies in particular also highlighted the way in which they used inventory data to help them monitor the stores and keep a close check on the movement of goods:

> LP own inventory management in the stores … [we are] experts at receiving trucks, transferring products, all the processes around billing. That's what my team does. Data integrity is our job and not just shrink control. Got to do cycle counts – stay on top of all the data that tells me I have a problem. Understanding what the barometers are telling us. Accuracy in inventory is about 90 per cent. Get your hands dirty – go and unload a truck, follow stock through the supply chain. Make the processes evolve as the business evolves. Control what you can control.

This quote is instructive for a number of reasons. First, that the loss prevention team clearly recognised the value of 'owning' inventory management, something which may not necessarily be seen by some as their responsibility. Secondly, that the loss prevention team are 'experts' in understanding the various steps in the movement of stock and are willing to go and get their 'hands dirty', again a skill perhaps not traditionally associated with people who are often seen as merely thief catchers. Thirdly, recognition of the importance of data integrity to the business as a whole and their responsibility for getting it right – the old adage of garbage in, garbage out is becoming even more pertinent as more data becomes available throughout retail businesses and poor quality information can undermine understanding (Howell & Proudlove, 2007).

What was also clear from all of the case-study companies analysed by Beck was that they not only prioritised the collection of data, but that they ensured it was analysed and used to guide not only the strategic planning of the company, but also the day-to-day work of the loss prevention team and store staff: '... keep a close eye on shrink ... weekly monitoring ... [we] watch the numbers very closely'. How this was done varied, but all continually stressed the importance of being guided by the numbers and not relying upon guesswork and hearsay. What was also stressed was the need for properly trained analytical staff whose exclusive role was to ask questions of the data:

> We also have a shortage analytics team comprised of three people ... do deep dives on the data to identify trends locally and nationally. They [the analysts] are new – recruited in the last 10 months. Business was very supportive of this move because they recognised that it enabled them to understand the risk to the business much clearer.

All five companies relied extensively upon some form of system that enabled them to 'data mine' their electronic point of sale (EPOS) data. This was seen as an extremely important part of not only identifying incidents of deviance by store employees, but also providing a viable deterrence to staff. Data mining software has been available for many years although early incarnations of these systems were inflexible, difficult to programme and required high levels of computing power and memory storage. Today these problems have largely been resolved and they now offer loss prevention practitioners the opportunity to monitor transactional data in real time and quickly identify exceptional incidents at the till.

It cannot be underestimated the value all five of these companies placed on the role of collecting and analysing as broad a range of data as possible. It enabled them to move away from guesswork and intuition and adopt an evidence-based approach to decision-making. It created credibility with the rest of the organisation as it could see the 'evidence' for engaging with loss prevention on particular issues. It enabled them to identify trends and develop a more strategic approach to shrinkage management, and it provided a rich source of information to guide the loss prevention team and store staff in their quest to reduce shrinkage.

In addition, work by ECR Europe has also highlighted the importance of using data to identify areas of risk in retail organisations – what they define as the 'Hot Concept' (Beck & Chapman, 2003). This suggests that through detailed analysis of shrinkage data, loss prevention practitioners can identify and then focus upon the particular products, places, processes and people most likely to generate shrinkage. As we detailed in Chapter 4, certain products are much more likely to be shrinkage prone than others. Similarly, certain stores within a retail estate are likely to have higher levels of loss than others. The Hot Concept takes this analysis further by suggesting that there are also certain processes more likely to cause shrinkage, such as the delivery of goods at the back of the store or the returns process. Moreover, particular types of people are more likely to be 'shrinkage prone', such as temporary or part time staff (Speed, 2003), or those who undertake certain functions, such as till operators or night shift shelf stackers. By using data to identify the various 'hot' elements within the business, retail loss prevention managers can then begin to formulate a strategy which focuses on the factors that require their attention – the vital few rather than the trivial many.

Operational excellence

As we detailed in the Chapter 7, the root cause of most forms of shrinkage can be linked to operational failures and recognising this is a key part of delivering *New Loss Prevention*. We see operational failures as creating the opportunity for much of the malicious shrinkage that retail businesses suffer from: deviant staff and dishonest customers are provided with an environment that minimises risk and maximises the perceived rewards. Staff in particular can quickly become aware of the opportunities that are presented for theft when parts of the organisation either no longer function properly, or existing processes become out of date or comprised by changes in the way in which the company operates. For instance, lax stock control processes can be exploited by staff who want to steal goods, while till operators who want to steal cash could be facilitated by managers no longer checking the level of cash in the till at the end of a particular employee's shift. Either way, as we detailed previously, the way in which the business is organised and operated can have a significant impact on the extent to which losses can occur, the likelihood of the incident being discovered in a timely fashion, and the ability to identify the perpetrator.

The flipside of this is developing Operational Excellence which is concerned with minimising the likely impact of operational failures on the business and at the same time ensuring the organisation is able to maximise its potential to satisfy the needs of customers and remain profitable. The case-study companies in Beck's research highlighted the importance of getting the balance right between sales and security through providing good service and manageable controls:

> [There is] a delicate balance between good service and proper amounts of control in your supply chain. Controls must compliment the service requirements of the business. Big priority is putting controls in place ... [this is] why it is important to have a diverse team because you have people who like doing auditing and examining processes. You can never apprehend your way out of a shortage. Cannot recover from a collapse in operational discipline – it is like the spine of the business breaking – all of a sudden we can't walk, we can't get motor function.

As can be seen, this respondent recognises the absolute value of having robust controls that are fit for purpose and compliment the overall functioning of the business. Another respondent noted how poor process adherence could be an indicator of a greater underlying malaise:

> [We] emphasise the importance of getting shrinkage right – poor process adherence tells you something else may be going on as well. Senior management has signed in to this.

Another company in this research explicitly stated the importance of making sure that procedures were followed: '[name of retailer] is focused on execution above anything else', while another used stock control procedures:

> They [store staff] track all the units as they come in to the store ... check all the boxes as they come into the store. [We] have good data to check what stock should be in the store. Organisationally, [name

of retailer] is very strong on process and have reduced failures to a minimum.

Achieving Operational Excellence is very much about the way in which the whole business is managed and how the problem of shrinkage is considered as part of this. Key to this is creating company processes and procedures which are well designed and implemented, are effectively monitored and controlled, and subject to periodic review. Detailed below is how we see this being done.

Design & implementation

Good processes and procedures need to be carefully *designed* and properly *implemented*. When developing any way of doing work it is important to consider whether the proposed actions are fit for purpose. In other words does the planned process or procedure actually deliver what is required from the staff who are intended to use and adhere to the new way of working? In part this is concerned with usability but it is also interested in understanding the context within which the planned process and procedure is intended to operate. For instance, if a new procedure is to be brought in which requires a member of store staff to put away all high value goods within 20 minutes of their arrival at the store, how likely is this to happen? For instance, what happens if the stock arrives late at night when there are few staff working or the secure cage is full of other stock? In these circumstances, the proposed procedure will not be able to be delivered consistently because of mitigating circumstances, such as a lack of coordination between planned delivery times with levels of staffing, or designated stocking levels for stores with low levels of available space.

In addition, have the staff who are supposed to implement any new process or procedure been given the necessary training to enable them to not only do the required task, but also appreciate the reasoning behind why it is being introduced? Like most people, retail staff will attempt to take the route of least resistance especially when any new work is viewed as not only additional to current duties but also potentially unnecessary. Moreover, the design and implementation of new routines need to take into account whether they are operable with existing systems and ways of doing work. For instance, it would make little sense bringing in a new process or procedure to capture data that is incompatible with other systems currently in place. Indeed, as detailed in the last example described above, the potential impact of introducing a new mode of operation needs to be clearly road tested to ensure that it has no unintended consequences, or if it does, then the savings outweigh the costs. For example, many larger retailers have moved away from checking stock at item level as it arrives at the back of the store because the saving in staff costs is considered to far outweigh the potential impact removing this process has had upon levels of shrinkage and stock accuracy.

So the first step in developing operational excellence is ensuring that the design and implementation of new processes and procedures is done in such a way as to be sensitive to the context within which they will operate, have been properly road tested to make sure there are no unintended consequences, and that they are fit for purpose and capable of being delivered by the staff tasked to implement them.

Oversight

The second component is oversight of operational excellence, which is made up of two elements: *monitoring* and *control*. While a company may spend considerable time designing and implementing a raft of processes and procedures, they are largely irrelevant if they are not being adhered to by staff tasked to abide by them. In many respects, this is one of the key reasons why operational failures occur and subsequently create the circumstances and opportunities for shrinkage. The pivotal role of monitoring and control cannot be underestimated and has been at the heart of effective shrinkage management for many years. Indeed, Curtis back in 1960 highlighted the critical role of control and its link with shrinkage: 'All stores and businesses have systems – without them they could not function – yet unfailingly when shortages show and large quantities of merchandise have mysteriously vanished, somewhere there has been a deviation from the established system' (1960: 10). He goes on to make the point more precisely: 'most of your store losses are caused by carelessness ... [which can] lead to theft. You should inject controls into your systems to keep errors at a reasonable level (1960: 806). Nearly 50 years later, his words seem even more salient as an ever more competitive retail environment seeks to reduce levels of supervision and control yet further within its operations. Good monitoring and control is as much about ensuring that procedures are followed as it is about creating accountability and transparency. Poor or absent controls create the toxic environment within which opportunity and carelessness can thrive.

In addition, the role of management and the way in which they behave with regards to following processes and procedures is critical. Again, it is worth quoting Curtis who makes this point extremely well: 'All levels of retail management must realise that they set the leadership example for their people' (1960: 814). If an organisation has a culture which condones rule breaking and employs a management team that overtly flouts established practices and procedures in front of other staff, then do not be surprised if this organisation struggles to ensure that staff adhere to the processes and procedures they are suppose to follow.

So the monitoring and control of processes and procedures is a fundamental part of achieving operation excellence – are staff doing what they are suppose to be doing and if they are not, what are the consequences for the business in terms of increased vulnerability to shrinkage? As one retailer member of the ECR Europe Shrinkage Group succinctly put it when describing his challenge in this area: 'we don't need anymore processes and procedures, – we have lots of really good ones – what we need is for our people to follow them!'.

Review

The final component of achieving operational excellence is having a mechanism for the continual *review* of current processes and procedures. Are they still fit for purpose as the business develops and adapts to new ways of working? As detailed early, modern retailing is a dynamic environment with continuing success premised upon an ability to respond to new challenges and opportunities. New products are constantly being developed as are new ways of handling them and marketing them to the public. In addition, new retailing systems emerge which require staff to work in different ways, and indeed the employment profiles of staff continue to change, with an increasing emphasis upon part time, contract and more mobile work forces. All of these factors can have a negative influence upon the capacity of a business to keep their processes and procedures in tune with the way in which the business needs to operate. A lack of a review process can lead to staff abandoning old ways of doing work or developing their own 'fixes' to ensure they are not either further burdened or penalised by the requirements of a changing retail environment.

Two simple ways can enable a business to review whether their retail operations are still fit for purpose. One is to talk to the staff who have operational responsibility for delivering on a day-to-day basis the processes and procedures currently in place – do they still think they are relevant and useful? The second, as we detailed in the previous chapter, is to undertake regular process mapping exercises based upon following the movement of particular products across the entire supply chain and closely monitoring whether the processes and procedures that are suppose to be followed are actually being adhered to. Finally, it is worth ending this section on Operational Excellence with another quote from Curtis, who summarised the importance of adherence to procedures back in 1960: 'We [also] need supervisors who will see that store procedures operate in reality as they are intended to operate in theory' (Curtis, 1960: 504) – wise words indeed.

Prioritising people

Any retail organisation can make substantial investments in systems, technologies and highly creative strategic plans, but without the right people who are properly motivated and trained to use and implement them, they will ultimately fail. Getting the right people engaged in shrinkage control is a critical part of delivering the Loss Prevention Pyramid.

We see this reflected in two broad areas: staff operating across the organisation and staff employed directly within the loss prevention team. The research work by Beck highlighted how the extent to which the loss prevention functions under consideration could influence the former varies, while for the latter all stressed the pre-eminence of getting a team that was multi-functional, highly motivated and clearly focused on delivering the strategic plan.

Organisational level

Much of the focus for the case-study companies was on getting the right people in the stores as this was seen as the most vulnerable part of the business in terms of staffing and shrinkage. Three of the five companies under consideration particularly emphasised the need to create stability in the stores and to try and reduce the churn and turn of managers. One had a strategy they called '216', whereby they tried to have stores where a manager had been in place for at least two years, an assistant manager for at least one year and supervisors for six months. This was seen as a key way to keeping store shrinkage low: 'these stores [the 216s] tend to have low shrink ... it's about stability in the store ... they get a chance to know the staff and the environment'. Similarly, other case-study respondents reflected upon the need to keep the turnover of managers to a minimum as this was often a bigger determinant of shrinkage than the location of the store:

> [we] believe it is all about the people and not where the store is located. Stop churning managers through high shrink stores – give them the support to deal with the problem. Our Los Angeles stores

are an example of low shrink stores in difficult areas where we have stability in store management.

This approach was tied into a policy of listening to store staff to make sure that they were given the help that they thought they needed, subject to improved performance on shrinkage: 'listen to the staff and meet their needs, such as extra labor ... but we then expect them to show it made a difference'.

A number of the companies Beck reviewed talked about the value of incentivising store staff although this was not a policy universal to all of them. One in particular had a policy whereby any reduction in store shrinkage was shared amongst all store staff, and this was seen as a particularly good way of keeping shrinkage on everybody's agenda. Other companies had tried out policies similar to this but for a number of reasons had decided to move away from it for all staff (store managers tended to remain incentivised on shrinkage and sales).

Three of the five companies had relatively recently moved towards the use of pre-employment screening for all staff joining their organisations. This was seen as a valuable way of reducing their exposure to risk, particularly in the stores:

> We have brought in a screening process for all staff ... [a] filter to help reduce the amount of poor staff coming into the business. We use the Esteem Database as well which eliminates some previously dishonest staff from entering the business. We have rejected 8,000 applicants so far .... Turnover has stabilised after introducing this system.

> We use pre-employment screening to work hard up front to make sure that person really wants to be in the organisation ... they have a predisposition to service and selling ... that they are not violent and so on.

The final area where the loss prevention respondents felt they had an impact on store staff was in education and training. Once again all five companies pointed to a range of ways in which they had developed programmes to ensure that store staff were kept aware of the current issues relating to shrinkage, and this was seen as important in building a 'culture of integrity' – a phrase that was used by four of the five companies.

The loss prevention team

In addition to trying to influence the way in which store staff were recruited, trained, monitored and motivated, the case-study companies observed by Beck also reflected in some detail on the importance of building their loss prevention team and the value in getting the right people focused on the challenge ahead and playing to their particular strengths. All five companies stressed the importance of creating a highly multi-functional team with a high degree of diversity:

> Our approach to recruiting is based around diversity ... like to have people on the team whose experiences are not related to LP ... have people at director level who used to run a store, worked in operations, audit. [They] bring the gift of really knowing the business ... understand how stores operate.

> We've developed a team that brings different skills to the table. Operations and HR [Human Resources] know how, supply chain experience.

> Developed a multi faceted team that has a range of skills including those with responsibility for safety and risk management ... most are not ex policeman but have experience in retailing or marketing or long term LP.

While they all recognised that they undoubtedly needed some members of the team who could offer a 'policing' function, particularly in terms of interviewing and carrying out investigations, they were seen as but one part of a broader more multi-skilled team. Awareness and experience of the retail environment, especially stores and the supply chain were considered highly important prerequisites for many of the posts within the loss prevention team. There was also a strong emphasis on staff who were capable of thinking beyond what were perceived as the traditional boundaries of loss prevention:

> We are looking for staff with an enterprise wide mindset – operate with a big screen TV set in their head – capable of looking at multiple channels simultaneously. We want people who can see the entire field and know what their role is at any point in time to have an impact on the problem.

Some of the respondents had set up specialist groups within the loss prevention department to deal with particular problems. For example, four of the five had set up organised retail crime (ORC) groups to respond to this seemingly growing problem. In addition, and as mentioned previously (see Data Management), the setting up of specialist analytical teams was also seen as a particular priority: 'we set up an analysts team to monitor data, dig into the data, carry out evaluations on new initiatives etc ... provide granularity to the data analysis'.

The final part of the picture was an emphasis on providing training for loss prevention staff and giving them the resources they need. This was seen as especially important in terms of retention and organic growth:

> They [the loss prevention team] are well resourced ... I believe that people are critical to dealing with the problem. Training is a high priority for the AP [Asset Protection] staff – helps with retention of staff.

> [It can be] tough to get the right people – best way to get them is to grow them organically – hire well at lower levels ... provide a good development programme ... more likely to get people who know the business and are well motivated.

Finally, a number of the heads of loss prevention stressed the critical importance of building a new team when they first joined the organisation, and how this, along with getting in place the mechanisms for data management, were the fundamental foundations for the success they had achieved in bringing shrinkage under control.

Over the last 20 or 30 years, the priority for many loss prevention functions has been to seek out yet more technologically refined solutions to the shrinkage problems they face – the 'appliance of science' to deal with an intransigent issue. However, what the experience of the companies studied by Beck reveals is that prioritising people within the business, especially in terms of those working within the loss prevention function and those operating in the stores, is an important aspect of developing an effective shrinkage management strategy.

Collaboration

The fifth element in the series of Organisational Factors in the Loss Prevention Pyramid is the importance of incorporating a collaborative approach to the work of the loss prevention function. This is not a factor that was highlighted by Beck's work on the best performing US retailers, although to a certain extent it is covered by one of the earlier factors (Organisational Ownership). It is, however, something which the numerous studies undertaken by the ECR Europe Shrinkage Group have identified as a defining element in delivering effective shrinkage management (Beck *et al.*, 2001; Beck *et al.*, 2003; Chapman, 2009). Collaboration can take place at two different levels: intra company and inter company, the former focused on how different functions within a business can work together and the latter on how different companies can collaborate.

Intra-company collaboration

As was detailed earlier, ensuring organisational ownership of the problem of shrinkage is an important foundation block upon which the Loss Prevention Pyramid is based. Different parts of the business need to recognise the value and importance of playing a role in minimising the losses incurred through shrinkage. *New Loss Prevention* sees the role of the loss prevention practitioner as an 'agent of change' orchestrating the company-wide approach to effective shrinkage management. This requires close collaboration with the other functions in the business. As we showed with the Shrinkage Road Map and its use in understanding the root causes of operational failures that can cause shrinkage, a cross functional team is much more likely to not only enable these root causes to be identified, but also develop suitable solutions to resolve them. As with ensuring senior management commitment to the problem of shrinkage, other functions within the business need to be persuaded of the value of contributing to the loss prevention cause. They need to be shown how minimising shrinkage can positively impact upon the overall profitability of the business, how it negatively impacts upon the ability of any given function to deliver their own objectives, and how they can be practically involved in the overall process. If this can be done, then a multi-functional, collaborative approach can be developed which is far more likely to deliver sustainable solutions to the shrinkage problem.

Inter-company collaboration

In addition to developing collaborative arrangements with other parts of the retail business, the loss prevention function also needs to reach out to other companies as well, such as manufacturers, logistics providers and technology providers. Again, the Shrinkage Road Map highlighted how this needs to be done if root causes of shrinkage throughout a supply chain are to be identified. In some respects this can be more challenging for at least two reasons. First, some retailers can have rather fraught relationships with their suppliers – a loss prevention manager working for one of Britain's largest supermarket chains once famously described three of their key suppliers as the 'axis of evil' when it came to discussions concerning shrinkage! While he was undoubtedly speaking in jest, his words will certainly resonate with many loss prevention managers who have sometimes found manufacturers to be less than interested in the way in which their products may suffer from shrinkage within the retail space. This comes in part from a school of thought that suggests that retail shrinkage is good for business for manufacturers – the retailers have to order more stock to replace that which has been damaged, lost or stolen. However, more enlightened manufacturers have begun to recognise that they can play a positive role in helping retailers to reduce shrinkage and that it does have an impact upon their profitability – empty shelves as a consequence of shrinkage are not good for anybody's profits. In addition, they understand that retailers may take actions (such as using defensive merchandising techniques to protect shrinkage prone products) that can reduce sales on their products. It is therefore in their interests to become engaged with the problem and collaborate with the retail community.

Secondly, inter-company collaboration can be hampered by concerns about the sharing of information relating to particular products. As we discussed in Chapter 6, the subject of shrinkage is considered to be highly sensitive and retailers rarely make information about its impact upon their business readily available. But as we showed earlier, the Shrinkage Road Map works best when as many data sources as possible are collected and shared with the project team (which could include manufacturers).

These stumbling blocks are not insurmountable and can be overcome through an open and honest dialogue. If they can, then the benefits of adopting a more collaborative approach to addressing the problem of shrinkage can be profound. It will enable a much more comprehensive root-cause analysis of operational failures to be carried out, which in turn will lead to the development of solutions that are more geared to genuinely fixing the problem rather than simply responding to the symptoms.

Prioritising innovation and experimentation

As anybody who has worked in loss prevention will quickly testify, the threats faced by organisations are rarely static and unchanging. Indeed, the field of loss prevention accurately mirrors the modern retail environment which can best be described as dynamic, evolutionary and increasingly challenging. Retail organisations that do not innovate and adapt are highly likely to quickly become footnotes in the history of commerce. The shrinkage survey undertaken by ECR Europe in 2004 highlighted the importance of innovation and experimentation in helping to reduce the cost of shrinkage. The survey showed that those companies which claimed to be highly prioritising this approach had levels of shrinkage 20 per cent below the average for all respondents (Beck, 2004a). Indeed, the various published Shrinkage Road Map case studies all show the value of adopting an experimental and innovatory approach to responding to the problem of shrinkage, with levels of loss consist-ently reduced at the same time as retail sales often being increased (Beck *et al.*, 2003).

A key feature of all of the loss prevention departments studied by Beck was their appreciation of, and commitment to, embracing inno-vation and experimentation. This often took the form of using cutting edge technologies (see Smith, 2006 for a review), but it also related to trying out new process and procedural approaches or a willingness to change strategies and think 'outside' the existing loss prevention box:

> We are an aggressive innovator willing to try things out ... [we] are benchmarking worldwide. Trying to keep improvement moving forward through innovation. [Got to] keep reinventing yourself over and over – keep modifying what is hot and what is not as the bad guys move focus.

For some of the respondents, but not all, being at the cutting edge of technology was very important to them. They want to be trailblazers and early adopters so that they will remain 'ahead of the game'. Views varied of what technology they adopted and supported. The value of EAS was considered very variable although all five used it in some way or other. One of the companies had recently made a significant invest-ment in source tagged EAS, moving away from a mixture of soft and hard tags to almost exclusively soft tags. They recognised that this had been a real challenge and it had impacted negatively upon their short term shrinkage figure. This was partly due to staff getting familiar with the new tags and the way they should be deactivated, but also the loss of the overt visible deterrence traditionally offered by hard tags. All five companies were quick to stress that while EAS had many limitations, not least because of the crying wolf syndrome (systems constantly being set off accidentally because of faulty tags, a failure to deactivate the tag, or exit gates being activated by non-tag devices or tags from other retail environments), they felt that it was important to be seen to be using it because virtually all other retailers had it – a sense that not having it would make them a 'soft' target on the high street. But they also agreed that their shrinkage strategy should not stand or fall on one approach (be it technological or otherwise) but that it should be seen as part of a broader multi-faceted approach where a combination of 'solutions' were used to meet the challenge.

All five companies made use of Closed Circuit Television (CCTV) although again, its coverage, type and purpose varied significantly. None felt that its sole purpose was necessarily to catch incidents of shop theft, indeed maintaining a monitoring presence was unrealistic for some of the case-study companies given the size of their stores and the limited presence of security staff. There was consensus that it did have a powerful role to play in ensuring that stores were perceived to be safe and that the organisation was acting responsibly in trying to ensure the safety of staff and customers in and around the shopping environment. One of the respondents noted how they used CCTV:

> Primarily use CCTV for safety – not a lot of shrink reduction with CCTV. It is good for procedure compliance and exception reporting which can impact upon shrinkage …remote monitoring is used to check on compliance.

While three of the five were highly committed to being early adopters of technologies, all five of the companies reviewed by Beck recognised the value of performing experiments and undertaking relatively rigorous evaluations of newly introduced interventions to ensure that future roll out decisions were based upon good quality test data. This links back to an earlier section on Data Management and the belief in having high quality data to inform decision-making. These companies were very willing to innovate and experiment, but they also wanted to make sure that the impact of this was carefully measured and evaluated.

Communicating shrinkage

A thread that runs through virtually all the other factors in the Loss Prevention Pyramid is the need to communicate about shrinkage, be it with store staff, the loss prevention team, supply chain logistics or the CEO; keeping the organisation informed is a vital part of *New Loss Prevention*. The five companies taking part in Beck's study recognised this and had developed a series of mechanisms to achieve this, which can be categorised under a number of different types of communication. The first is the need to generate *awareness* of the problem of shrinkage, particularly with store staff who may have just joined the organisation. This was done in a number of ways such as with videos and specific shrinkage information as part of the staff induction programme. Awareness was also created through the use of newsletters (one company had the wonderful title of 'shrink rap' for their newsletter), notice boards in staff areas, regular campaigns and focus days, competitions and so on. The degree of innovation amongst the companies was very high in terms of trying to keep the company aware of the problem.

Secondly, loss prevention teams need to communicate information about shrinkage to *influence* decision-making in other parts of the organisation. This could take the form of regular statistical updates on the extent of shrinkage and the way it is impacting on particular parts of the business. For instance, store planners may be provided with information on levels of shrinkage as they affect particular types of product, while broader trend data might be shared with the Board.

Thirdly, companies need to communicate about shrinkage to *direct* and *steer* the work of particular specialist teams for instance regional loss prevention staff, auditing teams, ORC groups and so on. This might take the form of comparative data or information about specific incidents that need further investigation. The use of bespoke databases for this purpose was used by some of the companies analysed by Beck which enabled staff to access the data directly and run reports specific to their particular needs. One respondent described this process:

> We have monthly reports for the management team ... [we] have empowered regional loss prevention managers to use the system and run their own queries ... developing an EIS [External, Internal and Safety] report that examines the risk of each store and develops an index for each store. It [EIS index] enables us to compare stores and allocate resources – this data is viewed by store managers as well.

The link between data management and communication about shrinkage was clear and explicit in all the companies looked at by Beck. The sense that there is no point in collecting high quality fine-grained data if it is not subsequently communicated to those that can use the information to help them impact upon the problem was very apparent. There was a sense that creating strategies and conduits to talk about shrinkage with the rest of the business was a priority and that it required innovation and energy to sustain it. It was also linked very closely with the process of embedding shrinkage management into the culture of the business. For instance, one respondent offered an interesting example:

> Every day the manager of the store gets the staff together for a huddle to discuss the things that are happening. We make sure they have information in the right format at the right time so that they can keep staff up to date with their shrink problems and give them some direction. It's a good way of keeping shrink on the agenda and making the staff keep thinking about it.

For this company it was simply a case of making sure shrinkage was on the agenda for the store huddle and also that the manager had timely data made available to them about what was happening specifically in their store.

So establishing and maintaining a series of mechanisms and methodologies by which shrinkage is communicated throughout the business is an important part of *New Loss Prevention*. It adds real value through keeping staff informed and aware of the problem, which in turn can act as a mechanism for creating focus and deterrence (Oliphant & Oliphant, 2001). It is also useful in keeping the issue of shrinkage on the agenda of other parts of the business as well as to steer the work of the staff directly employed by loss prevention. Keeping people thinking about shrinkage is not easy – it can quickly slip down or off the agenda – creating innovative and embedded means of communication is extremely important in ensuring that any organisation remains fully aware of the value of remaining focused on loss prevention.

Organisational factors: Developing a strategic framework

This second section of the Loss Prevention Pyramid has focused on a range of factors that can be seen as more or less under the direct control of the loss prevention team. The importance of a strong leader who can provide direction, focus and commitment; the development of a series of mechanisms for measuring the way in which shrinkage impacts upon the business; maintaining focus on operational excellence and a recognition of its role in minimising shrink; the need to get the right people involved within the business and the loss prevention team; the importance of engaging in intra- and inter-collaboration; the value of being innovative and willing to experiment; and the importance of communicating about shrinkage. All of these elements are important component parts that reside upon the Strategic Factors considered earlier and act as a broader organisational framework for the final factor discussed below.

The next section now looks at the final aspect of the Pyramid: Store Management Responsibility and how this Operational factor is the culmination of all the other elements discussed previously.

Operational factors

Store management responsibility

The 2004 ECR Europe shrinkage survey identified that over 75 per cent of all shrinkage was thought by respondents to occur in stores, perhaps not surprising given that this is the place where customers are allowed to interact with the product and staff have the greatest degree of autonomy and latitude in what they do and how they do it (Beck, 2004a). As we detailed earlier in this book, the scale and complexity of modern retailing is breathtaking and this is particularly apparent in the retail store. Large supermarket outlets can have in excess of 1.5 million separate items, the majority of which can be sold and replaced every week. They will have complex IT systems monitoring the movement of these products and employ hundreds of staff serving hundreds of thousands of customers. The opportunities for operational failure are many and varied but keeping direct centralised control of such a retail colossus is unrealistic on a day-to-day basis. Modern retail organisations rely upon the fact that for the most part the routine monitoring and control of all retail functions, including shrinkage management, is delegated down to store teams.

Research has shown that the risk of crime in general, and shrinkage in particular, is not evenly distributed across all places – some stores will have much higher levels of loss than others – what are termed 'hot stores' (Eck & Weisburd, 1995; Beck & Chapman, 2003). While some have argued that the primary contributory factor in explaining this difference is the location of the store itself – bad areas in terms of high levels of social deprivation and crime cause high shrinkage in retail stores, others have suggested that while this is a factor to be taken into account, the role of store management is equally if not more important. This is not a new idea, Curtis back in 1960 can be found referring to this when he said: '... good shortage results follow good executives' (Curtis, 1960: 178). More recently Beck and Chapman concluded much the same in their study of hot stores in European retailers:

> ... the way in which a store is managed is the key factor in explaining why some stores have higher rates of loss than others. Yes, the

environment within which the store is located does play a role, but good management teams recognise this and develop strategies accordingly to meet the challenge they face. As one of the managers interviewed for this study put it: 'This is a tough store but we know it and develop plans accordingly' (Beck & Chapman, 2003: 47–48).

Their research went on to identify four areas where store managers can play a major role in ensuring that their store does not have above average rates of loss: Accountability (the store manager recognises that shrinkage is a major priority for them); Action (commitment to make sure processes and procedures are followed) Attitude (show the rest of the store team that shrinkage matters); and Audit (prioritise measuring the problem of shrinkage in their environment).

Similarly, all five case-study companies analysed by Beck identified the importance of creating the right framework for ensuring that store management and their staff take responsibility for monitoring and controlling loss prevention at the micro level (the store): '[We] believe that the leadership in the stores is critical [to sustaining low shrinkage] together with clear rules and roles and appropriate rewards'. Another respondent identified how their role (loss prevention) was very much to support and guide the store staff in what they were doing:

> Store managers execute the plan at store level. Every day they have a meeting with all staff and shrink is a standing item. They have weekly data on shrink and talk to staff about this. We also monitor the numbers as well. We post the numbers on shrink in the staff areas. Field LP teams talk to managers and provide training, but it is very much hands off – give them the numbers.

Another respondent highlighted the need to provide support to store managers to control shrinkage, particularly those that might have above average levels of loss:

> Managers in 'target' stores get increased training. [There is] heightened expectations that they will follow procedures etc. I have seen too many stores in horrible areas have fabulous shrink levels – what was the difference, it was the management's level of engagement.

While creating support for the store management team was seen as important, for some of the case-study companies reviewed by Beck there was also a clear sense of creating a climate of responsibility through potential sanctions: 'a store manager knows that they can get sacked if they don't take shrink seriously – two over budgets and then they are in real trouble'; 'store managers are held directly accountable for their shrink, they are bonused on shrink'.

In addition, case-study companies recognised and prioritised the training and support of store staff to deal with the problem of shrinkage on a day-to-day basis. For some companies this included having a visible security presence in the store, such as a security guard or a loss prevention operative. But what was seen as critical was getting store management to 'buy in' to the shrinkage plan and to ensure that they became the devolved representation of the loss prevention department. All the companies were also united in creating mechanisms by which the store manager was sensitised to the problem particularly through incentives (bonus schemes) and potential sanctions (possible termination of employment). In a minority of cases this approach was adopted for all the staff in the store, and not just the store managers.

Modern retail companies are highly reliant upon store teams delivering the corporate plan, be it in relation to sales, marketing or shrinkage management. Ensuring that these teams have the right support network and organisational tools to enable them to deliver is a crucial part of the Loss Prevention Pyramid. Creating store management responsibility can only be achieved if the organisation provides the rest of the pyramid – if it does not, then store management teams will continue to have a plethora of excuses as to why their particular store has a shrinkage problem, all of which will have little to do with them and all to do with either where they are located or how they are treated by the rest of the business. But the business also has to make sure that store teams are not asked to take responsibility for shrinkage over which they have no control. For instance, shrinkage occurring in the supply chain can often only become apparent when products are audited in the stores. The assumption is then made that the losses happened where the stock was first identified as missing. The business needs to have mechanisms in place whereby shrinkage losses are more transparent and accountable otherwise store teams will become disillusioned when they are asked to control the uncontrollable or take responsibility for losses generated by others.

Placing store teams at the top of the loss prevention pyramid (when often their position within organisations is perceived as at the bottom of the pile) is important – they are the ones that ultimately deliver and they need to be given the recognition and support to enable them to achieve the overall goal of selling more and losing less.

New loss prevention: The loss prevention pyramid

The 11 factors outlined above come together to create the framework for what we see as *New Loss Prevention*. They are interlinked and dependent and we feel offer a viable means for effectively tackling retail shrinkage.

Setting the foundations

The bedrock for successfully implementing the Loss Prevention Pyramid is the ability to create, sustain and embed an organisational awareness of, and commitment to, dealing with the problem of stock loss. This starts at the very top of the company with senior management being fully committed to the concept of loss prevention being an important priority for all parts of the organisation. Without this level of commitment, the rest of the business will not be persuaded that shrinkage matters nor will the loss prevention department receive the mandate or resources necessary to implement new approaches to tackle the problem.

In addition, it is important to ensure that all parts of the organisation take ownership of the problem. Many organisations have traditionally viewed loss prevention departments as the sole arbiter on all issues relating to security and shrinkage. What we suggest is that they become the 'agents of change', working with other functions within the business to develop and operationalise a cross-company response to the shrinkage problem. This seems a far more realistic and sustainable approach given the limited resources available within most loss prevention departments.

Moreover, ensuring that this organisational commitment is embedded within the business practices, policies, procedures and strategic thinking is a vital component of *New Loss Prevention*. If this is not done, then the essentially ephemeral nature of organisational commitment to tackle shrinkage will quickly become apparent. Getting people to not only think about shrinkage but to take responsibility for it is a key part of the Loss Prevention Pyramid.

Without these three strategic level factors it is clear that any form of loss prevention approach will founder on the rocks of diffidence, marginalisation and under prioritisation. Getting a broader organisational framework that is conducive to taking loss prevention seriously is an absolute imperative.

Providing an organisational framework

The second group of factors that make up the Loss Prevention Pyramid relate to the way in which the loss prevention department can influence the functioning of the business through: ensuring strong loss prevention leadership; the creation of high quality data and data management systems; prioritising the development of operational excellence (through identifying and minimising operational failures); ensuring that, wherever possible, the right people work within the business as a whole and more specifically within the loss prevention department; the forging of intra- and inter-collaborative initiatives; the prioritisation of innovation and experiment-ation; and keeping shrinkage on everybody's agenda through various communication strategies. All of these factors are important in themselves, and require a specific plan to ensure they are properly developed and main-tained, but they are also highly dependent upon each other. For instance, it is difficult to conceive of an effective communication strategy without having access to high quality data. Similarly, it is difficult to be innovative and experimental (especially in such a competitive market as retailing) without firm and decisive loss prevention leadership.

Operationalising shrinkage

The final theme is that of store management responsibility: empower-ing store staff to take responsibility for dealing with the problem of shrinkage. Occupying the very top of the Loss Prevention Pyramid, this can only be achieved if the other factors outlined above are in place. If they are not, then store management will not only have a raft of ready-made excuses as to why shrinkage is a problem they cannot be expected to take responsibility for, but also they will not have access to the necessary resources and expertise to manage it effectively.

Operational failure and new loss prevention

As we detailed previously in Chapter 7, underpinning our thinking is the importance of recognising how operational failures are the root cause of most forms of shrinkage, and this should be viewed as a thread that runs through the Loss Prevention Pyramid. It can be seen explicitly in the emphasis upon ensuring Operational Excellence – the flip side of opera-tional failure – but it impacts upon many other areas as well. Perhaps more importantly, it is representative of a mind shift away from what we have defined as 'Old Loss Prevention', with its heavy reliance upon catch-ing thieves (primarily shoplifters), seeking out yet more technologically advanced panaceas focused more upon the symptoms of the problem rather than the underlying root causes, and viewing the store as the only place in which shrinkage occurs.

In the final chapter we reflect upon how *New Loss Prevention* can be used in practice and summarise some of the key themes discussed in earlier chapters.

10
Implementing New Loss Prevention

In this final chapter we will bring together the various themes covered in the previous parts of this book and seek to identify the key elements necessary for organisations to build, implement and sustain the Loss Prevention Pyramid. It is not meant to be a 'how to' guide to reducing stock loss within retail organisations – we leave that to others more qualified in the practicalities of operational shrinkage management. Our purpose has been to provide an overarching framework within which this type of work can be placed and to offer an alternative way of thinking about the shrinkage problems faced by retailers. In many respects what we are proposing is not radically different than that suggested by writers such as Curtis back in the 1950s and 1960s who espoused the importance of developing and monitoring effective retail controls as the primary means of minimising shrinkage (Curtis, 1960). Nearly 50 years ago he was making pertinent comments that fit neatly with our outlook on the problem: 'good store operations and low shrinkage go hand in hand' (Curtis, 1960: 802); 'most of your store losses are caused by carelessness ... [which can] lead to theft. You should inject controls into your system to keep errors at a reasonable level (Curtis, 1960: 806); and finally:

> Do you believe in gadgets? Today there is a dependence by many people on scientific things as a means of shrinkage control. This has often proved to be a false hope. In the end you still need sound operating systems and good supervision. Scientific devices have only a limited value... (Curtis, 1960: 811).

His last statement we feel is particularly relevant to the situation today and also explains to a certain extent why we feel the need to reiterate his points almost half a century later. The never ending search for the technological panacea has in some respects led the loss prevention industry down a path (some might view it as a cul de sac) which has meant that the role of retail controls (operational excellence) has (for many) become marginalised within the overall shrinkage management strategy. Some might argue that this is an inevitable consequence of the evolution of retailing which has produced an environment where controls are often viewed as costly and unnecessary. There is undoubtedly some truth in this statement, but we feel that there needs to be a balance struck between selling and security, between selling more and not losing even more. We certainly are not suggesting that technologies have no role to play in managing shrinkage in retailing – they most certainly do – but that they need to be viewed as just one of the options available, and that ensuring operational excellence (minimising operational failures) has a more important role to play.

Breaking the shrinkage 'life cycle'

The ever changing nature of the retail sector has meant that keeping shrinkage under control is not easy and constantly requires the development of new approaches, ideas and skill sets for those tasked to deal with it. What is clear is that many if not all organisations have strug-

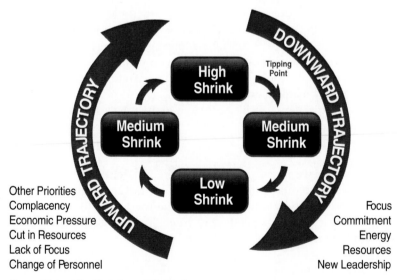

Figure 10.1   The Shrinkage Life Cycle

gled at some point to meet the challenges of this ever changing retail environment and have experienced what we term the 'shrinkage life cycle', where companies will experience times when levels of loss are relatively high and times when it is relatively low (see Figure 10.1).

For some companies the current trajectory could be one of a decrease in shrinkage as the problem receives new focus, commitment, energy, leadership and resources, enabling the organisation to effectively manage the problem. As we discussed in the previous chapter, this downward trend is often triggered by a 'tipping point' being reached in the business such as shrinkage reaching a particular value which is considered unacceptable by senior management. For other companies the trajectory of shrinkage could be upwards due in part to external economic pressures on the business leading to a cut in resources, a lack of continued focus on the problem, possibly caused by complacency, new priorities emerging or a change of personnel within the business (both at senior management level and within the loss prevention team). Either way, much like economic cycles, the shrinkage cycle is often an inevitable part of the retail landscape of most companies and many loss prevention managers may have been round this circuit many times in their career, particularly if they have moved between different organisations.

Maintaining low shrinkage is one of the most challenging tasks loss prevention practitioners have. Once the business feels it has 'done' shrinkage, it can be very difficult to maintain the energy and focus that was there on the downward trajectory and which drove much of the success in the first place. The inevitable upward slope awaits most companies and once again the loss prevention team will have to wait for a tipping point to arrive before shrinkage becomes a priority again. Part of what we would like to argue is that this cycle is not inevitable – that a wedge can be driven in to stop it happening and that *New Loss Prevention* through the use of the Loss Prevention Pyramid offers a framework to ensure that once low shrinkage is achieved it can be sustained over a long period of time.

Time for change

As we detailed in Chapter 2, retailing has changed dramatically in the past 100 years or so and created new and ever more demanding circumstances under which shrinkage needs to be managed and controlled. The turn of the last century saw the rise of mass merchandising which led to the development of many of the loss prevention practices we now see today. Over that time the need to protect products from a variety of threats has remained and the elimination of shrinkage will continue to be a chimera. But the growing obsession with the bogeyman of shrinkage – external theft – we feel has led to developments in shrinkage control that have created both a mind set and mode of operation which is increasingly focused upon the symptoms of the problem rather than the underlying causes – what we have termed operational failures. As one of the respondents to the research carried out by Beck on why some companies appear to have much lower levels of loss than others clearly concluded: 'you cannot apprehend your way out of shrinkage' (2007a: 29). They recognised that simply catching more shoplifters is not the answer to the problem but that you need to minimise the opportunities presented by the retail operation in the first place.

In Chapter 6 we offered a summary of the various ways in which the traditional approach to loss prevention has at best been keeping a lid on the shrinkage problem and for many retail companies this means that a substantial proportion of their profits are lost to shrinkage. We feel it is time for a change in the way in which loss prevention is viewed by the retail sector – to move away from the endless search for the 'bad guys' (be they errant teenagers, so called organised retail criminals or deviant members of staff) and to focus on the way in which business operations generate the opportunities and circumstances that create shrinkage. This requires a change of mindset (and indeed skill set) more focused on retail excellence than thief catching, more aligned with understanding operational failures than investigating criminal gangs. Undoubtedly, people will always try to steal from retail stores, and some will be highly successful, resourceful and determined, but it is time to recognise that not only are they a part of the overall shrinkage problem but that they can be limited through the effective design, implementation and control of retail processes and procedures.

Adding value to the business

One of the difficulties faced by many loss prevention departments is that they are often viewed as an inevitable but regrettable part of the retail operation by others working in the business. They are considered as a cost that wherever possible should be kept to a minimum and need only be involved when something has gone wrong. In part this is a consequence of the way in which traditional loss prevention has behaved and presented itself – 'we only come to see you when you have done something wrong!'. We feel this has had a major impact upon the ability of loss prevention practitioners to effectively engage with the rest of the business and persuade it that they can have a valuable role in contributing to overall profitability. As we detailed in Chapter 9, on average, a retailer operating in the European FMCG sector could increase its profitability by 30 per cent if it were able to reduce its shrinkage by 50 per cent. This is potentially a remarkable opportunity for any retail business, and especially so in a period of economic recession that many now find themselves towards the end of the first decade of the 21st century. There are few parts of a retail organisation that could potentially make such a contribution to the profitability of an organisation and yet loss prevention has this opportunity. In this respect, traditional loss prevention has been hiding its potential, underplaying a powerfully persuasive message that could be used to get the rest of the business to take it seriously and to secure the resources required to make shrinkage reduction a priority and focus of attention capable of delivering remarkable results. It is time that loss prevention made the rest of the retail organisation aware of what can be achieved through the development and implementation of a co-ordinated shrinkage strategy.

Loss prevention as agents of change

Traditional shrinkage management has often led to loss prevention teams being isolated within the business culminating in the introduction of 'solutions' that are piecemeal, partial and doomed to failure as they merely react to the symptoms rather than the root causes of the problem. As one of the respondents to Beck's study on low shrinkage retailers put it when describing how they had first set about dealing with a shrinkage problem that had reached crisis point (2007a: 15):

> For the first 6 months [after the tipping point] we tried 49 different programmes – most failed. We realised that we cannot do it ourselves – it's about retail owning shrink, it's about logistics owning shrink, it's about the organisation saying shrink is important. So we went to the business and asked for help. It worked and shrink has now become part of the culture of the business.

This is a quote that must resonate with many loss prevention practitioners that have tried to respond to the problem of shrinkage – keep trying lots of different programmes in the hope that one of them will have a successful outcome. What the respondent above recognised was that they could not address this problem on their own; they needed the rest of the business to work with them to develop lasting solutions that were embedded within the organisation. We therefore argue that the loss prevention function of the future must act more as 'agents of change' whose job is to motivate and co-ordinate the rest of the business to ensure that shrinkage is on everybody's agenda. As another respondent said: 'it is difficult to think of any part of the business that shouldn't be thinking shrink' (Beck, 2007a: 16). This requires loss prevention leadership that is focused on cajoling, convincing and co-ordinating other retail functions to put shrinkage on their agenda, accept responsibility and be held accountable. We recognise that this may not be easy as other functions will undoubtedly have their own agenda to pursue and will not necessarily welcome further responsibilities linked to shrinkage. Part of the solution to this is being able to clearly elaborate the value of tackling shrinkage to them (for instance buyers might be motivated through an explanation of how it impacts directly upon sales) and how particular functions can specifically help. This can in part be achieved through senior management establishing shrinkage as a cross functional business responsibility and by providing accurate, timely and focused data on the issue. Either way, the role of loss prevention needs to be one of liaison, communication and facilitation to ensure that all parts of the business work together to address the shrinkage problem.

Opportunity, shrinkage and operational failures

The role of opportunity in explaining why certain crimes take place is well documented in the world of criminology. Indeed, within retail loss prevention its role has been previously considered, certainly in terms of internal loss (Hollinger & Davis, 2006). Of course the idea that offenders will seek out, or take advantage of, attractive targets that are presented to them is common sense. We all engage in 'situational crime prevention' all the time – we make sure that our houses and cars are locked and that we do not leave valuables on display or unguarded. We know that by doing this we reduce our risk of becoming a victim because we are either making it harder for the offender to commit the crime in the first place (locked cars and houses require more effort) or the opportunity to commit a crime has been removed (there is nothing for the offender to steal).

One writer has described the retail environment as 'pregnant' with opportunities for crime (Pease, 1997) and he is correct. Indeed, much of the premise of modern retailing is to create as alluring and as tempting retail space as possible in the hope that customers will be persuaded to spend more money. Many retail spaces are purposively created to enable prospective customers to touch and smell the objects of their desire with limited levels of control and guardianship. This has been the bedrock of the success of mass merchandising – moving the goods from behind locked counters and into aisles where customers can 'serve themselves'. Given that some large retail stores may contain at any one time thousands of customers and hundreds of thousands of different products, with perhaps fewer than 100 staff to watch over them, the possibilities for deviancy are inevitably considerable.

In addition, staff who work in retail stores are not immune to the temptation created by modern retailing – they are constantly surrounded by desirable goods and indeed frequently have access to the most desirable product of all – cash. They will often work with minimal levels of supervision (particularly those working at night), be poorly motivated and paid, and hence may have little affinity with corporate goals of probity and profit protection. As Hollinger and Davis noted (2006), the plethora of opportunities available to retail staff to steal is considerable and it should not be viewed as surprising that so much internal theft takes place.

Given this landscape of opportunity presented by modern retailing, to both shoppers and staff alike, perhaps we should not be surprised by the eye watering levels of loss that some companies suffer – they are the victims of their own making (a view often put forward by those working in the criminal justice system). But some retailers are able to keep their losses low and we would argue that a large part of their success can be put down to how they operate – they have created a viable retail space that minimises these opportunities and this has been achieved in the main by creating methods of working that we view as 'operational excellence'. A key premise of *New Loss Prevention* therefore is acknowledging how the antonym of retail excellence – operational failures – provides the opportunities for a plethora of shrinkage events to take place. They are the root cause of most of the problems faced by retailers. In low shrinkage retailers, staff are less likely to steal because the opportunities presented by operational failures are not present. The excellence of the processes and procedures in place and the availability of timely and robust data make it more difficult to offend through increasing the amount of effort required and the risk of apprehension – less than highly motivated offenders will simply not bother. The same is true for most types of customers who steal – design a retail environment where the degree of effort and presumed likelihood of being caught are high and they will be deterred from offending. Through minimising the operational failures within the retail space the majority of the malicious shrinkage problems can be effectively managed.

Taking a journey on the Shrinkage Road Map

The Shrinkage Road Map developed by the ECR Europe Shrinkage Group has been designed to offer loss prevention practitioners a systemic and systematic approach to carrying out shrinkage reduction projects. Its purpose was to break the old cycle of retailers leaping to install yet another 'solution' when a shrinkage crisis emerged – selected more by blind faith and a persuasive sales pitch than rigorous analysis of the underlying reasons why the crisis emerged in the first place.

The six steps that together make up the Shrinkage Road Map: Plan; Map and Measure; Analyse; Develop Solutions; Implement; and Evaluate, are not revolutionary in themselves – it resembles many of the business analysis models developed in the past – but for the loss prevention industry it attempts to inject a degree of rigour into the process rarely seen before. The steps of Map and Measure and Analyse provide a means by which the root causes of shrinkage can, as much as possible, be clearly identified before any decisions are made about potential solutions. They purposively get the user to think about how existing operational failures can create the opportunities and circumstances for malicious and non-malicious forms of shrinkage to occur. It is prioritising this linkage that we feel makes the Shrinkage Road Map such a valuable tool for loss prevention practitioners.

Since its inception in 1999 the Road Map has been used by a wide range of companies around the globe including both retailers and manufacturers and to date the feedback has been, for the most part, highly positive. Partly this is because it is a relatively easy and quick tool to use – companies with access to reasonably good data can reach decisions about potential solutions to be implemented often within two days, But it has also be proven through numerous case studies to be effective in helping companies to develop shrinkage solutions that are often relatively cheap and sustainable. This is frequently because the proposed solutions are as much about making changes to the way in which the business functions (such as developing or adjusting existing processes and procedures) as they are about investing in new technologies.

The Shrinkage Road Map is also innovative because of the way in which it requires different parts of the business, and indeed different businesses, to come together to reflect upon the shrinkage problem that is trying to be addressed. It links in very clearly with our ideas on loss prevention leaders being 'agents of change', orchestrating a multi-functional (and in some cases multi-organisational) approach to understanding the problem and developing an appropriate solution. The Shrinkage Road Map purposively steers away from seeing shrinkage as merely a problem that is the sole responsibility of the loss prevention function and instead seeks to bring together a project team that can reflect upon the problem with a broad array of experiences and potential ideas as to how it may be resolved. We therefore see the Shrinkage Road Map as a powerful tool that can enable organisations to develop a new way of addressing their shrinkage agenda.

Getting started: Tipping points and securing senior management commitment

Introducing any new initiative or way of working into a business is not easy especially one that is as competitive, complex and dynamic as retailing. This is even more so when companies are in the grip of an economic recession as we find ourselves towards the end of the first decade of the 21st century. But as we outlined above, the economic case for prioritising the effective management of shrinkage is, we feel, highly persuasive. Getting started can be the most difficult part of the journey. Two factors seem critically important – one is an absolute prerequisite – securing senior management commitment – the other is making use of a key moment in a company's shrinkage life cycle – a tipping point.

As we have reflected throughout this book, getting senior management to recognise that shrinkage is a priority is a vital foundation block in developing the Loss Prevention Pyramid. Without it the other building blocks will not be able to be developed effectively and the entire structure is liable to collapse. In his work on low shrinkage US retailers, Beck's (2007a) respondents all elaborated in some detail on the extent to which senior management had 'bought in' to the idea of shrinkage being one of the key priorities for the business. Like the rest of the business, senior management need to be enlightened as to why shrinkage management matters to the organisation, and the most powerful way to achieve this is to instruct them on how it impacts upon customers and consequently business profitability. Shrinkage has a profound impact upon the consumer, most notably in higher prices (to cover the costs of shrinkage), out of stocks (product is missing because it has been stolen, damaged or mislaid) and inconvenience (such as retailers using defensive merchandising to protect products perceived as at risk). This in turn impacts upon the profitability of the business as unhappy customers go to other retailers where they think the products they want will be available, possibly cheaper and the shopping experience is likely to be less frustrating. Getting this message across to senior management can be a sufficiently sobering experience as to ensure their engagement.

In addition, and some of the case-study companies studied by Beck highlighted this, making use of a 'tipping point' in the shrinkage cycle of the business can also be a powerful mechanism for gaining the support of senior management. This is often a moment when shrinkage has reached such a critical high point that it becomes a reporting issue to senior management. This presents itself as an opportunity for the loss prevention team to make a case as to how the issue should be resolved by the business.

Either through presenting a case on how shrinkage is negatively impacting upon the business, or taking advantage of a tipping point (or a combination of the two), loss prevention executives need to ensure that senior management recognise the value of giving shrinkage control sufficient status within the organisation. Once this is achieved, then getting the rest of the business engaged becomes much easier, as does obtaining the necessary resources.

Collaborating on shrinkage

A key part of the work of the ECR Europe Shrinkage Group and a fundamental component of the Shrinkage Road Map is the way in which retailers need to engage with manufacturers, third party logistics suppliers, loss prevention solution providers, and other groups to both understand the root causes of shrinkage and develop appropriate and sustainable solutions. Sharing the problem of shrinkage with outside parties does not always come easy to retailers – there is a long tradition of keeping this information undisclosed and secret, fearing that its release will somehow undermine the competitiveness of the business or damage its reputation. The difficulties we outlined in detail in Chapter 4 of obtaining reliable information on the scale and extent of the problem certainly reflects this situation although an unwillingness to expose organisational deficiencies is perhaps understandable if rather regrettable. The first step on the road to recovery is often accepting that a problem exists in the first place and we feel that a greater degree of transparency within the retail community would be a positive step in the loss prevention industry attaining the recognition that it deserves.

But sharing the problems of shrinkage with trusted third parties is an important part of delivering the Loss Prevention Pyramid. We think this is the case for three reasons. First, by engaging with organisations that play a role in other parts of the retail supply chain, the genuine root causes of the problem are much more likely to be identified. In Chapter 8 we outlined how by using tools such as the Five Whys underlying issues can be uncovered which may be causing shrinkage much further down the supply chain, but are only being recognised and recorded in retail stores. It would be relatively easy to introduce a 'solution' in the store, but it is likely to be less effective than one proposed to deal with the root cause of the problem further down the supply chain.

Secondly, engaging with manufacturers and others gives retail loss prevention practitioners access to fresh insights into the shrinkage problem trying to be addressed. For instance, it could be that a manufacturer has recently worked with another retailer to address a similar problem and this learning could then be shared. Moreover, by engaging with third parties and including them in the decision-making process, agreed upon solutions (which may involve changes by all groups involved) are much more likely to be implemented effectively and efficiently – participants are much more likely to acquiesce to changes when they have been involved in the decision-making process.

Thirdly, engaging with third parties can help in the development of appropriate solutions. One of the criticisms of the loss prevention solution-provider industry is that they develop products and then go searching for retail problems for them to address. This in turn can lead to situations where a proposed solution is simply not economically viable – the cost of the intervention far outweighs the cost of the shrinkage problem it was designed to deal with – and retailers therefore are not willing to invest. In their defence, 'solution' providers will argue that this is because retailers do not effectively communicate their problems with them and therefore they have to second guess their demands. However, if retailers began to engage with such groups and share information on their specific shrinkage problems, then we are much more likely to get the development of solutions that are fit for purpose, both in terms of costs and benefit, and effectiveness.

Taken together, we feel these are powerful arguments as to why a central tenet of *New Loss Prevention* is the need for loss prevention practitioners to reach out to other organisations to help them respond more effectively to the shrinkage problems that they face.

The role of technology in shrinkage management

It would be easy to read this book and reflect that the authors are in some ways anti the use of technologies in loss prevention. This is most certainly not the case and there are undoubtedly swathes of technological innovations which are impacting effectively upon specific shrinkage problems in the retail sector. However, we feel that there is a pervasive sense present within the industry that the *only* answer to the shrinkage problem is technological. This is particularly evident in the various global loss prevention trade shows and conferences where the predominate sponsorship and advertising is dominated by solution providers seeking to offer yet more high tech panaceas to the apparent shrinkage problems faced by retailers.

We also feel that certainly in the past, technology providers have been overly aggressive, hopelessly optimistic and at times certainly disingenuous when it comes to reviewing the impact their developments may have on shrinkage. As part of the research for this book we spent a considerable amount of time collecting as much as possible the available information on the efficacy of a range of technologies, including Electronic Article Surveillance (EAS), Closed Circuit Television (CCTV) and data mining tools. This proved to be a largely fruitless task, certainly in terms of unearthing independent and rigorous reviews of the effect these types of technology have upon particular shrinkage problems. It was never the purpose of this book to offer a comprehensive review of the vast array of technological solutions currently available, our agenda was very different, but one conclusion would seem to be that much more research needs to be done to genuinely understand the impact these types of interventions have upon shrinkage. As things currently stand, most loss prevention practitioners are still very much in the dark about whether they should invest or not in any given technology.

In addition, the dominance of external theft – the bogeyman of shrinkage – has in part been driven by technology providers keen to sell yet more solutions to this particular problem. To a certain extent this is understandable as external theft seemingly offers the most controllable environment within which to create solutions. It has also created 'solutions' which have powerful business models, especially source tagging, where the cost can sometimes be 'passed on' by the retailer to their manufacturers and the requirement for the tags is endless (they are thrown away when the product is purchased). Keeping external loss high on the agenda is important if this model is to be maintained. But as we detailed in Chapter 4, perhaps as much as 80 per cent of the shrinkage problem retailers face could be internal (staff theft and process failures combined), with only a relatively small part being accounted for by external thieves. Such a message is often difficult to see when surveying the plethora of options presented to retailers by technology providers – for the most part the emphasis remains on yet more innovative interventions to deal with external threats, with the rise of organised retail crime in the US perhaps the most recent example of this. There is a sense that this is beginning to change (Levin, 2008) and solution providers are beginning to offer services much more geared towards responding to the specific needs of clients rather than simply offering a generic one size fits all approach. This is to be welcomed and can only lead to improvements in the industry.

We are not, therefore, anti technology, but we believe that three issues are important when considering the role of technologies in retail loss prevention. The first is that decisions about whether an investment should be made in any given technology should be premised by a detailed understanding of the root causes of the problem it is proposing to resolve – the technology itself should not be the starting point for understanding the problem. Secondly, all forms of technological intervention need to be viewed as merely another set of possible options available to the loss prevention practitioner, which may include alternatives such as better training, changes in working practices or perhaps the redesign of products or retail spaces. Finally, as discussed in the previous section, any technological innovations that are being introduced to deal specifically with shrinkage need to be able to offer a clear financial benefit to the retailer making the investment. Hard nosed retailers usually ask a deceptively simple question: how much will it cost and is it less than the amount we are currently losing? If it is, then they are likely to invest, if it is not, then the solution provider will need to go back to the drawing board.

One of the key steps of the Loss Prevention Pyramid is Innovate and Experiment and certainly a part of this is being open to trying out new technologies as they emerge. The loss prevention industry is awash with technologies and it seems clear that their development will continue at pace. The key to effective shrinkage management seems to be ensuring that any given technology is 'fit for purpose' premised upon a detailed understanding of the root causes of the problem under consideration. If it passes this test, then it has a role to play.

Breaking the Shrinkage Cycle: The loss prevention pyramid

It would be interesting research to find out whether the five low shrinkage companies selected by the panel of experts for Beck's research in 2007 are still regarded as 'best in class' or whether they have moved around the Shrinkage Cycle and are now experiencing higher levels of loss. The challenge for any low shrinkage retailer is maintaining their impressive performance – it is easy for companies to lose focus, reallocate resources and feel that they have defeated their problem of shrinkage. This is of course a mistake as shrinkage cannot ever be considered to be fixed – it needs to be constantly managed to keep it under control.

The purpose of the Loss Prevention Pyramid is, in part, to act as a wedge to try and resist the slide back to complacency and higher levels of loss. As we detailed in Chapter 9, each part of the pyramid needs to be in place in order for it to be successful – the whole is greater than the sum of the parts. Each of the 11 segments has a part to play – some acting as foundation stones creating the strategic bedrock, while others provide the organisational framework upon which shrinkage management is ultimately operationalised. Collectively, we believe, they offer an approach which is capable of enabling organisations to not only reduce their losses through shrinkage, but maintain them at a low and acceptable level.

New loss prevention

In this book we have tried to offer a different way of thinking about, and responding to, the problem of shrinkage in the retail sector. We do not claim to be revolutionary in our thinking – many of the ideas we have drawn upon have been around for over half a century. But what we have attempted to do is first of all challenge what we see as some of the failings of many of the current approaches adopted to try and manage shrinkage – approaches that seem to have at best kept a lid on a multi-billion dollar global problem. Secondly, we have suggested an overarching framework – the Loss Prevention Pyramid – underpinned by a rationale that operational failures create the opportunities and circumstances for most forms of shrinkage to happen, that offers loss prevention practitioners a structured, logical and sustainable way to begin to deal with their shrinkage problems. Above all, we hope we have made people think about the issue of loss prevention differently. It is all too easy to see loss prevention as being focused primarily on catching increasingly determined and wily thieves, when in fact it is much more about orchestrating an organisational approach with retail excellence at its core. To us, the former typifies the old way of doing things while the latter reflects what see as *New Loss Prevention*.

Bibliography

Abelson, E. (1989). *When Ladies Go A Thieving*. New York: Oxford University Press.

Akehurst, G. & Alexander, N. (1995). The Internationalisation Process in Retailing. In G. Akehurst & N. Alexander, *The Internationalisation of Retailing* (pp. 1–15). London: Frank Cass & Co Ltd.

Altheide, D. L., Adler, P. A., Adler, P. & Altheide, D. A. (1978). The Social Meanings of Employee Theft. In J. M. Johnson & J. D. Douglas, *Crime at the Top*. Philadelphia: JB Lippincott.

Association of Brazilian Supermarkets (2005). *Shrinkage in the Supermarket Sector*. Sao Paulo: Association of Brazilian Supermarkets.

Astor, S. D. (1971, January). Study of 1647 Customers Shows 1 in 15 a Shoplifter. *Stores*, p. 8.

Avoilo, B. & Yammarino, F. (2002). *Transformational and Charismatic Leadership: The Road Ahead (Monographs in Leadership & Management)* (Vol. 2). Oxford: Elsevier Science.

Bamfield, J. (1994). Article Surveillance: Management Learning in Curbing Theft. In M. Gill, *Crime at Work: Studies in Security and Crime Prevention* (pp. 155–173). Leicester: Perpetuity Press.

Bamfield, J. (1998). A Breach of Trust: Employee Collusion and Theft from Major Retailers. In M. Gill, *Crime at Work: Increasing the Risk for Offenders* (pp. 123–142). Basingstoke: Palgrave Macmillan.

Bamfield, J. (2006a). Sed quis custodiet? Employee Theft in UK Retailing. *International Journal of Retail & Distribution Management, 34* (11), 845–859.

Bamfield, J. (2006b). Management. In M. Gill, *The Handbook of Security* (pp. 485–508). Basingstoke: Palgrave Macmillan.

Bamfield, J. (2007). *Global Retail Theft Barometer 2007*. Nottingham: Centre for Retail Research.

Bamfield, J. (2008). *Global Retail Theft Barometer 2008*. Nottingham: Centre for Retail Research.

Barua, A., Mani, D. & Whinston, A. B. (n.d.). *Assessing the Financial Impacts of RFID Technologies on the Retail and Healthcare Sectors*. Austin: Center for Research in Electronic Commerce.

Baumer, T. L. & Rosenbaum, D. P. (1984). *Combatting Retail Theft: Programs and Strategies*. Stoneham: Butterworth Publishers.

Beck, A. (2002a, October). Auto ID and Stock Loss: Future Prospects, Problems and Priorities. *IDTechEx Web Journal* (21).

Beck, A. (2002b). *Automatic Product Identification and Shrinkage: Scoping the Potential*. Brussels: ECR Europe.

Beck, A. (2004a). *Shrinkage in Europe 2004: A Survey of Stock Loss in the Fast Moving Consumer Goods Sector*. Brussels: ECR Europe.

Beck, A. (2004b). *Questionnaire on Stock Loss Within European Food Retailers*. Leicester: University of Leicester, Department of Criminology.

Beck, A. (2006a). *Staff Dishonesty in the Retail Sector: Understanding the Opportunities*. Brussels: ECR Europe.

Beck, A. (2006b). Shrinkage and Radio Frequency Identification: Prospects, Problems and Practicalities. In M. Gill, *The Handbook of Security* (pp. 462–482). Basingstoke: Palgrave Macmillan.

Beck, A. (2007a). *Effective Retail Loss Prevention: 10 Ways to Keep Shrinkage Low.* Leicester: University of Leicester.

Beck, A. (2007b). The Emperor Has No Clothes: What Future Role for Technology in Reducing Retail Shrinkage? *Security Journal, 20* (2), 57–61.

Beck, A. (2008). *Preventing Retail Shrinkage: Measuring the 'Value' of CCTV, EAS and Data Mining Tools.* Brussels: ECR Europe.

Beck, A. & Bilby, C. (2001). *Shrinkage in Europe: A Survey of Stock Loss in the Fast Moving Consumer Goods Sector.* Brussels: ECR Europe.

Beck, A. & Chapman, P. (2003). *Hot Spots in the Supply Chain: Developing an Understanding of What Makes Some Retail Stores Vulnerable to Shrinkage.* Brussels: ECR Europe.

Beck, A. & Peacock, C. (2006). Redefining Shrinkage – Four New Buckets of Stock Loss. *Loss Prevention Magazine*, pp. 35–42.

Beck, A. & Willis, A. (1992). *An Evaluation of Store Security and Closed Circuit Television.* Leicester: University of Leicester, Centre for the Study of Public Order.

Beck, A. & Willis, A. (1995). *Crime and Security: Managing the Risk to Safe Shopping.* Leicester: Perpetuity Press.

Beck, A. & Willis, A. (1998). Sales and Security: Striking the Balance. In M. Gill, *Crime at Work: Increasing the Risk for Offenders* (pp. 95–106). Basingstoke: Palgrave Macmillan.

Beck, A., Bilby, C. & Chapman, P. (2003). Tackling Shrinkage in the Fast Moving Consumer Goods Supply Chain: Developing a Methodology. In M. Gill, *Managing Security: Crime at Work Series Volume 3* (pp. 195–212). Leicester: Perpetuity Press.

Beck, A., Bilby, C., Chapman, P. & Harrison, A. (2001). *Shrinkage: Introducing a Collaborative Approach to Reducing Stock Loss in the Supply Chain.* Brussels: ECR Europe.

Beck, A., Chapman, P. & Peacock, C. (2002). Shrinking Shrinkage: Developing a Systematic Approach to Stock Loss. *ECR Journal, International Commerce Review, 2* (2), 59–64.

Beck, A., Chapman, P. & Peacock, C. (2003). *Shrinkage: A Collaborative Approach to Reducing Stock Loss in the Supply Chain.* Brussels: ECR Europe.

Becker, G. S. (1968). Crime and Punishment: An Economic Approach. *Journal of Political Economy, 76* (2), 169–217.

Bernstein, J. E. (1963, October). Curbing Losses and Errors in Retail Store Operations. *New York Certified Public Accountant*, pp. 706–714.

Bicheno, J. (1998). *The Quality 60.* Buckingham: PICSIE Books.

Blythman, J. (2004). *Shopped: The Shocking Power of British Supermarkets.* London: Harper Perennial.

British Retail Consortium (2009). Retrieved February 18, 2009, from http://www.brc.org.uk/latestdata04.asp?iCat=52&sCat=RETAIL+KEY+FACTS

Brock, D. L. (2001). *The Electronic Product Code – A Naming Scheme for Physical Objects.* Auto-ID White Paper WH002. Boston: MIT.

Bryman, A. (1999). Leadership in Organisations. In S. Clegg, C. Hardy & W. Nord, *Managing Organisations: Current Issues* (pp. 26–42). London: Sage.

Buckle, A. & Farrington, D. P. (1984). An Observational Study of Shoplifting. *British Journal of Criminology, 24* (1), 63–73.

Buckle, A., Farrington, D., Burrows, J., Speed, M. & Burns-Howell, T. (1992). Measuring Shoplifting by Repeated Systematic Counting. *Security Journal, 3,* 137–146.

Burns, R. (2000). *Introduction to Research Methods.* London: Sage.

Butler, G. (1994). Shoplifters Views on Security: Lessons for Crime Prevention. In M. Gill, *Crime at Work: Studies in Security and Crime Prevention* (pp. 56–72). Leicester: Perpetuity Press.

Caime, G. & Ghone, G. (1996). *S(h)elf Help Guide: The Smart Lifters Handbook.* Toronto: TriX Publishing.

Cameron, M. O. (1964). *The Booster and the Snitch.* New York: Free Press of Glencoe, Collier Macmillan.

Carter, N., Holmstrom, A., Simpanen, M. & Melin, L. (1988). Theft Reduction in a Grocery Store Through Product Identification and Graphing of Losses for Employees. *Journal of Applied Behavior Analysis, 21,* 385–389.

Centre for Retail Research (2008). *Global Retail Theft Barometer Questionnaire.* Nottingham: Centre for Retail Research.

Chapman, P. (2009). *Addressing Retail Shrinkage Through Collaboration.* Brussels: ECR Europe.

Chapman, P. & Templar, S. (2006a). Scoping the Contextual Issues That Influence Shrinkage Measurement. *International Journal of Retail and Distribution Management, 34* (11), 860–972.

Chapman, P. & Templar, S. (2006b). Methods for Measuring Shrinkage. *Security Journal, 19,* 228–240.

Clarke, R. V. (1997). Introduction. In R. V. Clarke, *Situational Crime Prevention: Successful Case Studies* (2nd Edition ed., pp. 1–42). Albany: Harrow and Heston.

Clarke, R. V. (1999). *Hot Products: Understanding, Anticipating and Reducing Demand for Stolen Goods.* Police Research Series Paper 112. London: Home Office.

Clarke, R. V. (1980). Situational Crime Prevention: Theory and Practice. *British Journal of Criminology, 20,* 136–147.

Clarke, R. V. & Mayhew, P. M. (1980). *Designing out Crime.* London: H.M. Stationery Office.

Clinard, M. B. & Quinney, R. (1973). *Criminal Behaviour Systems.* New York: Holt, Rinehart and Winston.

Cohen, L. (2003). *A Consumers' Republic: The Politics of Mass Consumption in Postwar America.* New York: Random House.

Cohen, L. E. & Felson, M. (1979). Social Change and Crime Rate Trends: A Routine Activity Approach. *American Sociological Review, 44,* 588–608.

Cornish, D. B. & Clarke, R. V. (1986). *The Reasoning Criminal: Rational Choice Perspectives on Offending.* New York: Springer-Verlag.

Corsten, D. & Gruen, T. (2003). Desperately Seeking Shelf Availability: An Examination of the Causes, Extent and the Efforts to Address Retail Out-of-stocks. *International Journal of Retail & Distribution Management, 31* (12), 605–617.

Curtis, B. (1960). *Modern Retail Security.* Springfield: Charles C. Thomas.

Curtis, B. (1971). *Security Control: External Theft.* New York: Chain Store Age Books.

Curtis, B. (1973). *Security Control: Internal Theft.* New York: Chain Store Age Books.

Curtis, B. (1979). *How to Keep Employees Honest.* New York: Lebhar-Friedman Books.

Curtis, B. (1983). *Retail Security: Controlling Loss for Profit.* Boston: Butterworths.

Cusson, M. (1993). Situational Deterrence: Fear During the Criminal Event. In R. V. Clarke, *Crime Prevention Studies Volume 1* (pp. 55–68). Monsey: Criminal Justice Press.

Dabney, D. A., Hollinger, R. C. & Dugan, L. (2004). Who Actually Steals? A Study of Covertly Observed Shoplifters. *Justice Quarterly, 21* (4), 693–728.

Dawson, J. (1994). Internationalisation of Retailing Operations. *Journal of Marketing Management, 10*, 267–282.

Dawson, J. (2001). Is There a New Commerce in Europe? *International Review of Retail, Distribution and Consumer Research, 11*, 287–299.

Dawson, J., Findlay, A. & Sparks, L. (2008a). Introduction. In J. Dawson, A. Findlay & L. Sparks, *The Retailing Reader* (pp. 1–8). London: Routledge.

Dawson, J., Findlay, A. & Sparks, L. (2008b). Retail Strategy and Power. In J. Dawson, A. Findlay & L. Sparks, *The Retailing Reader* (pp. 273–284). Abingdon: Routledge.

Dawson, J., Findlay, A. & Sparks, L. (2008c). International Retailing. In J. Dawson, A. Findlay & L. Sparks, *The Retailing Reader* (pp. 342–354). Abingdon: Routledge.

DeHoratius, N. & Raman, A. (2007). Store Manager Incentive Design and Retail Performance: An Exploratory Investigation. *Manufacturing & Service Operations Management, 9* (4), 518–534.

DeHoratius, N. & Raman, A. (2008). Inventory Record Inaccuracy: An Empirical Analysis. *Management Science, 54* (4), 627–641.

DeHoratius, N., Mersereau, A. J. & Schrage, L. (2008). Retail Inventory Management When Records Are Inaccurate. *Manufacturing and Service Operations Management, 10* (2), 257–277.

Department for Environment, Trade and Regional Affairs (2000). *Second Report on the Environmental Impact of Supermarket Competition*. London: Department for Environment, Trade and Regional Affairs.

Dilonardo, R. (1997). The Economic Benefit of Electronic Article Surveillance. In R. C. Clarke, *Situational Crime Prevention: Successful Case Studies* (pp. 122–131). New York: Harrow and Heston.

Dilonardo, R. & Clarke, R. V. (1996). Reducing the Rewards of Shoplifting: An Evaluation of Ink Tags. *Security Journal, 71*, 11–14.

Ditton, J. (1977). *Part-time Crime: An Ethnography of Fiddling and Pilferage*. London: Macmillan.

Du Gay, P. (2004). Self-Service: Retail, Shopping and Personhood. *Consumption, Markets and Culture, 7* (2), 149–163.

Duffin, M., Gill, M. & Taylor, E. (2006). *Staff Dishonesty: A Report for Procter & Gamble*. Leicester: Perpetuity Research and Consultancy International.

Eck, J. E. & Weisburd, D. (1995). Crime Places in Crime Theory. In J. E. Eck & D. Weisburd, *Crime and Place* (pp. 1–34). New York: Criminal Justice Press and Police Executive Research Forum.

ECR Australia (2002). *A Guide to Collaborative Loss Prevention*. ECR Australia.

Edemariam, A. (2009, March 14). It all began in a small store in Arkansas. *The Guardian*.

Edwards, L. (1974). *Shoplifting and Shrinkage Protection*. Springfield: Charles C. Thomas.

Farrell, K. & Farrera, J. (1985). *Shoplifting: The Anti-Shoplifting Guidebook*. New York: Praeger.

Felson, M. (1986). Linking Criminal Choices, Routine Activities, Informal Control, and Criminal Outcomes. In D. B. Cornish & R. V. Clarke, *The Reasoning Criminal*. New York: Springer Verlag.

Felson, M. (1994). *Crime and Everyday Life*. Thousand Oaks, CA: Pine Forge Press.

Felson, M. & Clarke, R. V. (1997). The Ethics of Situational Crime Prevention. In G. Newman, R. V. Clarke & S. G. Shoham, *Rational Choice and Situational Crime Prevention* (pp. 197–218). Aldershot: Ashgate.

Fisher, M., Raman, A. & McClelland, A. S. (2000). Rocket Science Retailing is Almost Here – Are you Ready? *Harvard Business Review, 78* (4), 115–124.

Food Marketing Institute (2006). *Supermarket Security and Loss Prevention 2006.* Food Marketing Institute.

Food Marketing Institute (2007). *Supermarket Security and Loss Prevention 2007.* Food Marketing Institute.

Gartner (2008). *Over One Billion Computers now in Worldwide Use.* Retrieved November 14, 2008, from http://www.digitalhome.ca/content/view/2616/206/

George, J. & Jones, G. (2006). *Contemporary Management: Creating Value in Organisations.* London: McGraw-Hill Irwin.

Gilbert, D. (1999). *Retail Marketing Management.* Harlow: Prentice Hall.

Gill, M. (1998). Introduction. In M. Gill, *Crime at Work: Increasing the Risk for Offenders* (pp. 11–24). Basingstoke: Palgrave Macmillan.

Gill, M. (2007). *Shop Thieves Around the World.* Leicester: Perpetuity Research and Consulting International.

Gill, M. & Loveday, K. (2003). What Do Offenders Think About CCTV? In M. Gill, *CCTV.* Leicester: Perpetuity Press.

Gill, M., Bilby, C. & Turbin, V. (1999). Retail Security: Understanding What Deters Shop Thieves. *Journal of Security Administration, 22* (1), 29–40.

Gill, M., Hemming, M., Burns-Howell, T., Hart, J., Hayes, R. & Clarke, R. (2004). *The Illicit Market in Stolen Fast Moving Consumer Goods.* Leicester: Perpetuity Research and Consultancy International.

Glennie, P. & Thrift, N. (1996). Consumption, Shopping and Gender. In N. Wrigley & M. Lowe, *Retailing, Consumption and Capital: Towards the New Retail Geography* (pp. 221–237). Harlow: Longman Group Limited.

Global Commerce Initiative (n.d.). *Global Scorecard.* Retrieved October 28, 2008, from http://www.globalscorecard.net/

Grasso, S. (2003). *11th Annual Retail Crime Survey 2003.* London: British Retail Consortium.

Greenberg, J. (1997). The STEAL Motive: Managing the Social Determinants of Employee Theft. In R. Giacalone & J. Greenberg, *Antisocial Behaviour in Organizations* (pp. 85–108). Greenwich: JAI Press.

Greenberg, J. (2002). Who Stole the Money, and When? Individual and Situational Determinants of Employee Theft. *Organizational Behavior and Human Decision Processes, 89,* 985–1003.

Grint, K. (2005). Problems, Problems, Problems: The Social Construction of 'Leadership'. *Human Relations, 58* (11), 1467–1494.

Guthrie, J. C. (2003). *National Survey of Retail Theft and Security.* New Zealand Centre for Retail Research and Studies.

Guy, C. M. (1994). *The Retail Development Process.* London: Routledge.

Handford, M. (1994). Electronic Tagging in Action: A Case Study in Retailing. In M. Gill, *Crime at Work: Studies in Security and Crime Prevention* (pp. 174–184). Leicester: Perpetuity Press.

Hayes, R. (1999). Shop Theft: An Analysis of Shoplifter Perceptions and Situational Factors. *Security Journal, 12* (2), 7–18.

Hayes, R. (2003). Loss Prevention: Senior Management Views on Current Trends and Issues. *Security Journal, 16* (2), 7–20.

Hayes, R. (2007). *Retail Security and Loss Prevention*. Basingstoke: Palgrave Macmillan.

Hayes, R. & Cardone, C. (2006). Shoptheft. In M. Gill, *The Handbook of Security* (pp. 302–327). Basingstoke: Palgrave Macmillan.

Hennessee, T. (2003, January/February). Operational Shrink: There's More to LP than Preventing Theft. *Loss Prevention Magazine*, pp. 34–39, 61.

Hodges, S. & Harrison, M. (2003). *Demystifying RFID: Principles & Practicalities.* An Auto ID Centre White Paper. Boston: MIT.

Hollinger, R. C. & Adams, A. (2008). *2007 National Retail Security Survey: Final Report.* Gainsville, FL: University of Florida.

Hollinger, R. C. & Clarke, J. P. (1982). Employee Deviance: A Response to the Perceived Quality of the Work Experience. *Work and Occupations, 9,* 97–114.

Hollinger, R. C. & Clarke, J. P. (1983). *Theft by Employees.* Lexington: Lexington Books.

Hollinger, R. C. & Davis, J. L. (2006). Employee Theft and Staff Dishonesty. In M. Gill, *The Handbook of Security* (pp. 203–228). Basingstoke: Palgrave Macmillan.

Hollinger, R. C. & Langton, L. (2004). *2003 National Retail Security Survey: Final Report.* Gainsville: University of Florida.

Home Office (2009). *Crime in England and Wales 2007/08.* Retrieved January 5, 2009, from http://www.homeoffice.gov.uk/rds/pdfs08/hosb0708chap4.pdf

Horst, F. (2004). *Inventurdifferenzen 2003.* Köln: Verlag EHI EuroHandelinstituts GmbH.

Howard, E. (2000, March). Globalisation – Adaptation. *European Retail Digest,* pp. 6–9.

Howell, S. D. & Proudlove, N. C. (2007). A Statistical Investigation of Inventory Shrinkage in a Large Retail Chain. *The International Review of Retail, Distribution and Consumer Research, 17* (2), 101–120.

Hughes, A. (1996). Forging New Cultures of Food Retailer-Manufacturer Relations? In N. Wrigely & M. Lowe, *Retailing, Consumption and Capital: Towards the New Retail Geography* (pp. 90–115). Harlow: Longman Group Limited.

IGD (2009). *UK Food & Grocery Retail Logistics Overview.* Retrieved February 26, 2009, from http://www.igd.com/index.asp?id=1&fid=1&sid=3&tid=42&folid=0&cid=223

InternetWorldStats (2008). *Internet Usage Statistics: The Internet Big Picture.* Retrieved November 14, 2008, from http://www.internetworldstats.com/stats.htm

Ishikawa, K. (1990). *Introduction to Quality Control.* London: Chapman & Hall.

Jeffery, C. R. (1977). *Crime Prevention Through Environmental Design* (2nd Edition). Beverly Hills: Sage.

Jones, P. H. (1997). *Retail Loss Control* (2nd ed.). Oxford: Butterworth Heinemann.

Jones, T. (2009). *Using Contemporary Archaeology and Applied Anthropology to Understand Food Loss in the American Food System.* Retrieved February 4, 2009, from http://archaeologyandbotanyresearch.com/downloads/Overview%20of%20Findings%205-04.doc

Juran, J. M. & Gryna, F. M. (1988). *Juran's Quality Control Handbook* (4th Edition). New York: McGraw-Hill.

Juran, J. M. & Gryna, F. M. (1993). *Quality Planning and Analysis* (3rd Edition). New York: McGraw-Hill.

Kamp, J. & Brooks, P. (1991). Perceived Organisational Climate and Employee Counterproductivity. *Journal of Business and Psychology, 10* (4), 447–458.

Kaplin, R. S. & Norton, D. P. (1996, January–February). Using the Balanced Score-card as a Strategic Management System. *Harvard Business Review*, pp. 1–13.

Kent, T. & Omar, O. (2003). *Retailing*. Basingstoke: Palgrave Macmillan.

Kiesi, J. (2008). New Markets, New Opportunities, New Challenges: Developing Your Business in Global Market Place. *Loss Prevention Magazine*, pp. 58–62.

Kimiecik, R. C. & Thomas, C. (2006). *Loss Prevention in the Retail Business*. New Jersey: John Wiley & Sons, Inc.

Klemke, L. W. (1992). *The Sociology of Shoplifting: Boosters and Snitches Today*. New York: Praeger.

Kresevich, M. (2007). *Using Culture to Cure Theft*. Retrieved February 13, 2009, from Security Management: http://www.securitymanagement.com/article/using-culture-cure-theft?page=0%2C0

Levin, P. (2008). 40 Years of Change in LP ...and Beyond. *Loss Prevention Magazine*, pp. 64–68.

Loveday, K. & Gill, M. (2003). The Impact of Monitored CCTV in a Retail Environment: What CCTV Operators Do and Why. In M. Gill, *CCTV* (pp. 109–126). Leicester: Perpetuity Press.

Lyon, D. (2007). *Surveillance Studies: An Overview*. Cambridge: Polity Press.

Marcus, B. & Schuler, H. (2004). Antecedents of Counterproductive Behaviour: A General Perspective. *Journal of Applied Psychology, 89* (4), 647–660.

Mars, G. (1974). Cheats at Work: An Anthropology of Workplace Crime. In P. Rock & M. McIntosh, *Deviance and Social Control* (pp. 209–228). London: Tavistock.

Mars, G. (1982). *Cheats at Work: An Anthropology of Workplace Crime*. London: Allen and Unwin.

Mars, G. (2000). *Work Place Sabotage*. Abingdon: Ashgate.

Martinez, L. (2004). *The Retail Manager's Guide to Crime and Loss Prevention*. New York: Looseleaf Law Publications Inc.

Maslow, A. H. (1969). *The Psychology of Science: A Reconnaissance*. Chicago: Henry Regnery.

Masuda, B. (1992). Displacement vs Diffusion of Benefits and the Reduction of Inventory Losses in a Retail Environment. *Security Journal, 3* (3), 131–136.

McCahill, M. (2002). *The Surveillance Web: The Rise of Visual Surveillance in an English City*. Cullompton: Willan Publishing.

Mirrlees-Black, C. & Ross, A. (1995). *Crime Against Retail and Manufacturing Premises: Findings from the 1994 Commercial Victimisation Survey*. Home Office Research Study 146. London: Home Office.

Misa, T. (2004). The Compelling Tangle of Modernity and Technology. In T. Misa, P. Brey & A. Feenberg, *Modernity and Technology* (pp. 1–32). London: MIT Press.

Mitchell, V. W. & Kyris, S. (1999). *Trends on Small Business Retail Outlets*. Manchester: Manchester School of Management.

Moore, R. H. (1984). Shoplifting in Middle America: Patterns and Motivational Correlates. *International Journal of Offender Therapy and Comparative Criminology, 28* (1), 53–64.

Murphy, D. J. (1986). *Customers and Thieves*. Aldershot: Gower Publishing Company Limited.

Nagin, D., Rebitzer, R., Sanders, S. & Taylor, L. (2002). *Monitoring, Motivation and Management: The Determinants of Opportunistic Behavior in a Field Experiment*. NBER Working Paper No. W8811.

National Supermarket Research Group (2003). *2003 National Supermarket Shrink Survey*. National Supermarket Research Group.

Newman, G. (1997). Introduction: Towards a Theory of Situational Crime Prevention. In G. Newman, R. V. Clarke & R. G. Shoham, *Rational Choice and Situational Crime Prevention* (pp. 1–24). Aldershot: Ashgate.

Newman, O. (1996). *Creating Defensible Space: Crime Prevention Through Urban Design*. Washington DC: Office of Policy Development and Research, US Department of Housing and Urban Development.

Norris, C. & Armstrong, G. (1999). Introduction: Visions of Surveillance. In C. Norris & G. Armstrong, *The Maximum Surveillance Society: The Rise of CCTV* (pp. 3–12). Oxford: Berg.

Oliphant, B. J. & Oliphant, G. C. (2001). Using a Behavior-Based Method to Identify and Reduce Employee Theft. *International Journal of Retail & Distribution Management*, 29 (10), 442–451.

Parliamentary Office of Science and Technology (2004). *Radio Frequency Identification (RFID) Postnote*. London: Parliamentary Office of Science and Technology.

Pawson, R. & Tilley, N. (1997). *Realistic Evaluation*. London: Sage Publications.

Pease, K. (1997). Predicting the Future: The Role of Routine Activity and Rational Choice Theory. In G. Newman, R. V. Clarke & S. G. Shoham, *Rational Choice and Situational Crime Prevention* (pp. 233–246). Aldershot: Ashgate.

Peterson, R. A. & Balasubramanian, S. (2002). Retailing in the 21st Century. *Journal of Retailing*, 78, 9–16.

Planet Retail (2009). Retrieved February 18, 2009, from http://www.planetretail.net/CompanyAnalysis/RankingTop150CompaniesSelection.aspx

Purpora, P. P. (1993). *Retail Security and Shrinkage Protection*. Stoneham: Butterworth-Heinemann.

Quinn, B. (2000). *How Wal*Mart is Destroying America (and the World)*. Berkeley: Ten Speed Press.

Richardson, C. & Palmer, W. (2009). *Organised Retail Crime*, CRISP Report. Alexandria, VA: ASIS Foundation.

Ruggiero, W. G. & Steinberg, L. D. (1982). Occupational Deviance Among Adolescent Workers. *Youth & Society*, 13 (4), 423–428.

Sennewald, C. A. & Christman, J. H. (1992). *Shoplifting*. Burlington: Butterworth-Heinemann.

Sennewald, C. A. & Christman, J. H. (2008). *Retail Crime, Security, and Loss Prevention: An Encyclopedic Reference*. Burlington: Butterworth-Heinemann.

Sève, R. (1997). Philosophical Justifications of Situational Crime Prevention. In G. Newman, R. V. Clarke & S. G. Shoham, *Rational Choice and Situational Crime Prevention* (pp. 189–196). Aldershot: Ashgate.

Shackleton, R. (1996). Retailer Internationalisation: A Culturally Constructed Phenomenon. In N. Wrigley & M. Lowe, *Retailing, Consumption and Capital: Towards the New Retail Geography* (pp. 137–156). Harlow: Longman Group Limited.

Shapland, J. (1995). Preventing Retail-Sector Crimes. In M. Tonry & D. P. Farrington, *Building a Safer Society: Strategic Approaches to Crime Prevention* (pp. 263–342). Chicago: The University of Chicago Press.

Shury, J., Speed, M., Vivian, D., Kuechel, A. & Nicholas, S. (2005). *Crime Against Retail and Manufacturing Premises: Findings from the 2002 Commercial Victimisation Survey*. Home Office Online Report 37/05. London: Home Office.

Sieh, E. W. (1987). Garment Workers: Perceptions of Inequity and Employee Theft. *British Journal of Criminology, 27* (2), 174–189.

Simon, H. A. (1978). Rationality as Process and Product of Thought. *American Economic Review, 8*, 1–11.

Simpson, E. & Thorpe, D. I. (1995). A Conceptual Model of Strategic Considerations for International Retail Expansion. In G. Akehurst & N. Alexander, *The Internationalisation of Retailing* (pp. 16–24). London: Frank Cass & Co Ltd.

Slora, K. B. (1989). An Empirical Approach to Determining Employee Deviance Base Rates. *Journal of Business and Psychology, 4*, 199–219.

Smith, C. (2006). Trends in the Development of Security Technology. In M. Gill, *The Handbook of Security* (pp. 610–628). Basingstoke: Palgrave Macmillan.

Soliman, F. (1998). Optimum Level of Process Mapping and the Least Cost Business Process Re-engineering. *International Journal of Operations and Production Management, 18* (9/10), 810–816.

Speed, M. (2003). Reducing Employee Dishonesty: In Search of the Right Strategy. In M. Gill, *Managing Security: Crime at Work Volume 3* (pp. 157–180). Leicester: Perpetuity Press.

Stamatis, D. H. (1995). *Failure Mode and Effect Analysis*. Milwaukee: ASQC Quality Press.

Sutherland, E. H. (1949). *White Collar Crime*. New York: Dryden Press.

Sykes, G. & Matza, D. (1957). Techniques of Neutralization: A Theory of Delinquency. *American Sociological Review, 22*, 664–670.

Tesco PLC (2009). *Our History*. Retrieved February 26, 2009, from http://www.tescoplc.com/plc/about_us/tesco_story/#

Tilley, N. (1997). Realism, Situational Rationality and Crime Prevention. In G. Newman, R. V. Clarke & S. G. Shoham, *Rational Choice and Situational Crime Prevention* (pp. 95–114). Aldershot: Ashgate.

Time (1998). Retrieved April 16, 2009, from http://www.time.com/time100/builder/profile/walton.html

Tonglet, M. (1998). Consumers' Perceptions of Shoplifting and Shoplifting Behaviour. In M. Gill, *Crime at Work: Increasing the Risk for Offenders* (pp. 107–122). Basingstoke: Palgrave Macmillan.

Tse, K. K. (1985). *Marks & Spencer: Anatomy of Britain's Most Efficiently Managed Company*. Oxford: Pergamon.

Turbin, V. (1998). Shrinkage Figures and Data Corruption: Lies, Damned Lies and Statistics. In M. Gill, *Crime at Work: Increasing the Risk for Offenders* (pp. 25–34). Basingstoke: Palgrave Macmillan.

University of Florida (2007). *2007 National Retail Security Survey*. Gainsville, Florida: University of Florida.

Upchurch, A. (2002). *Cost Accounting: Principles and Practice*. Marlow: Financial Times Prentice Hall.

Wal-Mart (2009). *About Us*. Retrieved February 18, 2009, from http://walmart-stores.com/AboutUs/

Walton, S. & Huey, J. (1993). *Made in America*. New York: Bantam Books.

West, D. J. & Farrington, D. P. (1977). *The Delinquent Way of Life. Third Report*. London: Heinemann Educational Books Ltd.

Winstanley, M. J. (1983). *The Shopkeeper's World 1830–1914*. Manchester: Manchester University Press.

World Bank (2009). *Total GDP 2007*. Retrieved February 18, 2009, from http://siteresources.worldbank.org/DATASTATISTICS/Resources/GDP.pdf

Wortley, R. (1997). Reconsidering the Role of Opportunity in Situational Crime Prevention. In G. Newman, R. V. Clarke & S. G. Shoham, *Rational Choice and Situational Crime Prevention* (pp. 65–82). Aldershot: Ashgate.

Wrap (2008). *Non-Household Food Waste*. Retrieved June 18, 2008, from http://www.wrap.org.uk/retail/food_waste/nonhousehold_food.html

Wrigely, N. & Currah, A. (2003). The Stresses of Retail Internationalisation: Lessons From Royal Ahold's Experience in Latin America. *The International Review of Retail, Distribution and Consumer Research, 13* (3), 221–243.

Yake, T. (n.d.). *Business Abuse: A Major Factor in Retail Failures*. Retrieved October 29, 2008, from http://www.yake.com/sentry/index.htm

Yin, Y. K. (1993). *Application of Case Study Research*. London: Sage.

Young, W. (2004). *Sold Out: The True Cost of Supermarket Shopping*. London: Vision Paperbacks.

Index

Shrinkage Road Map Solution Matrix
124
Sieh, E. W. 68
Simon, H. A. 105
Simpson, E. 23
Situational crime prevention 100,
103, 105, 107–8, 111, 168
Slora, K. B. 68
Smith, C. 154, 185
Soliman, F. 119
Solution providers *see* Shrinkage
management, and role of
technology
Source tagging *see* Electronic Article
Surveillance (EAS)
Speed, M. 72, 143
Spoilage 31, 45–6, 53, 59, 79, 81,
110 *see also* Wastage
Staff discounts 74, 85
Staff theft *see* Internal theft
Stamatis, D. H. 121
Steinberg, L. D. 68
Stock loss *see* Shrinkage, definition of
Stock taking *see* Audits
Store detectives 49, 84–5, 90
Store transfers 33, 67
Supermarkets 11, 46, 78
Supply chains *see* Retailing, supply
chains
Sutherland, E. H. 67
Sykes, G. 14, 70

Tags *see* Electronic Article Surveillance
(EAS)
Technology *see* Shrinkage
management, and role of
technology
Technology providers *see* Shrinkage
management, and role of
technology

Templar, S. 28, 35, 39
Tesco 15–18, 23, 127
Theft *see* External theft and
Internal theft
Thomas, C. 76–7
Thorpe, D. I. 23
Thrift, N. 10
Tilley, N. 98, 103, 106, 108, 116,
126
Tonglet, M. 64
Tse, K. K. 9–10
Turbin, V. 80, 89

Uniform Product Code (UPC) 79
University of Florida 31, 35, 45,
47, 69
UPC (Uniform Product Code) 79
Upchurch, A. 39

Vendor fraud *see* Inter-company
fraud
Violence 63, 90

Wal-Mart 11, 15, 17, 23
Walton, S. 11, 26
Wastage 31, 45–6, 54–5, 58–9,
78–9, 91 *see also* Spoilage
Weisburd, D. 158
West, D. J. 64
Willis, A. 96
Winstanley, M. J. 9–10
Wooden dollars *see* Process
failures
World Bank 1, 11, 48
Wortley, R. 106–7
Wrap 55
Wrigely, N. 23

Yake, T. 35, 80, 82
Yammarino, F. 139